'til the fat girl sings

From an
Overweight Nobody to
a Broadway Somebody
—A Memoir

Sharon Wheatley

Adams Media
Avon, Massachusetts

Copyright ©2006, Sharon Wheatley.
All rights reserved. This book, or parts thereof, may not be reproduced in any form without permission from the publisher; exceptions are made for brief excerpts used in published reviews.

Published by
Adams Media, an F+W Publications Company
57 Littlefield Street, Avon, MA 02322. U.S.A.
www.adamsmedia.com

ISBN: 1-59337-543-3

Printed in the United States of America.

J I H G F E D C B A

Library of Congress Cataloging-in-Publication Data
Wheatley, Sharon.
'Til the fat girl sings / Sharon Wheatley.
p. cm.
ISBN 1-59337-543-3
1. Wheatley, Sharon. 2. Overweight women--United States--Biography. 3. Overweight children--United States--Biography. 4. Women singers--United States--Biography. I. Title.

RC628.W45 2006
362.1'963980092
[B 2
2006005005

This publication is designed to provide accurate and authoritative information with regard to the subject matter covered. It is sold with the understanding that the publisher is not engaged in rendering legal, accounting, or other professional advice. If legal advice or other expert assistance is required, the services of a competent professional person should be sought.
—From a *Declaration of Principles* jointly adopted by a Committee of the American Bar Association and a Committee of Publishers and Associations

Many of the designations used by manufacturers and sellers to distinguish their products are claimed as trademarks. Where those designations appear in this book and Adams Media was aware of a trademark claim, the designations have been printed with initial capital letters.

The following story is true. However, some names, places, and dates have been changed to protect the privacy of those involved.

Part opener photo © www.istockphoto.com.

This book is available at quantity discounts for bulk purchases.
For information, please call 1-800-872-5627.

contents

For Rob and Charlotte.

Your love is magical.

"The opera ain't over
till the fat lady sings."

—*Daniel John Cook*

overweight

adj. Weighing more than is normal, necessary, or allowed.

underestimated

v. An estimate that is, or proves to be, too low.

acknowledgments

Oh my. Wow. This is so exciting! Please, everyone, take your seats. There are so many people who have supported me along the way, and I'd like to take a moment to acknowledge them.

I'd like to start by thanking my parents. You have been such great sports throughout this entire process and I really appreciate your love and support. I hope I made you proud, and I hope you know how much I love you both. Many thanks to my sister, Susan, who has been a fantastic aide as I wrote this book, and who has always seen my potential no matter what I weighed. Thanks to my partner in crime, my brother, Buzz, and all of my extended family, including Tony, Maryday, and all of my aunts, uncles, cousins, nieces, nephews, and in-laws.

Thanks to everyone at Adams Media, especially my spectacular editors, Danielle Chiotti and Paula Munier. This book was totally Danielle's idea, and I'd like for her to stand up and take a quick bow. Paula gave the book the polish it needed; I am very grateful for your clear organizing principles. Thanks to Frank Rivera and Karen Cooper for the inspired cover design, and Laura Daly for overseeing the entire process.

Thanks to my agents June Clark and Peter Rubie, and especially Melody Rubie who "discovered" me in our *Phantom of the Opera* dressing room.

I'd like to acknowledge several of my teachers who made such a positive impact on my life, including Judith A. Brown, Carol Dettenwanger, Cathy Ogden, William Perry, Kathy Wade, Catherine Schellhous, Michelle Mascari, Cathy Creason, Kim

Iscman, Don Stringfield, Shirley Speaks, Barbara Honn, Terry Labolt, and Aubrey Berg. Thanks for supporting me and thanks for passing me through school. Sorry I didn't study more, but I hope I made you laugh. I know I didn't always make your jobs easy. Thanks to my acting teacher Joan Rosenfels, who encouraged me to write down my stories.

Thanks to all my great friends along the way: Allen (Karpe) Kendall, Missy Trautmann, Meredith Potter, Mimi and Kip Pritchett, Carloyn Kraft, Lauren Russ, Nina Naberhaus, Peggy Merrick, Kim Altenau, Andy Thaman, Todd Gessner, Tony Perrazzo, Hylan Scott, Jon Carver, Matt Farnsworth, Eileen Tepper, Traci Lyn Thomas, Michael and Sarah Uriarte Berry, Lucy Vance, Liz McCartney, Chris and Catherine Peterson, Debbie Himmler, Kathryn Schwarz, Emma Atherton, Jacob Brent, Susan Owen, Linda Balgord, Jane Orans, Amy Rogers, James Hadley, Lisa Queen, and Amy and Vince Luce DeGeorge. My life has been better because of all of you. Thank you.

To my generous, kind, and loving mother- and father-in-law. Thank you for taking care of Charlotte and supporting me in ways I couldn't even imagine. I love being a member of your (big) family.

Thank you to every producer, director, and general manager who ever gave me a job. Special thanks to Cameron Mackintosh, who unknowingly paid every bill in my household for a ten-year stretch of employment. Also thanks to Kristen Blodgette, Robert Nolan, Richard Jay-Alexander, Peter Von Mayrhauser, Craig Jacobs, Richard Stafford, Vinnie Liff, Geoffrey Johnson, Andy Zerman, my agent Craig Holzberg, and my most recent family at *Avenue Q*, including Jason Moore, Kevin McCullom, Evan Ensign, Jen Bender, David Benoit, Jeff Whitty, Bobby Lopez, Jeff Marx, and the entire cast and crew at the Wynn Casino in Las Vegas.

A big thank-you to Marg Hainer for your endless support and long hours. I hope you know how much you've helped me.

Last, but certainly not least, I'd like to thank my husband, Rob, and my daughter, Charlotte. You have suffered through months and months of me digging through every emotional skeleton in my closet, and it has been tough on all of us. Thank you for understanding why this is important, and thank you for giving me the space to succeed. Many years ago when I wished on a star to have a wonderful adult life, I could not have ever imagined being blessed with anything as wonderful as the two of you. I love you both so much. Thank you, everyone, for this fantastic honor. I'll meet you all at the party!

overture

"I just couldn't write anything without hope in it."
—*Oscar Hammerstein II*

"Sharon, I have an audition for you."

My agent, Penny, talked at lightning speed, and I knew from past experience that she would not slow down or repeat the information. I looked around frantically and grabbed the nearest writing supplies: a purple crayon and a Cinderella coloring book.

Calls from Penny were few and far between after I got pregnant. That didn't surprise me then, but now, a year after I'd had Charlotte, I was still having trouble getting auditions. There are thousands of actors in New York City, and getting auditions is always tough—but I'd heard through the grapevine that most producers didn't believe I'd accept work, assuming that I'd prefer to stay home with the baby. I'd planned on being a working mom, and I hate it when people make assumptions, so I made a point of pride to go to every audition I was offered, no matter what it was.

"What's it for?" I asked, crayon poised.

"The Broadway production of *Cats*. Jennyanydots, the Gumbie Cat."

"Mmm-hmm." I wrote *Cats Broadway Jennysomething* next to Cinderella's pumpkin. I knew very little about *Cats* except that it was a dance show that had been running on Broadway forever. As primarily a singing actor, I never thought I'd get an audition for it, so I'd never paid it any mind. But any Broadway audition is a good thing, and I was desperate for a steady job.

"Your audition is on Tuesday, May 31, at 10 A.M. at the Winter Garden Theater. Bring two contrasting songs, and be prepared to dance."

"Dance?" I stopped writing. "I have to *dance?*" I was thrilled at the idea of auditioning at the famous Winter Garden Theater, but that one terrible little word caused my heart to race.

"It's *Cats*." Penny sighed her *I hate stupid actors* sigh. "That's what the cats do. They dance. Now, there will be a jazz combination followed by a tap combination, and then they will make a cut. Those asked to stay will sing and then dance again. They said to be prepared to—"

"I have to dance *two* combinations, and *then* there's a cut?"

"Yes." Sigh again. "That's what they said."

I'd been to dance auditions before, but only after I'd had the chance to win them over with my acting and singing first. Called "movement" calls, these post-singing dance auditions are filled with a bunch of nervous singers in dance clothes unworn since theater school. Movement calls are pretty easy, since the choreographer is just checking to make sure that we won't fall down. Usually the "dancing" is simple, limited to a "step, touch" while we snap our fingers.

But this wasn't a movement call. This was *Cats*—real live Broadway dancing—and I'd have to dance first. I'd have to buy real dance clothes, crawl around on the stage, and remember complicated dance combinations that I didn't have the skills to execute.

"I can't do this." The real dancers would trample me. I pictured myself in a lumpy, sweaty mess on the stage. "You know I don't turn down auditions, especially for Broadway, but I'll make a total ass out of myself. Tell them thanks, but no thanks."

"You should go." Penny was adamant.

"They'll never hire me. They're looking for a *dancer.*"

"It's a job on Broadway," Penny said. "You could be home with Charlotte."

I knew Penny was frustrated with me, but that couldn't be helped. "I'm not what they're looking for. This would be a waste of time."

I hung up, feeling depressed. It had been so hard getting auditions lately, and it killed me to have to turn something down—especially a job on Broadway. The phone rang again. It was Penny, talking faster than ever in her *I have important information* speed. "Okay, look. I called and told them you said no, and they said they want you to come in anyway. Apparently dance skills aren't that important. They are looking for personality."

"Penny, you know why I can't do this audition." It was my turn to sigh. "I'm too fat to be a cat!"

"What are you talking about?" Penny sounded astounded. "You look great! You've lost all your baby weight."

True, but this was different. This was *Cats.* The cast members had a median weight of about twenty-seven pounds and they'd been in dance class since the age of two. These cats wore slinky, figure-hugging spandex from head to toe. Even at my prebaby thinnest, I didn't have a gorgeous dancer body worthy of display in spandex. "*Cats* is different."

"Okay," said Penny in her *I'm staying calm with this neurotic actor* voice. "You have some weird hang-ups about this. I'm going to call back and tell them you're coming. You spend the weekend clearing your head. If you really don't think you can do it, I'll call and cancel on Monday." I heard the phone ring in her office.

"I've got to get that. Talk to you Monday." And she hung up.

I pushed the off button and resisted the urge to throw my phone out the window. I looked at Charlotte, who was trying to force a square toy from her shape sorter into a round hole. She banged it over and over again, and then grunted in frustration.

"Hey kiddo, try this." I flipped the toy and showed her the match, the square hole. Charlotte grabbed the toy and went back to her square peg–round hole combination, banging it over and over again, trying to make it fit. I gave her a big kiss and said, "Oh, baby. I know just how you feel."

act one

"Sometimes I am so sweet
even I can't stand it."

—Julie Andrews

chapter 1
do re mi

Admiring my ballet slippers, I crossed and uncrossed my pink legs in anticipation.

When I was a little girl I wanted to be a dancer. I begged my mother to take me to ballet like all the other girls in my kindergarten class. The local ballet class was held in the basement of a nondescript 1970s building in Cincinnati, Ohio, where I grew up. In the back seat of my mother's Oldsmobile Cutlass, dressed in brand-new pink tights and a black leotard, my long dark hair shellacked into a bun, I felt feminine and beautiful. Admiring my ballet slippers, I crossed and uncrossed my pink legs in anticipation.

At the school, my new ballet teacher welcomed me and my sister future prima donnas. Lining us up at the bar, she taught us first position.

Eagerly I checked out the line of ballerinas in the big mirror. Each one was pink and perfect; then I saw myself in the mirror and I felt my heart jump. Different. I looked different. What was it? I looked again. Hair? Check. Leotard color? Check. Tights? Uh oh.

It was the tights. Just below where my leotard stopped, you could see my Scooby Doo underwear through my tights. No one else's underwear was showing. Embarrassed, I tugged the Scoobys back into hiding while attempting a grand plié. With a smile, I checked myself out again, only to find, I was still different! I couldn't figure it out. I had the ballerina hair, the ballerina clothes, and the ballerina shoes, but something was off.

The elderly teacher sashayed over to my side of the room and spoke to us in an exotic accent. "Nice, girls. Very good. But remember, ballet is all about the line of the body. Think tall, like a giraffe. Suck in your stomachs!"

I sucked in. She walked the line, one by one, saying, "Good . . . good." Then she got to me. She stopped. "Suck in your stomach."

I sucked in harder.

She poked me near my bellybutton with her ballet cane. "From here."

"I'm trying."

"*Tsk, tsk.* No more cake for you, hmm?" She patted my head and moved on.

The girl behind me, whose name was also Sharon, snickered and whispered, "No more cakes for you, fatty!"

A few of the girls around us laughed. My body was hot all over with embarrassment, and I glanced back into the unforgiving mirror. I knew what was different: I was fat. In ballet, I couldn't make long, lean lines like a giraffe, because I was a hippo. I sucked in my stomach as best I could for the duration of the forty-five minute class, until we were finally released back to our parents.

"See you next week, ladies!" the ballet teacher called after us.

In the car on the way home I told my mother I didn't like ballet. I didn't tell her the truth. I was too fat to dance.

The car was freezing.

"Dad, can we please have some heat on?" begged my sister. "It's about twenty degrees back here."

My mom, my sister, Susan, and my brother, Buzzy, had been asleep since 3 A.M. when we pulled out of our Cincinnati driveway to start our nineteen-hour car trip to Ft. Lauderdale for Christmas break. I was glad to hear my older sister's voice. I'd been awake the entire trip.

I felt my stomach rumble. I tapped my mom's shoulder. "Mom? Are we going to stop for breakfast soon?"

Mom reached down and shuffled through a shopping bag at her feet. "Here. I brought some breakfast for the car. We'll stop for lunch when we get near Atlanta."

My mouth salivated at the thought of breakfast. "Did you bring Pop Tarts?" I loved strawberry frosted Pop Tarts with tiny sprinkles.

"No, I brought grapes, bananas, and a box of Cheerios." I wrinkled my nose in disgust. "Don't make that face, Pop Tarts are fattening. Take a banana and give one to Susan and Buzzy. When we stop for gas you can pick out something else."

My dad reached over and flipped on the radio. "Well, since everyone is awake I'm going to catch up on the news." The sound of loud static filled the car, and my sister covered her ears, annoyed. "Wait a minute, wait a minute, let me find a station. . . ." He began to search the stations, momentarily taking his eyes off the road.

"*Chuck!*" my mother yelled as the car swerved toward the median. She pushed his hand away from the dials and took over. "You drive. I'll find something on the radio."

"Turn on something good," my brother requested. I knew that meant anything with electric guitars.

My sister covered her ears in the back seat. "Can we please just turn it off?"

In the front seat, an argument was brewing. "Slow down, you are turning the dial too quickly!"

"No I'm not. We're just too far from anywhere to pick up a station." My mother continued to search. Soon the car was filled with the sound of James Taylor singing "You've Got a Friend." "This is the only channel we can get this far out in the sticks. Do you want it on or off?"

"*Off,*" my brother and sister said in unison.

"*On,*" I yelled. "I love this song!"

"You don't even know this song," my brother sneered.

"I do too know this song. Me and Mom listen to it in her car, don't we, Mom? Listen. I even know the words." I started to sing along loudly to prove my point.

My dad turned down the volume. "Listen to her!"

I kept singing, thrilled that everyone in my family focused on me. I sang as perfectly as possible. When the song ended, I smiled and looked at my sister. "See? Isn't that a good song?"

"Hey," she said with admiration, "you can really sing."

My dad agreed. "Well, how about that? How long have you been able to sing like that?"

"I like to sing."

"I've been telling you, when she sings along with the radio, she sounds exactly like the singer. I can't tell who's who!"

"Cool." My brother didn't sound annoyed at all. "You sound really good."

Flattered and a little embarrassed, I handed him a Ken doll. "Will you play now?"

"Nah. I'm gonna read. Get your feet off my side." He pulled out a battered copy of *Rolling Stone* magazine and buried his head.

I pulled my feet back up on the hump and looked out the window. I was happy, but hungry. I grabbed the Cheerios box and crunched big handfuls into my mouth. I didn't really like Cheerios, but I needed something to hold me over until something familiar came on the radio. My family liked my singing! Sweet thoughts of strawberry Pop Tarts and James Taylor songs filled my head as I filled up on Cheerios, my head straight back, both feet on the hump.

Life would never be so simple again.

Ayer Elementary School was an experimental school, designed without internal walls to reflect a modern, freeform style of teaching. From the very first day, I loved the expansive, friendly feeling of the building. I loved the teachers, who focused on my outgoing personality rather than my size. My fellow first-graders, however, were not so forgiving.

My weight locked me out, almost from the beginning. I dreaded recess, where out on the playground out of earshot from the teachers, the kids were free to hurl words like *fat* and *cow* at me with impunity.

I decided that if my classmates were going to treat me like that, then I would make friends with grownups.

My first conquest: Dolly, the elderly woman who drove the school bus. I loved to sit in the seat right behind her so I could watch her shift the tall gearshift as she pumped the pedals. While she drove, I told her all about my day at school. I sang her songs I'd learned in music class and brought her the watercolors I'd painted of her big, yellow school bus. She entertained me by turning on the big windshield wipers and telling me about her grandchildren, who lived hundreds of miles away. Dolly was my protector; sitting upfront by Dolly saved me from the boys in the back of the bus, the same boys who teased me on the playground. Once at school, I stayed as close as possible to the grownups. Adults saw past my fat in a way that kids couldn't. I just needed to be outgoing, funny, and happy—and I succeeded so well that I was known as "Little Miss Sunshine" by most of the faculty.

But there was one teacher who wasn't fooled by my sunny persona: Mr. Ritter. As a first-year teacher, he was given the grunt work of "recess moderator" on top of his normal teaching duties. During recess, I'd hang around Mr. Ritter and he'd tell me stories about how much he had hated recess when he was a kid.

"I was teased a lot, Sharon, just like you," he'd tell me as he brushed my hair. Mr. Ritter ran an imaginary "hair salon," and I was his best customer.

I couldn't understand why anyone would tease him, and I begged him to tell me what the kids had said, but he shrugged it off.

"It's not important. All I'm saying is, I know how mean kids can be. What would you like today? A French twist?"

I thought Mr. Ritter was the nicest man on the planet— a fact that I shared enthusiastically with my mother on many occasions. In fact, I raved about him so much that she invited him over to our house for a drink one Friday, late in the school year.

The day of the visit, I was ecstatic that Mr. Ritter was actually *in* my house. I ran in and out of the room where he and my parents were having a drink, showing him all my toys, pointing out our swimming pool, dragging in my dog and my cat. Finally, my enthusiastic interruptions annoyed my dad enough to order me out of the room. I stomped away, but after a few minutes, I crawled back to listen at the doorway. They were talking about me, as I hoped they would be. I lay just outside the doorway, thrilled to be the center of attention, even when I wasn't in the room.

I heard Mr. Ritter's high voice first. "I know I said this at the parent-teacher conference, but Sharon is a really special girl."

My mom, who'd gotten a lot of mileage out of the "Little Miss Sunshine" story with family and friends, was clearly thrilled to hear more good reports. "Well, she certainly likes you, too! Sharon has always had a very special relationship with her teachers."

"Actually, I've been kind of concerned about Sharon." Mr. Ritter's voice dropped; he suddenly sounded very serious. "I was wondering if you've noticed if she's been a bit depressed."

"Depressed?" My father jumped to my defense. "What are you talking about? Sharon's the least depressed kid I know."

"It has to do with Sharon's obsession with the color purple." Mr. Ritter cleared his throat. "I'm assuming that you've noticed it?"

Everyone knew my favorite color was purple; it was practically the only color I wore. My room, my notebooks, and even the gym shoes currently on my feet were purple. I looked down to admire them and wondered what the color purple had to do with anything.

"There have been a lot of studies in the past couple of years about why certain children are strongly attracted to certain colors," Mr. Ritter continued. "It turns out that an attraction to purple, especially deep purple, is a warning sign of depression."

Mr. Ritter paused, and waited for my parents' reaction. Still in hiding, I held my breath.

My father spoke first. "Are you serious? Are you diagnosing my daughter with depression because she likes the color purple?"

"Sharon sometimes struggles socially in school," said Mr. Ritter. "I think that's contributing to her depression. I've become increasingly concerned about her."

"I haven't ever seen a single sign that Sharon is depressed," said my mother, echoing my father's disbelief. "I think she is just the opposite. She's our Little Miss Sunshine! Ask anyone who's ever met her."

My father changed the subject then, and Mr. Ritter left shortly thereafter.

I was too young to really know what they were talking about, but I knew enough to understand that I had somehow dodged a bullet.

Later that night I heard Mom and Dad laughing about it through their bedroom door.

"Can you believe that?" My father was incredulous. "That's the problem with teacher training these days. They spend time learning what colors mean instead of how to control their classrooms. Bunch of flaky damn liberals."

I couldn't see my mother through the closed door, but I knew she was nodding in agreement.

Things were never the same with Mr. Ritter after that. Our beauty salon–chat sessions came to an end—due as much to my ambivalence as Mr. Ritter's. I wasn't sure if I should like him since my parents thought he was a "flake." But, at the end of the school year, when he announced he was moving to San Francisco with his roommate Jeffry, I cried and cried.

My purple story from second grade quickly made it into family lore, repeated countless times to friends and relatives. The way my parents told it, I was outgoing and happy, and all little girls loved purple. Case closed.

But I knew that Mr. Ritter had discovered my secret: that I was sunshine on the outside, and deep purple on the inside.

In third grade, just when I thought I'd never make a friend, just when I thought the boys would tease me forever, and the girls would ignore me forever, the most popular girl decided I was funny. Madison Pepper was one of those wonderkids who excelled at everything from grades to sports to music to art class. Everyone wanted to be her friend. She was effortlessly popular, and to make her even more perfect, she laughed at my jokes. Once I had her attention, I cracked her up as often as I could by impersonating our teacher behind his back.

Our social studies teacher, a well-traveled man named Mr. Bencher, had a habit of gesticulating wildly from the elbows down in a circular helicopter propeller motion while talking to the class. My brother had also taken Mr. Bencher's class, and he'd shown me the way he had made fun of him by pretending to "take off" in flight while talking in an exaggerated way about the great pyramids of Egypt. I liked Mr. Bencher, but one rainy Tuesday, I decided to re-create my brother's impersonation for my own social gain.

"Hey, Madison. Guess who I am," I whispered one day during class. I waited until Mr. Bencher had his back to the class and I whispered in a deep, authoritative tone while slowly propelling myself out of my seat. "*The great pyramids were built to house. . . .*" Midway through I noticed several sets of laughing eyes looking in my direction, so I flapped harder. Wanting a dramatic climax, I flapped myself out of my seat and landed in a dramatic crash on the floor to peals of laughter. The commotion of my classmates attracted Mr. Bencher's attention. He motioned crazily for me to get up, which I mimicked as soon as he turned around, causing the class to laugh harder. Their laughter was like a drug, especially when Madison flashed me a thumbs up. "*You're funny,*" she mouthed. I propelled my arms back at her and crossed my eyes. I was *funny*!

My comedy routine continued until Mr. Bencher caught me midflight, and I was warned that I'd be sent to the principal's office if I didn't calm down.

Getting in trouble was well worth it. Later that day in the cafeteria, Madison decreed to a big group of kids, "Hey, you guys, Wheatley's funny!" And, as easy as that, I was invited to sit with her. No one could command a luncheon of Sloppy Joes with style and panache like Madison. I was thrilled to have such a famous friend. By the time I'd sat at her table for a week straight, I was telling everyone that Madison was my best friend.

Of course, Madison already had loads of best friends. She tried to make sure that we all got a turn. Still, I struggled not to be jealous. Madison had elevated me from being just the fat kid. I still got teased, but not nearly as much, especially when I was with her.

Since I didn't live near Madison, I had to cement my friendship with her while we were at school. My big chance came in chorus. Third-grade chorus was a mandatory part of the curriculum at Ayer Elementary. Mr. Wilder, the music teacher, was a small, sweet man with a neatly trimmed moustache and large, round glasses that gave him a mouselike appearance. His expectations of us were low, which matched our expectations perfectly. We liked art class, where we could mash our fingers in clay. Music class was stupid.

As a student who didn't really excel at anything, I was surprised when Mr. Wilder started singling me out in class for my singing. It was the first time anyone outside my family had ever remarked on my singing—and I loved it. The more Mr. Wilder praised me, the closer I sat to the front of the room and the more my musical confidence grew. I started to look forward to music class, and I worked hard to earn more compliments from Mr. Wilder.

do re mi

"Sharon, you really have a knack for singing. Has anyone ever told you that?" he said one day after class. "I've never had a student with such an excellent ear."

I didn't know what that meant, but it sounded good. I asked my sister Susan about it that night at dinner, and she confirmed it was a good thing. The very next day, I went to the library, checked out the soundtrack to *Oliver*, and sang every word to every song while I was alone in my bedroom. Music quickly became my favorite class. I even started hanging around after class to help Mr. Wilder wipe down the chalkboards—just in case he had anything else to say about my good ear.

With music class and Madison Pepper on my side, my confidence grew. I held late-night interviews in my bedroom with my stuffed animals, pretending I was a guest on the *Tonight Show*. When my interviewer asked me what I liked best about school, I'd reply, "Oh, well, that's an excellent question. I guess I'd have to say music class. I have a really good ear, you know. I might be the best singer in the world."

A couple of weeks before the Fall Concert, Mr. Wilder approached Madison and me as we were leaving class. "Girls. You are both doing very well in class, showing a lot of potential." He waved a piece of sheet music at us. "I was wondering how you would feel about singing a duet for the Fall Concert."

The number, "Where Is Love?" from *Oliver*, was beautiful, sad, and difficult to sing. It was one of my favorite songs; I knew every word by heart. I was ecstatic.

"You mean you want us to sing this song all by ourselves, in front of everyone?" Madison looked less than thrilled. "The whole school?"

Mr. Wilder nodded. "You're doing very well in class, Madison. Your singing shows promise. I thought that you might like an opportunity to show everyone what you can do." He paused for a minute before adding, "You too, Sharon."

I wished that Mr. Wilder had been talking to me, telling *me* that I had a lot of promise. But even being a late addition to Madison's compliment was a thrill. I was being singled out for something good, and I would get to stand in front of the entire school as Madison's best friend and partner. It was a dream come true.

As Madison stood fidgeting with her hair, it dawned on me that she could say no, and I experienced several seconds of crushing terror.

"Okay." Madison shrugged her narrow shoulders in agreement. Even though inside my heart was screaming with joy, I feigned Madison's indifference, and shrugged too.

We practiced for the next few weeks with Mr. Wilder, and the sound of our voices blending together gave me chills. I wanted to practice every minute of the day, and I was annoyed when unimportant things like classes and homework got in the way.

The day before the concert, I was so excited that I called Madison three times. "Do you want to practice over the phone again?"

She refused; I begged her. By the fourth call, her mom got on the phone and told me to stop calling because it was past Madison's bedtime and she needed her sleep. I, meanwhile, hardly slept a wink.

The next day, Mr. Wilder separated the folding walls that divided the music room and the cafeteria, combining them into one gigantic room. My first venue.

Madison and I watched the parents file in for the show.

She looked great. All in white, with her bright smile and blond hair, she looked like a model from a toothpaste ad.

"You look great." I felt dumpy standing next to her in my navy corduroy pants and a sweater.

Madison smiled but didn't say anything.

"Do I look okay?" I asked her.

"Yeah, sure." Madison seemed distracted. "Are you nervous?"

"A little," I admitted. But it was a good nervous, that adrenaline state of fear and excitement. I knew that I was ready.

Madison, on the other hand, was white as a sheet. That surprised me. I'd always considered her, in addition to her celebrity at Ayer Elementary, a show business professional. Her parents were divorced, and her father lived in Hollywood. He produced a major musical television show, and everyone said that she'd appeared on the show on one of her trips to see him. By birthright alone, Madison Pepper was destined to be a star.

Mr. Wilder took up his position in front of the band, and the concert began. In what seemed like a flash, it was time for our duet.

As I stood in front of the school with my best friend by my side, I saw the whole room in a hazy, hushed shadow. I looked for everyone—my parents, my brother and sister, my grandma and papa, my aunts, all of them. It was the first time I had ever seen an audience from a performer's perspective. As I scouted the crowd, I leaned over to point out Madison's mom and brother. But Madison didn't really care.

"I can't do this." She sounded as if she were choking.

"You'll be great," I whispered.

Why was she so upset? She was Madison Pepper—like Mary Poppins, she was practically perfect in every way. If anyone screwed this up, it would most certainly be me. As we took our places at the microphone, she looked okay, and during the opening bars of the song, she flashed her famous bright smile at the audience.

And then it was showtime, and we were singing the opening lines together.

It was one of the best moments of my life, and I drank it in as best I could—the sound of my voice from the microphone as it echoed throughout the carpeted cafeteria was thrilling. It was the first time I had ever felt like I belonged somewhere.

I was so intoxicated by the experience that it took me a minute to realize that only one voice was booming through the room. Mine. Madison had hopped back a step or two and was smiling a wild, panicky smile. I couldn't believe it. Madison Pepper had stage fright.

I faltered for a second. Surely, if the girl wonder couldn't sing the song, then I couldn't do it either. I almost stopped and walked off the stage at that very moment. But as the piano played on, I realized something. I knew the words. I knew the song. I wanted to do this more than anything in the world, and I could do it just as well without Madison Pepper.

In that moment, I chose my path. I stepped forward and finished the song with no problem. My life changed course that night. Standing there on the dividing line between the music room and the cafeteria—an appropriate combination for me— the applause from the audience washed over me, planting seeds of confidence. I wasn't just the fat girl. I could sing.

Given my moment of glory singing "Where Is Love?" it was only fitting that my first glimpse of a professional musical was the Cincinnati theater company Playhouse in the Park production of *Oliver*. I begged my parents to take me, and they finally agreed. For years I'd watched my mom get ready for the theater—and now it was my turn. On the night of the show, I dressed in my fanciest dress, wore pantyhose, and even sprayed on a little of my mom's perfume. Our exciting Saturday night of culture also included dinner at a restaurant that had an all-you-can-eat make-your-own-sundae bar, which I thought was fantastic. On my second trip to the sundae bar, I hummed a little *Oliver* as I ladled hot fudge over my ice cream and thought about what fun it was going to be to see the big hits "Food Glorious Food" and "Consider Yourself" performed onstage with live actors. I knew that *Oliver* had kids my age in it, but I was not prepared—not at all—for what was coming.

That night, as the house lights dimmed, I sat on the edge of my seat listening to the orchestra play the overture. It sounded so different from my recording, so crisp and exciting, that I felt the hair on my arms stand up. When the curtain went up, and I saw those real-life kids just like me on that stage, I started to cry—and I didn't stop until the show was over and we were in the car on the way home. It was the most complicated emotion I had ever felt—a mixture of awe, love, magic, longing, and good old-fashioned jealousy. If a person could actually turn green from envy, a hysterical, pudgy, freckled nine-year-old, the color of the Wicked Witch of the West, would have occupied my seat at *Oliver* that night.

I've heard that show-biz people have it in their blood, and I am here to tell you that during that performance of *Oliver*, I got a complete show-biz blood transfusion. I cried myself to sleep that night, furious at the injustice of a life that had made me a mere audience member. *Never again*, I vowed to myself. From that day forward, I was an actress.

chapter 2

the sound of music

I knew from the beginning that if I was going to have a theatrical career, I was going to have to do it on my own.

If I had been born into a vaudeville family like my idol, Judy Garland, I would have been the perfect show-biz kid. My parents were supportive, but they weren't exactly helpful in a Mama Rose from *Gypsy* kind of way. With absolutely no connections to anyone famous, and stuck in Ohio, I knew my chances of appearing on the *Tonight Show* were limited. It was a huge cross for a nine-year-old to bear. I knew from the beginning that if I was going to have a theatrical career, I was going to have to do it on my own.

Despite my geographical challenges and the fact that my weight was a huge handicap in my social life, my recent cafeteria-singing debut had proven to me that I had the ability to overshadow my girth with song. I invented elaborate fantasies of being swept away to Hollywood in a limo and plunked down in the middle of my own variety show—*The Sharon Wheatley Variety Hour*—complete with backup dancers. Naturally, in my fantasy, I was pixie thin with straight blond hair and galloped around the Hollywood sets on a white horse named Sunshine. Every couple of months, I would fly out one lucky student from my former grade school in boring Cincinnati, Ohio, and we'd play tetherball on the playground built just for me. Then I'd send them home with a glossy black-and-white photograph endorsed "Friends forever, Sharon Wheatley."

My ambitions found their greatest expression in my obsession with *The Sound of Music.*

Some kids are addicted to video games. Others are addicted to soccer. I was addicted to *The Sound of Music, SOM* to us dedicated fans. Some of my earliest and fondest *SOM* memories are from the chopped-up televised version that aired every year on Easter night. I would curl up in front of the TV with my new best friend, my Easter basket, to gorge on chocolate bunnies and the von Trapp Family Singers. Most kids who love *SOM* want to be a character their own age, maybe the cute Gretl, or the feisty Brigitta, but not me. Don't get me wrong. I liked the kids, but they weren't the character I identified with. It was spunky, irrepressible Maria who caught my eye. I loved that she was always late, always in trouble, always saying the wrong thing, but she still managed to get everyone in the movie to fall in love with her. I'd march around during the commercial breaks, swinging my Easter basket and singing Maria's anthem "I Have Confidence." If Maria, orphaned and stuck in a locked abbey could get out and get a life, I could too.

I listened to the soundtrack constantly, performing Maria's songs, complete with staging, to an adoring Friday night theater crowd comprised of an army of stuffed animals.

Imagine my delight, one Saturday morning when I was ten, when I discovered this small ad next to the kids' pages in my local paper:

Auditions

Indian Hill Community Theater is holding auditions for their upcoming production of *The Sound of Music*. Seeking children of all ages who can sing to play the von Trapp Family Singers. Please bring sheet music to the audition and be prepared to sing from the show. No experience necessary.

I knew that there was no one else, not in the entire city of Cincinnati, nor the entire state of Ohio, nor the vast United States of America, who was better suited to play a von Trapp Family Singer than I was. I immediately cut out the ad and took it to the one person I knew could help me: my sister Susan.

Susan was the smart one in the family. She was so smart that she was going to be the first female U.S. president, and she studied all day, every day. She spent hours locked in her bedroom with her homework, books, and music. I was usually forbidden from even knocking on her door, but I didn't care. This was an emergency.

I banged on her door, clipping in hand. When she threw open the door, ready to yell at me, I thrust the paper at her. Unable to resist reading anything, ever, she took the bait—and took up my cause. Just why, I'm not sure. Maybe it was because her room was close to mine, and she heard my daily *SOM* concerts. Maybe she knew how miserable I was at school. Whatever the reason, she took it upon herself to train me like Rocky for the *SOM* audition. Together, we tackled the audition head on.

Susan could play the piano, so we sang every song in the *SOM* vocal selections, trying to decide what my piece should be. We finally settled on "Edelweiss," which sounded rich and pretty in my voice. I loved singing with a piano instead of with the record, and I begged my sister to play it over and over again.

Throughout our days of practice, I could see Susan's opinion of me changing. For the first time, I was more than a little sister to her. I was a person with a talent of my own, a talent that she admired. She told me over and over that I had a natural ability to phrase and match pitches. I'd spent so many years longing for her attention that I basked in the glow of our new relationship. I felt as if I were finally interesting to her, and that fueled my desire to win a part in the show even more.

An organizational wizard, Susan overlooked no detail. She orchestrated a fashion show of all of my dresses, so she could help me pick the best one. Together we chose my Easter dress, a pink and pouffy number with a cross-up lacing in the front and an apron. She even enlisted my mother to help with my hair. Mom braided my thick brown hair in two stiff plaits that she curled up and pinned under, à la Gretl. I checked myself out in the mirror and smiled. I looked completely Austrian.

After six days of intensive training, which concluded with a wildly successful dress rehearsal for my parents, I felt confident. Susan drove me to the audition, and we agreed that I was ready. But when I walked into the gymnasium of Indian Hill High School and saw how many children had shown up, my excitement faded. My stomach heaved. The gym was a madhouse full of kids in mock lederhosen being cajoled by their pushy parents— the theatrical equivalent of soccer moms. Hairspray and nerves were flying everywhere.

Despite the chaos, I studied each singer as closely as I could. My sister, ever the helpful coach, read my mind and elbowed me a little. "These kids can't sing. You've got this in the bag."

It felt good to hear her say that. The other kids really *weren't* doing so great. They either couldn't match the notes or they rushed ahead, leaving the piano accompaniment behind and sounding like a skipping record. With some sense of relief, I realized my sister was right. I really had a shot.

One girl with sandy blond braids and knobby knees did fairly well. Her voice was husky, though, and she missed a couple of the higher notes. But at least she kept time with the piano. They asked her to sing a second time, and she did a little better. When her turn was over, the producers called my name. Suddenly I felt very damp in my pink Easter dress, and I noticed my hands were trembling. If she noticed my terror, Susan didn't let on.

"Go knock 'em dead," she whispered, and gave my arm a light squeeze.

I walked to the piano, gave my music to the pianist, and turned to face the grownups at the table. They sat in folding chairs under the basketball net, identical notepads laid out on the table. Little did I know at that moment that I was experiencing what would become my version of a job interview for the rest of my life.

The judges were busy writing, and I wasn't sure if I should just start singing or wait until they were finished. I waited for someone to look up, trying not to appear uncomfortable as I did so. A baby started to cry, and I prayed his mother would take him outside.

An athletic man in the middle looked up first. He was very tan and dressed in white, with a pink sweater slung around his neck. He looked as though he'd stopped by between sets on the tennis court. His smile was friendly and his voice was encouraging.

"Hi, honey," he said. "What's your name?"

"Sharon Wheatley," I said, noting that my voice sounded strong and confident. The other four observers scribbled furiously on their pads.

"And what are you going to sing for us today, Sharon?"

"I am going to sing 'Edelweiss.'"

"Okay, great. Hit it."

The baby was now shrieking, and I could barely hear the piano start. I focused on Mr. Tennis, and started my song. "Edelweiss, edelweiss. Every morning you greet me." The first part of the song was low, and a little hard to project, but I did my best. Thankfully, the baby stopped crying a few seconds later, and I sang my heart out, lost in the Austrian Alps.

When I got to the most difficult part of the song, the verse, I felt the room grow quiet. I could hear my voice booming out across the gymnasium. I liked how it sounded.

When I finished singing, the room was silent. The notebook women stopped writing. Mr. Tennis stared at me for a long moment, scratching his eyebrow with his pen. His next reaction provided me with years of encouragement, even in my most hopeless moments.

"Wow."

One glorious word, and I let it wash over me. "Wow" was better than opening presents on Christmas Day, and much better than singing in the crummy school cafeteria.

"No, I mean it. Where did you learn to sing like that?"

I shrugged. Mr. Tennis shuffled his papers and asked me to come back at six o'clock to read some of Brigitta's scenes.

I was shaky with excitement as I made my way back to the waiting area. Susan was ecstatic. She took me to McDonald's, where we wolfed down Big Macs and worked on Brigitta's big monologue at the end of the first act. As I gobbled my French fries, I fantasized about my star dressing room.

Back at the auditorium, I was delighted to see there were very few kids left. They had only called back two kids per part. It was down to Knobby Knees and me for the role of Brigitta. My sister was right. I had it in the bag.

After more singing and reading, we were grouped, cattle like, into two opposing von Trapp families—from Liesel to Gretl. It was like being on an episode of *Family Feud.* I wanted a buzzer so I could buzz in and say, "Pick us! We're the real von Trapps!"

As we stood there, Mr. Tennis and his buddies walked the lines and looked us over, whispering and pointing. I'd never been sized up like that by anyone before, and it made me feel even more self-conscious than usual. The kid next to me (Kurt von Trapp) kept clearing his throat and shifting his weight from one foot to the other. His eyes bulged out of his head and he was grinning like a Cheshire cat. By contrast, I tried to look talented and well behaved.

The judges stopped in front of me; the whispers grew more intense. I smiled at them, then did my best Brigitta look—bratty and know-it-all, yet with a hint of adorable sneer.

"Sharon, we'd like you to try the other line," said Mr. Tennis.

I walked over to the other line and switched places with Knobby Knees. I smiled at my new family of von Trapps. Of course this was my family. I couldn't believe I had even considered the other counterfeit von Trapps for a second.

I was just making myself at home when I got moved back to the other line. This time, they told me I would be Louisa, and I felt my heart sink. As an *SOM* expert, I knew this was a totally wrong move. Louisa was older and blond. I was too short and too dark.

As I took my place in line as Louisa, something else dawned on me. Everyone else in line had one common denominator. They were all thin. No matter where the judges moved me, I didn't match up. I looked like the outcast von Trapp cousin who had just come in from the farm where my parents had raised me on whole cream instead of skim milk.

On my third move, the whispering intensified, and I started to panic. They couldn't take Knobby Knees over me! She couldn't even sing. I was born to play Brigitta. I was the "Wow" girl!

Mr. Tennis called me out of line, and I could feel both families of von Trapps watching us as he put his arm around me and walked me to the exit. He gave my shoulder a squeeze and said, "Thanks a lot for coming in. You did a really nice job. You keep singing, okay?"

I was the first one eliminated.

Looking back at the skinny families of von Trapps perfectly lined up, I felt ashamed. I didn't look like any of them. I wasn't thin. I wasn't blond. I was all wrong for everything. I wasn't cute enough to play the von Trapp dog. My throat started to burn, and I blinked away tears.

I was afraid Susan would be disappointed in me, but she ranted the whole ride home about narrow-minded people who only cared about face-lifts and tans. "You're better than any of them, Sharon. Did you see those idiots? They were all dressed like they were doing the country club version of *The Sound of Music*. They are so into looks. They wouldn't know talent if it hit them over the head! You're special. We just have to find the right thing to feature you."

I didn't feel very special. I just felt fat and miserable, and I wanted to burn my stupid, stupid pouffy dress and hide out in my room with the bag of Oreos my mom had tucked away on top of the fridge.

That night I dreamed of heaven. In my version of heaven, I got to play every role I was too fat to play in real life. I was Annie in *Annie*, Nancy in *Oliver*, and of course, in back-to-back productions, every female von Trapp family member, including Maria. The tickets were free and there was a new show every night. I had a big dressing room with a stocked refrigerator full of delicious food with no calories, and my sister was in the front row, cheering for me, Sharon von Trapp.

chapter 3
ain't misbehavin'

This summer I will get thin. I will listen to all of my mother's diet advice and I WILL NOT SNEAK MY FATHER'S FOOD.

The summer before middle school was the longest summer of my life. I was determined to start my new school with no handicaps; the "new" me would be a skinny, likeable girl with endless social and theatrical potential. I'd sit out by our pool late at night and make passionate wishes to the summer stars as bats flew overhead. This summer I will get thin. I will listen to all of my mother's diet advice and I WILL NOT SNEAK MY FATHER'S FOOD. Cross my heart and hope to die. Even as I made my devout pledge to the stars, I knew I had my work cut out for me. My legacy was undeniable. I was born with my father's love of all things fattening and my mother's lousy metabolism. This combination, coupled with my weight problem, caused a lot of tension in my house.

My parents were great friends, but as different as night and day—and that difference extended to their relationship with food. My mother considered food the enemy—and keeping trim a fight to the death. Mom was a champion dieter. If there were

'til the fat girl sings

a Diet Olympics, my mother would take the gold in every event. Her unsolicited weight loss advice was a constant conversation throughout my childhood. She could tell me, in two seconds flat, which was more fattening: a slice of Cheddar or a slice of Swiss. She'd tell me why the backstroke burns more calories than the breaststroke, why lifting weights could speed up my metabolism, why eating grapefruit for breakfast is the best way to start my dieting day. My mother, who is *always* on a diet, lost and regained the same ten pounds for my entire childhood, without ever going above a size 8. I, on the other hand, outgrew my mother's size 8 clothes by the fourth grade.

My mother has strict philosophies that rule her chronic dieting. Every morsel that she puts in her mouth is discussed and analyzed for its caloric content and its impact on her hips. Throughout my childhood, my mom had the power to turn any family event into an impromptu Weight Watchers' meeting. Her typical line at any gathering, from Christmas to Easter to the Fourth of July, was, "Well, okay, I'll try your cake. But I only want a little tiny sliver. *No*, no, not that big. I just can't eat like a normal person. It goes straight to my hips!" Then, suddenly, everyone wanted only a tiny sliver of cake, and the conversation veered from how the kids were doing to the nutritional value of butter cream icing.

My father is a "glass half full" kind of guy who likes to say things like: "Sharon, some people might look at a half-full glass and describe it as half empty. I feel sorry for those people. They aren't going to get anywhere in life. You and I are the kind of people who look at that glass and ask why that glass is only half full. How can I fill that glass up all the way? That's how you need to live your life, kid. You gotta figure out how to fill that glass up all the way till it pours over the rim."

Dad was a swimming pool contractor, but his real passion was inventing. Living with him was like living inside the movie *Chitty Chitty Bang Bang*. His gadgets filled our house, and his dreams of making millions dominated our family conversations. "Did you see the floating solar bricks I invented for the swimming pool? It's going to make us millions. Let me tell you how I did it. . . ."

Every morning around 11:30, fantastic smells began to waft through the house, seducing me away from the sensible tuna sandwich my mother planned for me to eat, and filling my head with dreams of a fried egg sandwich with a pickle. No matter how much I tried to resist, I inevitably ended up in the kitchen, my nose leading the way, my stomach right behind it. Even before I crossed the threshold, I knew exactly what he was cooking, just from the aroma, and all my willpower flew out the window.

"Hi ya, Dirtball. I'm just whipping myself up a little egg sandwich. So what has a rotten kid like you been up to today?" Dad swirled a huge lump of butter around the frying pan.

My father slept until eleven or so most days, so I'd catch him up on the morning's events.

"I swam laps this morning." This was a lie, but as my father was a late riser, he didn't know that. "Twenty-five of them."

My dad hated exercise, and he always sympathized with those who tried to do it.

"All that swimming sure makes you hungry." I waited, hoping he'd take the bait

"Are you hungry?"

I played it cool. "Yeah, I'm hungry. I think that Mom left some tuna in the fridge. I can just eat that, I guess." It was a fine line I walked. Despite my dad's opinion that I shouldn't eat his way, I knew he hated dry, diet food, a fact I could use to my advantage.

He narrowed his eyes. "Do you want tuna?"

"Not really."

"Would you like me to make you a sandwich?"

"Do you mind?"

"Hell, no, I don't mind. What do you want? Grilled cheese? Scrambled egg? Hot dog? I can make it just like Howard Johnson's. I'll grill the bun, just a touch. You don't get as much butter as I do—you're just a rotten kid." He smiled at me. "But I'll make it taste good."

"Scrambled egg sandwich," I said, as he reached for a frying pan.

I loved these late mornings in the kitchen with my father. My dad manned the stove, while I watched, both of us giddy from the scent of the rich, sweet butter.

He was organized and efficient, easily juggling many tasks at once, a trait that did not extend beyond the kitchen. His ingredients never varied: eggs, bread, butter, mayonnaise, milk, salt, pepper, pickles—all lined up like willing soldiers ready for a mission.

"You have to use butter. None of this margarine crap." He spread a generous amount on his bread, adding even more to the frying pan. "We're going to make you a low-cal version."

I happily agreed. My father, who knew next to nothing about dieting, still used more butter than a family of four could consume in a day, even on his "low-cal" versions.

When the sandwiches were ready, he swept them onto the table with a flourish. "Look at that; look at that!" And we dug in.

Egg sandwich days were the good days—we were silly and loud, full and happy.

But this summer the "swimming lap" story didn't buy me nearly as many egg sandwiches. The pressure was on for me to lose weight. And it didn't let up. My father had decided he was a bad influence on me. "I'm not cooking for you anymore, Sharon. Your mother and I have talked about it, and you've got to get your weight under control. I know you have all these big show-biz dreams, but none of them will come true with you looking like this. From now on, you are to eat like your mother. No more egg sandwiches."

I missed the egg sandwiches, but I more than made up for it by sneaking food. My favorite food to sneak was my Dad's Soft Batch chocolate chip cookies. I heated them in the microwave for five seconds each, one by one, while I watched *Gilligan's Island.* But I didn't eat them all. I made sure I stopped before *The Beverly Hillbillies* came on, so there would be some left for Dad.

"Sharon!"

I heard my dad yell from his big chair in the garden room.

"What happened to the cookies your mother bought this morning?"

Dad was spread out on his chair, the newspaper in his lap, with the TV blasting. I stood in the doorway between the garden room and the living room trying to block out his fury while he screamed. I focused on the doorjamb with the peeling white paint and struggled to stop the tears from spilling over. It didn't work; it never did. Fat tears rolled down my cheeks. Dad hated it when I cried; it made him angrier.

"Look at me when I'm talking to you!" he bellowed. "Do you want us all to have to eat carrot sticks because of you? Your mother and I have told you this a million times! You cannot act like me! You cannot just eat whatever you want!"

"I'm sorry." My hands were cold; the doorjamb was peeling white; the latch was gold. I stole a glance at this angry person—this person who was usually my funny dad, my buddy, the one who knew every dream in my head. I felt transparent, as though he was yelling right through me. I wanted to stop him and ask, "Can you still see me?"

But I couldn't. I couldn't breathe. I couldn't even hear what he was saying anymore; it was like he was talking underwater. I stared at the doorjamb; peeling white and gold, familiar, it anchored me. I took a few deep breaths.

"I understand," I heard myself tell him. "It won't happen again." I climbed the stairs to my room and read *Little House on the Prairie* for the tenth time, losing myself in that happy family, with Laura and Pa, who never talked about weight or diets or Soft Batch cookies.

I ate carrots and swam laps for a few days as a peace offering, but soon I was back to my sneaky ways. I thought I was in trouble again when my mother urgently knocked on my door one late afternoon.

She burst into my room while I was reading *Caddie Woodlawn* and eating a bag of nacho cheese chips, which I had swiped from the kitchen.

"Guess what, Sharon? Just guess what I'm going to do this summer?"

"Umm, let me think. Don't tell me." I thought that if I made her laugh I could get her out of my room before she noticed the chips. "You are going on a trip to Egypt."

"Egypt? What are you talking about?" She looked around the room in motherly disdain. "Sharon, your room is a pigsty." She started picking up clothes. I knew that she expected me to get up and help her, but I stayed where I was.

My mother picked up a bathing suit and hung it on my doorknob. "Sharon, this is still wet! It smells musty in here. You should leave your door open."

I didn't point out that my door was closed for a cheesy, delicious reason.

"I give up. Tell me where you're going."

"I'm going to fat camp!" she said with the excitement that a normal woman might use to say, *I'm going on a luxury cruise!* "Doesn't that sound like fun?"

"Fat camp? *And what,* I wondered, *could possibly be fun about it?* "What's fat camp?" *Whatever it was, it didn't sound good.* And what if it were a mother/daughter fat camp? I shuddered, picturing us eating celery sticks and Jazzercising every day, so we could win the trophy for best mother/daughter campers.

"Do I have to go?" I braced myself.

"No. You can't go. It's for adults only. I'm taking Nancy."

Nancy was my mother's sister and my favorite aunt, and the only person who let me eat anything that I wanted. I loved having sleepovers at her house on Saturday nights. She stocked her cabinet with "crap" and we ate bags of Cheetos and watched Cary Grant movies all night.

"Aunt Nancy?" I couldn't believe she'd want to go. Like my mother, Aunt Nancy was thin; but unlike my mother, she never obsessed about her weight. I loved this about her.

My mom began fussing with my clothes again. "Sharon, these clothes are clean! They're still folded. Why are they under this pile of dirty things? This room is disgusting!" As she opened my drawer to put my shorts away, she unearthed a pair of khaki shorts with purple embroidered flowers that I had "accidentally" pushed to the back. They were horribly wrinkled and still had the tags on. "Why don't you ever wear these? They're so cute."

"I'll wear them soon. Promise." If she saw me in those shorts, she would definitely find a fat camp for me. The shorts were a husky size 12, and I'd never worn them because they didn't snap or zip.

"Good." She smiled at me as she folded the shorts and put them back in my drawer. "I've noticed all the laps you've been swimming. As long as you keep up with your healthy eating, I think you can go down a whole size by the time school starts. Hopefully I'll get some new healthy recipes for us at camp." She smiled at me before she walked out the door. "Don't worry, honey, we'll get you out of that husky department yet. I promise I'll teach you everything I learn, and who knows! Maybe I'll even get your Dad on board!"

By the time Mom came back from fat camp, prettier than ever, I'd eaten my way through another size. Fresh from her triumph and full of new ideas for losing weight and keeping it off, Mom renewed her efforts on my behalf. But her resolve was equaled only by my considerable ability to manipulate her.

Her first move was to take me to see a doctor. When she first told me that I had an appointment with Dr. Greely, a pediatrician in Northern Kentucky, I was confused. I told her I didn't feel sick at all. She explained that I had to talk to her about going on a diet, and I instantly contracted an anti-talk-to-anyone-about-dieting flu, with symptoms ranging from severe embarrassment to an intense desire to run away from home and hide out among the Entenmann's snack cakes in Aunt Nancy's pantry. I *hated* to talk about my weight. Some people might think the worst thing about being a fat kid is getting teased. I'm here to say that it isn't. The worst thing about being a fat kid is being forced to listen to an adult's opinion of why you are fat, and then the brilliant solution of how to solve it. Teasing I could run away from; but there was no escape from the calm, rational discussions with grownups about my weight.

The day of my appointment I was so nervous that I had diarrhea. The diarrhea actually gave me a little bit of hope. If I could lose enough weight before my one o'clock appointment, then my mom would be happy with how I looked and we could cancel; then I remembered that pretzels were supposed to be easy on the stomach, so I wiped out half a bag with some Coke I found in the basement refrigerator.

I didn't know what a person wore to discuss dieting with a total stranger, so I decided to go for the sporty look. I chose plaid pants and a tennis shirt for the appointment, hoping it looked like I was dropping by right after my tennis game.

My mom drove me to the doctor's office, but I insisted that I go in by myself. My weight was a highly guarded secret, and having my mother next to me while I was weighing in was like my own personal version of hell. When I signed in, the receptionist asked me to fill out some papers. After writing down my name and address, I got to the line "Reason for your visit today." After much deliberation, I wrote, "I *might* need to lose some weight." I thought that summed it up without going into detail, and it didn't commit me to anything.

When the doctor came into the room, I was surprised. I realized that I had been picturing diet doctors from Hollywood, someone beautiful and extremely fit. She would take me under her wing and gently talk me through the dangers of food while gossiping about the love lives of our favorite stars. Instead, I got Dr. Greely.

Dr. Greely wasn't fit. She was fat. As if that weren't enough, the poor woman had a huge purple birthmark that covered half of her face.

"So," she consulted my chart. "Sharon. You *might* need to lose weight. Why don't you hop up on the scale and let me be the judge of that?"

Everyone in my life thought they were the judges of my weight loss. I didn't need another judge, especially when I knew what her verdict was going to be. Too fat. I heard it all the time and I was sick of it. Still, I did as I was told and "hopped" onto the scale.

The scale confirmed what we both already knew. As I climbed back onto the papered exam table, I came up with a brilliant and glamorous solution to my weight problem. "You know, Dr. Greely, when Judy Garland was filming *The Wizard of Oz,* she was prescribed diet pills by her doctor to keep her weight down. You could give me diet pills."

I pictured myself taking a pretty red pill every day in my kitchen with my orange juice. I imagined my mother smiling as she waved goodbye to the new, thin, popular me as I left for school.

"Is that why you're here? For diet pills?" Dr. Greely reached her hand into the top drawer of a cabinet, presumably to get her prescription pad. This was so easy! I was so smart, so medically brilliant, that I momentarily considered a career as a doctor. But instead of a prescription pad, she pulled out a chart of the food pyramid.

"I don't prescribe diet pills to little girls who just need to learn to eat less." She handed me the chart. "Tell me which of these foods you like the most."

Naturally, I preferred the minuscule "sweets and fats" corner, but I knew that answer wouldn't fly. I pointed to the larger fruits and vegetables corner instead. "This one. I just love fruits and vegetables!"

"Hmm. Are you telling me that your favorite foods are fruits and vegetables?" She peered at me over her glasses.

"Oh yes. I love fruits and vegetables." I tried not to stare at her purple birthmark. "The problem is, I eat so many salads, that I tend to bloat."

"*Mmmhmm.* That's what all this weight is? Too many salads?"

I nodded and almost told her that I also grew my own fruits and vegetables, but her look stopped me cold.

"This is going to be a total waste of time if you are going to just sit there and lie to me. Your mother asked me to help you because she doesn't know what to do. She's worried about you. Is that what you want? To have your mother worry about you because you can't stop eating?"

I looked at the floor so I didn't have to see her purple face. Suddenly my tennis outfit seemed like a bad idea. I could feel my fat spilling over the waistband of my plaid pants and I felt hideous. Like a joke. And before I could stop them, the words came out:

"The kids at school tease me."

"Kids are mean."

I thought about her birthmark and realized that Dr. Greely must have been teased too. I started to feel a kinship with her. From now on, it would be birthmarked Dr. Greely and fat me against the world. We would take on those mean kids, one by one.

"They are so mean! There is this one kid in my class and he follows me through all of recess *mooing.* For twenty whole minutes, he *moos* at me. One day he got six other boys to do it too! And then this one time, in gym class. . . . " I let it pour out of me. In that moment, I loved Dr. Greely. I wanted to be her favorite patient. I wanted to come back every week and give her updates.

"Hey, hey, hey," she said, raising a hand to stop me. I realized I had talked too much and hadn't given her a turn. I waited for her to share a terrible story about her childhood.

"So, do you like dessert?"

"Oh, yes!" I replied.

"Do you like ice cream?" Oh. This was going to be a lunchroom story. I knew from experience how bad the teasing could be during lunch. Maybe they had thrown ice cream on her.

"Very much," I said.

"When you get ice cream out of the container, do you put some in the bowl and then stand in the kitchen and eat it right out of the container until it's gone?"

I was caught off guard by the question, so I answered it honestly. "No, I don't usually eat it until it is gone. I leave a little because I don't want to get in trouble for finishing it." Suddenly I realized that Dr. Greely didn't want to share teasing stories with me. My heart started to race. She'd tricked me into talking about food, and I didn't want to talk about that. Ever.

She snapped my chart closed and took off her glasses. I could see her whole birthmark. It was slightly raised from the rest of her face.

"That's the problem," she said. "That's why you are getting so fat. Stick to eating what you put on your plate, and eat things according to the food pyramid. Try to exercise instead of watching TV. That should take care of it. Make an appointment with the receptionist and I'll weigh you again in a month to see how you're doing." Then she shook my hand. "Nice meeting you, Sharon. Good luck." And she walked out.

I sat on the papered table for a long time after she left. I had gotten what I deserved. I was a fat kid, and the only thing that people wanted to talk to fat kids about was how to lose weight. The only antidote to teasing at recess was less ice cream, more exercise.

I walked out to find my mom sunning herself in the car. She was so thin and pretty, and I wanted to curl up next to her and tell her everything. About how the boys *mooed* at me and about how worried I was that maybe I really was a cow because I couldn't seem to stop eating.

"So," she said, "how'd it go?"

I wanted to tell her that I hated Dr. Greely and her big, scary purple scar. I wanted to tell her that I was sorry that I wasn't skinny like her and that I thought she was so beautiful. But I didn't. Instead, I stayed on my side of the seat and told her about the food pyramid and the exercise.

"We'll go to the grocery store on the way home and pick up some good food for your new diet." She smiled at me. "Have you ever tried spaghetti squash?" There was no way I was going to live on spaghetti squash.

Let me clarify something: Being an overweight kid is very different from being an overweight adult. To get fat as an adult, basically you need to have money and a car, and you are free to do and eat whatever you want. To get fat as a kid, however, you have to manipulate an adult with money and a car to get the food you want. My dad had little idea of what was healthful and what wasn't, so he was easy to trick. But my mother, the dieting champion, was much more difficult. I had to have on my game face at all times, and I became a master manipulator.

Getting the food I wanted meant winning at a game I thought of as "How to Get It Anyway." To play this game with my mother, who herself is a master game player, I had to be in tip-top form, fully prepared to pull out my bag of tricks at a moment's notice. One of the best places to play this game was at the Stale Store—a heavenly little shop that served as the final resting place for the expired Hostess products of the world. Bins and bins of bread, Twinkies, Suzy Q's, Sno Balls, Crumb Cakes, Ho Hos, and hot dog rolls all ready for the taking—buy one, get one free. Since my mother loved a good sale, we spent a lot of time at the Stale Store, which was just fine with me. I couldn't imagine a better way to spend a hot, end-of-summer afternoon than rooting through bins of cupcakes and fruit pies. As we pulled down the steep driveway, my mother did her best to put a stop to my game before I started it. "*No treats today.* I mean it."

"I wasn't even going to ask! Jeez, Mom."

As we pulled to a stop in the parking lot, I resisted the temptation to sprint into the store. Instead, I tried a new, risky move by staying put, seatbelt on, eyes downcast. If I played it just right, I might be able to get results. Mom got out of the car and was halfway in before she noticed I wasn't with her.

"I'm not going in," I announced.

She looked surprised. I never, ever stayed in the car. I went everywhere with her—it was my sister Susan who usually brought a book and stayed in the car.

"What's the matter with you?"

"I don't always want a treat, you know. Sometimes I just want to be with you." I wished that I meant this a little more, but the truth was, my brain was screaming *Treat! Treat!*

"Oh, Sharon, why don't you come in with me and we'll both get a little something for the ride home."

"Okay, if you want." In my mind I ran through fields of chocolate cupcakes with squiggly white piping.

Once inside, a crucial decision determined the scope of our shopping experience. Basket or shopping cart? In my head I chanted, *Shopping cart, shopping cart, shopping cart.*

"Sharon, grab a cart. It looks like they just got a shipment." My wish was granted.

My mother was a Hostess expert, trained by her father who had driven a Hostess truck throughout much of her childhood. Other shoppers, novices, might settle for any old loaf of bread, but not Mom. I stood back and watched as she rooted through the bins, explaining, "They always put the freshest bread in the back so they can sell the older stuff first." She unearthed four loaves and placed them in the cart with an air of triumph. "These don't even expire until tomorrow."

When she moved on to the dinner rolls, I saw my chance and wandered over to the snack cake aisle. Once there, I inhaled deeply. Even through the boxes and the cellophane wrappers, the snack cake aisle had a distinct, sugary, cakey, plasticy smell—the Hostess equivalent of Grandma's cookies fresh from the oven.

The Stale Store always had oodles of Twinkies in stock, and Suzy Q's were in good supply as well. Ho Hos and Ding Dongs were plentiful, but the Holy Grail of the Stale Store was undoubtedly the chocolate cupcakes. They were a rare find, indeed. This popular offering didn't need a twofer sale at the Stale Store, not when it could sell out full-price at the grocery store right up the street. Sure, I enjoyed a Ho Ho or a Ding Dong as much as the next girl (the crunch of the Ho Ho icing had a certain appeal), but if I could eat one thing every day for the rest of my life, it would be the Hostess CupCake. With its sticky, gooey, white cream filling and delectable chocolate frosting that was so waxy you could peel it off—if you wanted to—and eat it first, the chocolate cupcake had a special place in my heart. When I was alone, I peeled off half the frosting, just to the white squiggle, and ate it, saving the other half as the finale. Sometimes I broke the cupcake in half like an Oreo and licked out the creamy center. But if anyone was around, I just ate it like a normal person, so I didn't draw any attention to the fact that I was eating something fattening.

I had to search quickly because my mother would never, never indulge a hunt for my cupcakes. She'd grab two boxes of Twinkies (yuck!) and quickly wheel away, as if she didn't like to be spotted among so many calories.

In the center of the aisle, an employee was unpacking a shipment box that had CUPCAKES stamped on the side. My pulse quickened. I had hit the mother lode; then I hesitated. Asking for a box from an adult was different from picking one up off the shelf, because it invited them to comment on whether I should have the treat or not. I didn't like the "hot lunch" line at school for the same reason: I was afraid the woman serving up the fries would comment on my weight. Taking a second helping of mashed potatoes at dinner was also risky business. If I did it while my mom was out of the room, I could get away with it. But if she caught me, she would move the zucchini bowl closer. "Why don't you take some vegetables instead?"

I appraised the woman in the blue polyester apron unpacking the boxes of cupcakes, trying to work up the nerve to reach past her and take one for myself. Her red stretch pants were tight, accentuating a very large and lumpy butt. I knew Mom would say, "Those pants are terrible. No one over 100 pounds should ever set foot out of the house in them." I decided that I was probably okay asking for a box of cupcakes (or two or three) from a woman with a lumpy butt. I walked over to her: "Excuse me? Could I have a box of chocolate cupcakes?"

"Sure. Here you go. We just got these in. They'll be gone by the time we close. How many do you want?"

I pondered. How many could I get away with? If I told my mom that they were part of a new shipment, she might buy a lot of them because they were fresh, and she would definitely like the fact that they were hard to find. It was risky, but I made an impulsive decision. "I'll take six boxes."

"That's smart. I got myself a few boxes in the back. I get first dibs on the shipments."

As she handed me the boxes, I noticed her nametag: *Kathy, Asst. Manager.*

She saw me looking. "I just got promoted."

I walked away thinking about Kathy and her cupcakes. I pictured her sitting at a TV tray watching *Jeopardy!* and eating cupcakes, one right after another. I wondered what it would be like to be an adult, to eat as much food as I wanted, anytime I wanted. The idea both excited and worried me. I had just heard a story about a woman who was so fat that they had to use a crane to get her out of her house when she died. As I carried the six boxes to my mother's cart, I vowed that no matter what, I would never work at the Stale Store.

My mother was not impressed with my find. "I am *not* buying six boxes of cupcakes. I don't care how fresh they are! Put them back." She said this a little too loud.

I was embarrassed but not willing to give up. "Why do I have to put them all back? I thought that we were here to get stuff for lunches."

"You may keep one box. You're not going to have one at your lunch every day, Sharon. They're fattening." *As if I didn't know that*, I thought. "Otherwise I will give you a choice of fruit as your dessert." *Which will go straight into the trash*, I answered in my head.

"They're buy one, get one free. It seems silly to just get one. Right? I mean, then why even come here?"

"All right. You can get two. I'll give them to your brother and sister too." With this comment, my unsuspecting mother had opened the door wide for more snack cake purchases.

"But Buzzy likes Suzy Q's. Do you want me to get some?"

"Go get two boxes of Suzy Q's, but that's *it*. I mean it."

"You got it. I'll be right back." I skipped off to exchange the goods. Suzy Q's weren't my favorite, but at least they were big. I had one more trick up my sleeve. On my way back to the register, I picked up an individual cherry fruit pie and a two-pack of crumb cakes. I loaded everything onto the belt by the register, beaming up at my mom.

My mom didn't notice my additions until they had been rung up. "What is that? I am not getting you a fruit pie and a crumb cake. Put it back. You are really pushing me today, Sharon."

I feigned surprise. "What do you mean? *You* are the one who said that we could both have a little treat for the car. I got your favorite. A crumb cake."

"That was before we got four other boxes of crap." She looked at the cashier. "Have you already rung it up?" The cashier nodded.

"Okay. Let's just go."

I bagged everything, strategically placing the crumb cake and fruit pie close to the top. I had them out and unwrapped before we even pulled out of the parking lot, but my mom's mood had turned sour. When I offered her a crumb cake, she waved it away. "Oh, the whole thing is too much. Just break off a little piece and put the rest in the bag."

I knew my mom's pinch-and-eat technique. She pinched away at things, never taking them out of the wrapper, until they were gone. I hated it. I tried to ignore her and started in on my cherry pie. It was a little runny and I had on a white shirt, so I held the wrapper under my chin to catch the drips.

My mother glanced over at me. "You are *not* going to eat that entire thing. It's big enough for a family of four. Eat a few bites and put it back in the wrapper."

I rolled my eyes and did as I was told. I decided that I would sneak it up to my room and eat it by myself. It would taste better if I wasn't being *watched*. I sighed loudly.

"Hey! Don't give me that attitude. You're the one who hates the clothes in the husky department. If you want cute clothes like your friends have, you have to cut out the junk."

Junk was a general word that my mother used to describe any food that wasn't a fruit or vegetable. Candy? Junk! Pizza? Junk! Spaghetti-Os? Junk! I was sick of it. Everything I liked, she considered crap. I was silent for the rest of the ride home and then raced up to my room and slammed the door. I had hidden the pie under my shirt when I made the dash for my room, and now I pulled it out. I turned on *Annie* as loud as I could and ate every last bite of my cherry pie as I commiserated with Annie's hard-knock life.

I managed to forget about the chocolate cupcakes for most of the afternoon. But as the evening turned to night, I battled between the logical side of me who did not want to weary husky clothes anymore, and the hungry, sneaky side of me who wanted that cupcake.

The good side told me to go into the bathroom, have a Dixie Cup full of water, and brush my teeth. The bad side told me to find those cupcakes. I decided to sneak downstairs. My brother, Buzzy, was a first-class sneak, and he had shown me how to get all around the house without being heard. We lived in a creaky, old house, and it took me awhile to memorize which stairs and floorboards squeaked, but by now I had it down in every room. To steal money from my father's dresser for extra treats at school lunch, I had to walk along the right edge of their bedroom floor early in the morning, avoiding the middle, squeaky, floorboards that would wake him up. If I stuck close to the edge, it was possible to get to his dresser, slide the change silently off, and get back out with enough pocket change for an ice-cream sandwich. Buzzy was so good he could sneak Dad's wallet out of his pants as they hung on the end of the bed and swipe actual dollar bills.

Unfortunately, Buzzy wasn't a food sneak, so he was no help in the kitchen. Over time, I mastered the kitchen on my own, studying which cabinets squeaked, how to silently remove a spoon, and (the hardest and my personal favorite) how to silently open a Doritos bag (do it slowly). Before heading to the kitchen, I had to do a parent check, which involved crawling quickly to the door of the garden room and peeking in. My mom and dad were watching their favorite Wednesday night show, and Mom was knitting, so I was probably safe.

I searched the cabinets, turning up nothing except for a bag of ruffled potato chips that were hidden in a stockpot. I took a few and moved on. Chips were a good find, but that night I wanted cupcakes. I pulled out a stool and started rooting around on top of the refrigerator when the garage door opened. Terrified, I stopped midair, racking my brain for an excuse. Buzzy walked in and greeted me with a lopsided smile. "Hey. What are you doing?"

"I'm looking for the stuff we got at the Stale Store today. Have you seen it?"

Buzzy got out a glass and poured himself some milk.

"Who's in the kitchen?" my dad yelled from the garden room.

I crouched on the stairs while Buzzy yelled back, "It's me. I'm getting a glass of milk. Do you want anything?"

Dad declined, but reminded Buzzy to wash out his glass. Buzzy drank his milk and put his glass in the sink without rinsing it out. "Mom put everything in the freezer in the garage. She told me not to tell you."

"Thanks. If I eat a cupcake, will you cover for me? She won't care if she thinks it's you."

"Yeah, okay. But make it a Suzy Q. I don't like the cupcakes that much."

Even though my brother clearly had no taste, I was grateful for his help. As I made my way to the garage, he stopped me.

"Hey. Mom took the phone out of my room when she grounded me. Do you know where it is? I need to make a call."

I did know. I'd seen it earlier today. "It's under the sink in Mom and Dad's bathroom."

"Thanks, Sis." And then we were off, sneaking in opposite directions.

The garage was cool and echoey. I discovered the Stale Store boxes hidden behind stacks of frozen chicken and steak. I opened the box of Suzy Q's, took one out, ripped it open, and looked for a place to sit down. There was a potato chip can from a Super Bowl party, and I pulled it up next to the freezer, opened it to see if there were any chips left (there weren't), put the lid back on, and sat down. Usually, when I ate a Suzy Q, I first pried it open so I could lick out the cream center, but this one was frozen solid.

I was licking the crumbs from the wrapper and contemplating how to eat the frozen treat when the door to the house flew open.

My dad's head popped into the garage. "Anybody in here?"

I froze. There was nowhere to go. Then, as fast as he had appeared, he disappeared, turned off the light in the garage, and shut the door, leaving me in total darkness.

I heard him yell up to Buzzy, "Buzz, did you leave the light on in the garage?" There was a pause while my brother answered. "Well, get down here and wash out this milk glass!"

My brother came into the kitchen, and I could hear him arguing with my father. While they fought, I worked my way through two Suzy Q's. Knowing that I shouldn't, I opened the cupcake box and dug in. I sat on that potato chip can for a long time, eating frozen cupcakes and waiting for my dad and Buzzy to leave the kitchen.

Over the next couple of weeks, I snuck down to the freezer in the garage every day, and then twice or three times a day. I had perfected a ten-second microwave-thaw technique that allowed me to eat a Suzy Q without breaking my teeth, and by the time school started, I had cleaned out every box in that freezer. I had also eaten all of the potato chips out of the stockpot. I had even eaten the dusty crumbs out of the potato chip can in the garage.

When my parents discovered it, my mother cried and my father screamed at me and sent me to my room. I was so ashamed of myself, but no matter what my parents said to me, I knew in my heart that nothing would change. I was doomed to be a fat grownup. I would never, ever, be able to stop eating. In fact, I'd just grow fatter once I had my own money and a car. I would get a job at the Stale Store, get promoted to assistant manager, and have a bunch of cats that would eat the few crumbs that dropped to the floor. Eventually, I would die alone, too fat to leave the house. My body would have to be lifted out by a crane, and the people who teased me would tell their skinny kids, "I knew her once. She was a really great singer. I remember how she got every solo in the school concerts. We all thought she'd grow up to be really famous. Problem was, she just couldn't stop eating."

chapter 4
dreamgirls

For me, Anderson was more prison than school—a jail custom-made to torture me for my cupcake-eating crimes.

If the teasing was bad in elementary school, it reached a fever pitch in middle school. Anderson Middle School collected kids from five different grade schools; it was huge and intimidating. The doors closed behind you as soon as class began, every class began with rules and threats, and a piercing bell told us when to change classes, eat lunch, and go home. For me, Anderson was more prison than school—a jail custom-made to torture me for my cupcake-eating crimes.

On the first day of school, I looked around my homeroom and realized I hardly knew anyone; then I spotted Jodi. She was one half of a set of antagonistic twins I knew from grade school. I'd gone to the twins' birthday slumber party in fourth grade. At the party we played a game where everyone wrote down what they really thought of each person there, and then, of course, we read them out loud. My sheet, decorated in twelve different little girl scripts, told me that I was fat but nice. I ended up crying in the bathroom. The twins told their mom that I was sick, and

I ended up going home before the first bowl of popcorn was popped. I hadn't spoken to either of them since. But now, on the first day at Anderson Prison, Jodi was the only person in homeroom I recognized.

I walked over to her desk, where she was putting animal erasers on top of her pencils, a flamingo, a gorilla, and a parrot. She ignored me until I said, "Hi, Jodi. I like your erasers. They're cute." Jodi took the flamingo eraser off and put it on, off and then on. She said a brisk hi, hardly glancing up at me.

Still, it felt good to be talking to someone I knew. "So, how was your summer?" I asked.

The girl sitting at the desk next to her looked over and said, "Hey. Who's your friend?" I noticed that she had the same animal erasers Jodi had. They were also both wearing lip-gloss. I made a mental note: *Get lip-gloss. Tonight.* Jodi looked over at the girl and said, "She's not my friend."

I stood there for a minute, looking at the brick-colored floor, trying to think of what to do next and waiting for someone to speak. No one did. Eventually I sat back down at my desk and waited for the bell to ring, reminding myself over and over that it would be a really bad idea to cry on the first day of school.

By lunchtime I was desperate for a friendly face. I spotted Madison Pepper paying for her lunch, and I rushed over. She'd spent the summer in Hollywood with her dad, and I'd missed her. I'd mailed her tons of letters, but I hadn't heard from her once.

In typical Madison fashion, she was perfectly dressed and it looked like she hadn't thought about it at all. She'd just rolled out of bed and put on her jeans and T-shirt like it was any other day. Standing there in my new jeans, new shirt, and new shoes, everything so new, new, new, I suddenly felt ridiculous. My outfit screamed *trying too hard.*

"Hey—you look great," I told her. "I'm so glad to see you! I tried to call you last night, but your line was busy. I was so nervous about starting classes today."

"It's just *school*." She put her change away and picked up her tray. "Do you have your lunch?"

I held up my brown paper bag, full of lunch, minus anything Hostess.

"Where do you want to sit?" she asked.

Someone yelled Madison's name. We looked around and spotted Robby Coy, who was waving his arms wildly from the corner.

"Yo, Hollywood. Sit over here!" Robby was at a table with a bunch of his friends, which included every cute boy in the sixth grade. As Madison approached the table, they catcalled and whistled.

"Look, it's Coy's girlfriend!" I heard one of them say.

"In his dreams." Madison snorted and turned to me. "Come on."

I followed right on her heels. All the guys moved down one space to make room for Madison in the center of the table—right next to Robby. Madison sat down and I looked up and down the table for a seat. I finally spotted one at the far end of the table, about eight seats from her, next to a cute and funny kid named Kevin Smits. His dad owned the dry cleaner my parents used and I'd seen him there, working behind the counter.

As I started toward the empty chair, a boy I didn't know yelled, "Boom! Boom! Boom!" shaking his chair from side to side. At first I didn't get it. He glanced around like he was terrified and didn't know what was happening. When I started walking again, he started up again, even louder. "*Boom, boom, boom!*" Then he yelled, "Oh my God! It's an *earthquake*! Everybody hold on!" He grabbed onto Kevin Smits's shirt like he was clinging for his life.

I couldn't figure out what was happening, but I had a feeling it had to do with me. All the boys cracked up.

As I got closer to Kevin Smits, he started shaking his chair, too. Kevin looked up at me, his eyes wild, and said, "Jesus, woman! Stop walking! You're causing an earthquake in here!"

The boys broke out in peals of hysterical laughter. I stood like a statue, not daring to move, not daring to cry. In my mind, I felt as if I'd been sucked out of the room, as if someone had opened the door on an airplane 30,000 feet in the air. As I looked around the cafeteria, I saw everything as if from a great distance, and in slow motion—the boys laughing, and Madison calling them assholes, but smiling like she thought it was kind of funny.

The cafeteria monitor, Mr. Penwell, came over and told the boys to quiet down or they would get detention. He told me to take a seat. I wondered if the boys would still *boom* with him standing there, but they didn't. I took a step toward the empty seat. Quick as a flash, Kevin Smits threw his backpack on the chair and said, "Sorry. This seat is saved." Laughter traveled up and down the table.

I knew what he was doing, I knew it wasn't saved, but I didn't know what to say. I looked to Madison. She was always the smart one at times like this, always jumping in with a clever comeback that would put everyone at ease. But she was deep in conversation with Robby and oblivious to my struggle. I was on my own. I tried joking with Kevin.

"Very funny. That's not really saved, right?" I smiled. "Can I sit down?"

Kevin looked at me with puppy dog eyes. "Sorry, it's saved for people who weigh less than 800 pounds. You'll have to look for a different chair."

I walked away, pretending not to notice the chorus of *booms* and the laughter that followed me. I found an empty chair at a remote table in the lunchroom, next to a pasty-white girl named Marla Twine I knew from the bus. Madison and I called her Casper the Friendly Ghost because she was so pale. When I sat down she smiled and tried to talk to me, but I completely ignored her and choked down my lunch in silence.

Later that night, I called Madison. "Hey."

"Hey. I'm on the other line with Robby. Can I call you back?"

"Yeah, sure." I twisted the phone cord around my finger. "I just wanted to talk about what happened at lunch."

"What do you mean?"

"Madison! Those guys were so mean. I ended up sitting next to Casper."

"Sharon, they were just kidding. You are way too sensitive; you have to learn to laugh about it. That's how those guys are. They didn't mean anything by it. I swear. Look, I've gotta go. I'll call you back."

Madison always said that she would call me back, but she never did. I thought about what she said. Was I too sensitive? Were they just kidding? I was certain Madison was right. There was a right way to handle it, but I didn't have a clue what it was. I vowed to try harder.

I eventually found a lunchroom seat at the end of a long table of girls—the most popular girls in the sixth grade. They were the girls Madison would probably sit with if she weren't sitting with Robby, so I figured if I waited long enough she would come back. These girls were important—and even though I only had a fringe position at the table, I was happy to be there. I knew they allowed me to sit there because I was friends with Madison.

There was one girl at the table, Angela, who utterly fascinated me. She was clearly overweight, almost as big as I was; but for some reason her size was universally ignored. She never got teased. I watched her every move. I figured if I watched long enough, I would understand how she got away with it. I cataloged all of the little differences between us. She was slightly thinner than me, and that difference allowed her to barely squeeze into regular-sized clothes. This instantly made her look more like everyone else, only slightly larger. And she actually seemed to compensate for her difference by making everything larger. For starters, she dyed her big hair bright blond, so she stood out. She also had big, straight, white teeth, so when she smiled, it was like watching a toothpaste commercial. Her voice was big too, echoing throughout the lunchroom.

But the biggest difference between us was that most of her extra weight settled on her chest, giving her the biggest knockers in the sixth grade. That, I decided, was why she got to sit in the middle of the lunch table while I was relegated to the end. I briefly considered stuffing my newly purchased bra and dying my hair blond, but I just couldn't bring myself to do it. Instead, I tried to survive sixth grade as the fat girl who wanted to be liked.

Meanwhile, the teasing never stopped. One day our science teacher, Mrs. Smithwick, wrote a list of vocabulary words on the board and told us to look up the definitions and use them in a sentence for our homework that night. When we came back to class the next day, Mrs. Smithwick selected volunteers to read the sentences out loud to the class. One of the boys, a spunky, popular kid named Tony Conner, waved his hand wildly when we got to the word *heifer*.

He was very serious as he read from his notebook, "Heifer. H-e-i-f-e-r. The definition of heifer is a young cow. My sentence is 'Sharon Wheatley is a heifer.'" There was a short silence in the classroom before loud laughter erupted.

It felt like someone had snuck up behind me and slammed a frying pan into my head, just like in the cartoons. If I had been a cartoon, little animated birds would've been circling my head as the class roared with laughter. I watched Mrs. Smithwick, a timid woman, and wondered what she would do. She turned to the chalkboard and did some frantic erasing as she waited for the laughter to die down. It was very rare that a teacher actually heard teasing, as it was usually whispered, passed in a note, or saved for an unsupervised time like at recess or on the bus. I held my breath, not sure what I wanted more—for her to punish him or ignore him. After Mrs. Smithwick finished her very thorough erasing, she simply turned around and called for the next word as if nothing had happened.

Such was my life at Anderson Middle School.

With no support from faculty, I tried to join in the fun, as Madison had advised. When Tony Conner hatched a plan to throw unpopped popcorn around Mrs. Smithwick's room during class, I brought in a big bottle of Orville Redenbacher's kernels, and passed them out to the whole class. It was fun tossing those popcorn kernels with everyone else in class, hearing them *ping* on the linoleum floor and metal desks. When I handed Tony his popcorn kernels, he said, "You're cool, Wheatley."

I smiled to myself. Madison was right. I was learning to play the game.

When a popular boy named Chris Frost started calling me Whale, I shrugged it off, even as the name caught on and spread like wildfire through the sixth grade student body. I realized that if I didn't cry, and instead laughed along with them, they treated me like a friend. I never answered to it, but I got used to it.

At the end of the year, Chris asked me if he could sign my yearbook. Here is what he wrote:

Sharon,

To a girl who hated my guts in the first half of the year. Now that we're pretty good friends, that's all that counts!

Luv ya, Chris.

On the page he had signed, and on all the blank pages after that, Chris drew whales, big whales and little whales, as if it were a sign of affection. My own personal icon. But soon, being on the fringe of popularity wasn't good enough. I wanted more. And I vowed to get it.

In my new quest for popularity, I examined the various cliques at the school. I soon realized that the silver bullet that would propel me to instant popularity was being a cheerleader. I would become a cheerleader.

The six newest squad members had catapulted directly out of obscurity and into unqualified popularity. I, too, could harness the power of the pompom—and transform myself just as these girls had done. Meanwhile, I carved out a position for myself as the person who did favors for the more popular girls. "Sharon? Would you mind giving this note to Jeff for me?" *No problem!* "Sharon? Would you get me an ice-cream sandwich?" *Yes, of course I will.* Anything to keep my place at the table until I became a cheerleader myself.

Throughout the seventh grade, I concentrated on my goal. I went to every game, I learned every cheer, and I scored a pair of saddle shoes and wore them every day. I practiced jumps, cartwheels, and splits in front of a mirror in my parents' room every night. On really good weekends, I convinced Madison to spend the night so she could teach me cheers and critique me, which she did grudgingly. She was the reigning captain of the squad, so I figured there was no better person to get direction from than my future captain. She sat patiently on my parents' bed and watched as I rehearsed again and again.

"I don't get it, Wheatley," Madison said. "Why is this so important to you? It's just jumping around in a stupid skirt."

Since the first grade I'd watched Madison get everything she'd ever wanted. Boys, popularity, cute clothes, good grades, art shows, select soccer team, student council president, captain of the basketball team, captain of the cheerleaders—she got it all. If I got even *one* of those things, I might have a fighting chance at being treated like a normal person.

I wanted to scream at her, "Of course you don't understand! You have it all! Did you ever, for even *one second* think about how easy you've got it?" But I didn't say a word. Madison Pepper was my lifeline to friends in this school, and it was risky to fight with her. "Yeah. Cheerleading is kind of drippy," I lied, "but it's really important to my mom. She's pushing me really hard." As the tryouts for the eighth-grade squad approached, I felt ready. Madison had taught me every jump, coached me on my tumbling, and critiqued the cheer I'd composed myself, which was required for the tryout. The energy on tryout day was at fever pitch. Even though the tryouts weren't until after school, we all showed up for school that day adorned with our best "cheerleader hair," which included various braids and ponytails, tied up in black and orange ribbons.

At lunch as Madison wolfed down her sandwich, I confided to her how nervous I was. I watched her eat, wondering what it must feel like to be so calm. I hadn't eaten in two days.

"I think everyone in this school has gone insane." Madison rolled her eyes and sighed heavily, in a way that implied the entire subject of cheerleading bored her to death. "It's really no big deal."

"That's easy for you to say; you're a shoo-in. Do you even have to try out?"

"Yeah, I have to try out, but I'm not going to. I don't want to be a cheerleader next year." She ignored my shocked expression and continued. "I don't want to be a cheerleader anymore. It's stupid. We only get to go to some of the away games and when we do, we have to go on a separate bus from the guys. Hey. I'll be right back, okay?"

With a toss of her perfect hair, she got up and joined the guys at the next table, leaving me alone with my nervous stomach and sweaty palms.

By the three o'clock dismissal bell, the entire school was buzzing. We all raced to the locker rooms to change clothes. I wore a new pleated "skort," a white T-shirt, and a light pullover sweater that my mom said made my eyes look really blue. She'd also French-braided and lacquered my hair with enough hairspray to make the braids last until I was ninety-seven. I was ready.

First, Miss Renner, the cheerleading coach, taught us a cheer to perform for the judges. They always did this cheer at the home games, so I already knew every word of it. I was going to be great.

They lined us up for tryouts in alphabetical order, which meant I had to sweat it out for hours until they got to the Ws. I tried to study for my science test the next day, but it was impossible to keep the laws of gravity straight when I was so focused on the more unforgiving laws of popularity.

When it was finally my turn, I ran into the gym and did a one-armed round-off on my way to the judges' table, deciding that a little enthusiasm was a great way to start. Behind a folding table in the center of the room sat every member of the current eighth-grade squad, clad in their uniforms and looking pretty and very official, pens and pads at the ready. I wished I were singing instead of cheering. I took a deep breath and got started.

"Ready? Okay," I yelled as loud as I humanly could.

Madison had told me that the thing that I had over everyone else in my school was a really big voice. "All that a cheerleader needs to be is loud. That is the entire point of you being there, to get the crowd worked up. With your voice, you're going to get everyone within a ten-mile radius to cheer at the game. Scream your guts out!"

As I belted out the cheer, I felt myself transformed. I could feel the soft turf of the football field beneath my saddle shoes, smell the bite of the autumn air, and feel those pompoms in my hands. As I came into the last lines of the cheer, I knew that the elusive black sweater with the big orange *A*—the calling card to my new life—was within my grasp.

The judges gave me an enthusiastic "That was great, Sharon," and I flashed them my best smile before prancing to the exit. Maybe they would let me replace Madison as the captain. And then Madison would realize she had made a huge mistake and would beg me to take her back. As the captain, I would pull strings to get her back on the squad. She was my friend. It was the least that I could do.

My mom was waiting for me in the parking lot. "How did it go?"

"I'm pretty sure that you are looking at an eighth-grade cheerleader!"

My mom beamed at me. She had been listening to me practice for the past six months. She knew how badly I wanted this, even if she didn't entirely understand why. She didn't understand that it wasn't about becoming a cheerleader. It was about leaving the heifer behind.

Once we got home, I began the long and torturous wait for *the call*. As soon as I walked through the door of the house, the first question out of my mouth was "Has anyone called for me?" I knew that there were still tryouts going on, but I wanted to make sure that I had not missed a thing.

I sat by my Snoopy phone for hours. I willed it to ring. At least a dozen times, I picked up the receiver to make sure that it was working, and every time I heard the dial tone I was both relieved and distraught. I rushed through dinner and then locked myself away in my room to attempt to study for my science test.

Finally, the Snoopy phone rang. I heard a perky, singsong voice.

"Sharon? This is Theresa Nobel, the captain of the eighth-grade cheerleaders."

She didn't need to tell me—I knew exactly who she was. Not only was Theresa the captain of the cheerleaders, but she also had the best hair in the entire school. It was naturally light blond, the color movie stars spend hundreds of dollars to achieve. It hung down her back like a thick, shimmering curtain, the envy of every girl who sat behind her in class. My stomach did flip-flops, and my hopes began to rise. Maybe Madison was wrong.

"About your tryout today. You did a really great job. In fact, a lot of us thought that you were the best person we saw all day."

For a moment, my hopes lifted. I had visions of Theresa helping me with my hair and makeup before a game.

"Thanks, Theresa." Despite my inner panic, I sounded remarkably calm. "I practiced a lot."

"Yeah. We could tell, and that's really great. The thing is, Sharon, we can't make you a cheerleader."

I opened my mouth to say something, but nothing came out. I tried again.

"Why?" I managed to croak.

"Well, see, cheerleaders have to look a certain way. I'm sure you understand. And if I'm being totally honest, and Madison said that I should be, we don't have a uniform that would fit you. I'm really sorry. Be sure to come to the games, though, okay? Bye!" And she hung up.

I was still a heifer, and nothing I did, no matter how well I did it, was going to change that. My dreams of football games followed by large group outings to Pizza Hut were dashed. My dreams of boy/girl parties, three minutes in the closet, spin the bottle—dashed. I was stuck being a person I hated forever. All my energy drained out and I lay face down on my bed. A few minutes later, Snoopy rang. I ignored it, and soon I heard a knock on my door.

"Hey." It was my brother Buzzy. "Madison is on the phone."

"I don't want to talk to her." I thought about that for a second and caught my brother as he was walking back to his room. "Tell her I'm in the shower." He nodded. I'd never turned down a phone call from Madison before. She called me so rarely that I usually did a backflip on my way to the phone. Tonight I couldn't face her and all her popularity; it was just too much to bear. I'd never be Madison Pepper, ever, no matter how hard I tried, and talking to her made me feel terrible. I didn't want to annoy her, but I didn't want to be her friend anymore, either.

That said, I knew Madison was right—this cheerleading thing was stupid. But I wanted it. I wanted to be the stuck-up one, the popular one, the pretty one. I wanted my Snoopy phone to ring too much. I wanted everyone to sign my yearbook until all the empty pages were gone and they had to sign over photographs, squeezing words into the margins. I wanted to go to the movies with Glen Fox or Kevin Smits and wear lip-gloss and wonder if they were going to kiss it off. I wanted it, right or wrong, crazy or sane—I wanted it desperately.

I stayed in my room for a long time. Late that night when everyone was in bed, I went downstairs to the kitchen where I collected four things. A jar of peanut butter, a full-size bag of Nestlé Toll House Chocolate Chips, a spoon, and a garbage bag. I walked back up to my room, locked the door, and ate spoonfuls of peanut butter dipped in chocolate chips.

While I ate, I collected every single cheerleading item in my room and threw them in the garbage bag. Pompoms, skort, blue sweater, saddle shoes, Madison's wallet-size picture—I threw everything away. Except the food.

chapter 5

kiss me, kate

It was the first time I'd ever realized my body could be anything besides fat.

One of the few people who accepted me unconditionally in seventh grade was the music teacher, Cathy Thomas. She'd singled me out on the first day of music class, teaching me a harmony part to "The Age of Aquarius" from the musical *Hair,* and I'd been attached to her side ever since. Miss Thomas was young, right out of music school, and she was devoted to her students in an "I'm more than your teacher, I'm also your friend" kind of way. She let me talk her ear off about my huge plan to be on Broadway someday.

"I think I will be more like Ethel Merman and Mary Martin," I told her. "I'm not going to run off to Hollywood the minute I become successful like Barbra Streisand. I'll stick around because Broadway is really my passion. What do you think?"

"It's good to have passion, Sharon." Miss Thomas looked at me with a kind of admiration. You hold onto that. It will get you places."

While other girls in my class were boy-crazy, I was Miss Thomas–crazy. With her I felt talented, little, and cute. I wanted her to pack me up in her backpack and take me home, so we could have sing-alongs and bake cookies.

Toward the end of the year, I walked into Miss Thomas's classroom, all ready to launch into whatever huge injustice had happened to me that day, when I saw a little blond girl erasing the chalkboard. Miss Thomas must have seen the expression on my face—a "back away from that blackboard, little girl, and no one will get hurt; Miss Thomas is mine" kind of look—because she immediately put her arm around me.

"We have a new friend today, Sharon. This is Trisha Luce."

As I looked at Trisha, I realized I knew who she was. A sixth-grader, she had a reputation for giving boys blowjobs at the bus stop. I hadn't really believed it at the time, but I'd never seen her up close, either. Yeah, I thought as I looked at her, it could be true. She looks like she'd do that.

Trisha became a regular in Miss Thomas's classroom. She didn't talk very much, and when she did, you could barely hear her. I interrogated her to bring her out of her shell, and I was fascinated by what I found. "What are your plans? What are you going to be when you get older? What do you mean you don't know? What are you going to study in college?" I'd ask. She liked the attention, and over time she opened up, first just the basic facts like she had an older sister named Debbie, then more details. Her mother, it turned out, had recently died of cancer. Her dad drank all night and passed out on a chair in front of the TV. This baffled me.

"You mean he doesn't sleep in a bed? Not ever?"

"Never," Trisha told me. "Well, sometimes he does when his fat girlfriend, Mrs. Bell, spends the night on the weekends."

Trisha's tragic life sucked me in. I'd never met anyone my own age who'd lost a parent. Even in the throes of preteen disdain for my own mother, I couldn't imagine losing her.

kiss me, kate

Trisha's motherless future made me want to mother her myself, and that's exactly what Miss Thomas and I did on those days after school as we cleaned the chalkboards. She had these soft brown eyes that looked sadder than any orphan on TV, even the starving ones. She didn't have any friends, and she and her sister fought all the time.

"Who do you talk to?" I'd ask.

"You," she'd say. Trisha was a walking soap opera. I was hooked.

Miss Thomas had decided to leave Cincinnati and return to Utah to marry the man she loved. She invited Trisha and me to the wedding. Even though we were happy for her, Trisha and I cried every day during Miss Thomas's last week of school.

"Sharon, I need you to watch out for Trisha for me," Miss Thomas told me when we said our final goodbyes. "She's the kind of kid who could get into a lot of trouble. I think a good friend like you, a good influence, could really save her. Will you do it?"

I nodded solemnly and sincerely. I hadn't ever been asked to take care of anyone before, and I certainly hadn't ever been told that I would be a good influence. As the youngest child, I was accustomed to being the needy one, not the one being needed. Knowing that someone thought I was able to take care of Trisha made me feel important and grown-up. I took what she said very seriously, and as the school year ended, Trisha and I became close friends.

Trisha lived five miles away from me, so it was difficult for us to see each other once school let out. She never had a ride anywhere because her dad worked all day, and my mom tired of playing taxi after a few visits. So I did something totally out of character—I pulled out my bike.

I could ride a bike, but I was not a kid who went on bike rides. The first time I rode my bike to Trisha's house, I about had a heart attack. I remember telling her about it in detail: "Oh my *God*. There were like a zillion hills. I think it was all *up*hill. And on top of that it's about twenty-five miles." I lay down, my large legs and arms spread on her driveway, and proclaimed, "I'm never riding home, ever. I'm going to sleep right here." She laughed at me and brought me a big glass of water, which she dumped on my head.

"Don't go home, ever," Trisha said. "I like that you're here."

My mom didn't really like Trisha, but she was so happy that I was actually exercising by riding my bike that she let me go to Trisha's house every day for the entire summer. If she'd had any idea what we were up to, she happily would have let me sit on the couch and watch *Brady Bunch* reruns all summer while hand-feeding me Suzy Q's.

Trisha lived in a subdivision called Hilltop, which was a rundown development. Trisha was, in effect, a blue-collar version of Madison. But the greatest difference between Madison Pepper and Trisha Luce was how Trisha treated me. I'd spent years chasing Madison around, agreeing with her, idolizing her every move, and expecting nothing in return but a seat at the lunch table. But Trisha admired me; her intense loyalty and affection—something I'd never experienced with a friend before—helped me overlook the differences between us.

Trisha wasn't a cheerleader, she wasn't popular, she wasn't what my mother would call refined—all the things I'd looked for in a friend before. Trisha was tough and had a reputation for being a slut. Usually my friends liked to come to my house, since we had a swimming pool and a tennis court in my backyard. But Trisha and I spent every day of the summer at her house, for one simple reason: total freedom. I'd never spent any time in a house when there were no parents around, and I reveled in it. We could come and go as we liked. We made unlimited and elaborate prank calls. We scoured the house for money and then walked down a four-lane highway eating pizza we paid for with pennies in little plastic bags. With no one around to say no, our options were endless. Once school let out, we settled into a daily routine. First, we listened to music as loud as we could and gave head-banger rock 'n' roll concerts for each other, using Trisha's curling iron as a microphone. Then, we got out Trisha's dead mother's makeup and applied as much of it as possible.

We stole her sister Debbie's bras, stuffed them, and pranced around the neighborhood in short-shorts and tank tops with our chests sticking out. It was the first time I'd ever realized my body could be anything besides fat, which fascinated me. I wore crop tops and cut my jean shorts shorter. As we walked, I could feel the breeze on parts of my body that had never been exposed before. Both exhilarating and terrifying, it was fun to act sexy. The boys in the neighborhood whistled at us. I wondered what being slutty really meant and if, given the opportunity, I could really do it.

"Do you really give boys blowjobs at the bus stop?"

"No," Trisha told me, "but don't tell anyone that. It's better if they think I did."

Trisha's dad and his girlfriend, Mrs. Bell, were smokers, and Trisha and I stole their cigarettes and smoked all day, walking around the house like we were adults. When her fifteen-year-old sister, Debbie, caught us, all she would say was, "Can I have one?"

"Get your own," Trisha would snarl at her.

"Yeah." I'd add. It was fun to be nasty.

As June turned to July, I settled into a new attitude, one that was totally different from my former Little Miss Sunshine self.

I'd always been the good girl, the reliable, upstanding kid, but with Trisha I discovered that I loved being bad. I shed my goody-goody, self-conscious skin and tried on rotten for a change. Like a hologram, my new rotten self only appeared within a one-mile radius of Trisha's house, when I was far away from everyone I knew. I lived in terror that my parents would catch me.

Trisha and I did not spend time with anyone else. We were a two-person, self-reliant team, and I loved the exclusivity of it. When we needed something we didn't have at the house, we'd walk up to the gas station and steal it. Trisha was a good thief—she could rip off two candy bars and two cans of Coke at a time. We worked out a system. Because I was so good at talking, I distracted the cashier. I'd ask for directions, ask about the weather, ask if there was a nearby pizza place, anything that came to mind, while Trisha shoved our loot up her shirt. We were way too scared to make a regular thing of this, but we did it often enough that I never lost a pound that summer, even with all the aerobic bike rides.

Once the allure of smoking and stealing wore off, we started to chug her dad's booze. I don't remember what we drank—only that it burned. We poured ourselves drinks in highball glasses, using a lot of ice and a lot of Coke to mask the taste. We pranced around the house in our makeup, drinking our drinks and smoking, and pretending that we were incredibly grown-up and sophisticated. Toward the end of the summer, it had gotten to the point that I had to wash my face with cold cream, take a shower, and gargle with Scope before I left her house, weaving my way five miles on my bike. Trisha was clearly the best friend anyone could ever have, and I couldn't believe I'd *ever* wasted my time wanting to be a stupid, snooty cheerleader. I stopped pining for Madison's friendship; instead, Trisha and I mocked Madison and her superficiality.

Besides, we got a lot of attention from the boys in her neighborhood. We'd lie out on her driveway, Trisha in a bikini, me in my version of a bikini—cutoffs, and a low-cut T-shirt—and the boys would visit. These boys were different from the boys I knew. They weren't interested in talking or in my jokes; instead, they were excited by what my overweight body might give them. They circled us on their bikes like vultures. Nervous, I wanted to grab a beach towel and cover my big body from their view. Trisha, on the other hand, would pull her bathing suit straps down so they got a little show. They knew what they wanted, and they thought that Trisha and I would give it to them.

Trisha taught me the art of flirting. "Be kind of nasty to them," she told me. "Don't talk too much. Make them uncomfortable. That's what guys like."

While Trisha was a master at this technique, I was terrible. I talked constantly, made jokes, asked them details about their bikes, their haircuts, their favorite class at school—as if I cared—anything to avoid flirting, which took body confidence that I simply didn't have.

I don't know what Trisha did with those boys, but whatever it was, it made me jealous. I didn't want her to spend time with anyone else. I knew there were meetings in the woods after I had gone home in the evenings, even though I didn't ask, and she didn't tell. It upset me that Trisha was giving someone else attention in such a private way.

"Those boys are mean!" I told her. "They only want you because they think you'll put out. They don't care about you the way I do."

Knowing that I was around a girl who "put out" made me wonder if I wanted to be a girl who "put out" too. Maybe if I participated in the meetings in the woods, then I wouldn't feel so jealous. I'd spent so much of my life in friendships in which I gave and got nothing in return; I suspected that that's what it would be like to "put out" with those boys. I knew I didn't want that.

But Trisha's open sexuality woke up my sexuality, and it confused me. I felt as though I understood Trisha better than anyone in the world, and I wanted our friendship to be enough for her. I told her I loved her. I wanted to prove it; I wanted to show her I cared.

We began to explore new ways to show affection for each other. It started in the bathtub. Trisha and I loved to take bubble baths. We would fill the tub with hot water and long squirts of Dawn dishwashing detergent until it overflowed with bubbles, and then we'd hop in with our bathing suits on. We washed each other's hair, washed each other's backs, washed each other's feet, and then one day, something more happened, both of us daring to go further.

"Do you want me to wash your fronts?" Hysterical laughter, followed by a hushed, "Okay." And then, "Turn off the light." Our wet bathing suits hit the floor. We were only twelve, but we knew what to do. I knew it was wrong, and part of me was ashamed, but like the thrill of the booze and the rush of stealing, the aphrodisiac of someone—anyone—liking me so much won out over the voices that said "don't do it." We were two lonely, needy, little girls playing grownups. I'm sure this kind of friendship wasn't what Miss Thomas had had in mind, but it was our interpretation of how best friends should show affection. It gave our friendship a secret power; we thought we were like Clark Kent, ordinary citizens with a secret superhero identity.

Trisha and I did not fool around often—twice, maybe three times the entire summer—but we talked about it a lot. Right before school started again, she ended it during one of our marathon phone conversations. I was reading her a sexy story I had written about her, and she interrupted my racy twelve-year-old Harlequin novel prose.

"Sharon?" Trisha said. "I don't want to do this anymore. I think we should stop."

"Stop everything? Like not be friends anymore?" I panicked, afraid I'd ruined everything.

"No. Not everything, dummy, just this part. I don't like it anymore."

"Okay." I tried to make it sound as though I didn't care, but I wasn't sure I was ready to stop. "But we're still friends, right?"

"Best friends forever," she vowed.

"Best friends forever," I vowed back. But even as the words left my mouth, I worried they were not true.

After that phone call, I kept my distance for a few days. In that time, I thought about everything I'd done that summer. With a sinking feeling, I admitted to myself that I'd crossed over about a million lines, lines that made me someone else. And I didn't like the person I was becoming—a person who stole things, a person who smoked and drank, a person so caught up in someone else that I'd lost sight of everything I'd really wanted for myself. I'd become a person who didn't feel like me—and I knew I needed to find my way back. I found my *Annie* record buried deep underneath my bed and turned it on full blast, soaking in the music, remembering how much I loved it. I turned up "You're Never Fully Dressed Without a Smile," and sang along. After a summer of head-banger rock 'n' roll, I'd forgotten how much I liked Broadway.

As it turned out, I was the one who ended our friendship. I wanted to distance myself from the summer person I'd become. When we returned to school that fall, I stopped calling her, and I didn't return her calls. Her brown eyes held too many private memories, and I could never really meet her gaze after that.

I ignored her. Keenly aware of her cheap clothes and trashy reputation, I told myself we were too different to sustain a real friendship. I didn't want to become any more like her than I already had. I missed her, but I couldn't handle my guilt. I felt I'd failed Miss Thomas—I hadn't helped Trisha. I'd only corrupted her more.

I went back to dressing in my normal, conservative clothes and makeup. Feeling a little lost, I tried to hang out with the cheerleaders again, but it wasn't the same. In my desperate attempt to fit in, I'd lost myself. I wasn't a cheerleader, I wasn't a bad girl, I wasn't even really a singer anymore—I hadn't sung in front of anyone for my entire three years at Anderson.

My sister, Susan, noticed my depression during her trip home over the Christmas holidays, and she became concerned. Because Susan is the kind of person who likes to "fix" things, she hatched a plan that I would come to visit her at Yale over my spring break. I'm not sure how she convinced my parents to let me fly to LaGuardia Airport alone at the age of thirteen, but I was thrilled to go. I followed Susan's directions, caught a shuttle bus to New Haven from LaGuardia, and spent a week hanging out with her and her very cute new boyfriend, Tony. They let me wander around on campus, and sustained me by filling me with French fries and chocolate milk smuggled from the dining hall. While they were off at classes, I entertained myself by playing my sister's albums, and soon I discovered a singer named Bette Midler. "Susan, she is the greatest singer *ever*!" I screamed over the scratchy recording of "Lullaby of Broadway," which I'd played over and over. Susan smiled at me, happy for my enthusiasm over something more than cheerleading as I continued my rant. "You know what your friend Ken told me? He said that Bette Midler was in the Broadway show *Fiddler on the Roof* before she made this record. Did you know that?" My sister shook her head "no," unable to make herself heard over the girl group arrangement with blasting horns. "I'm going to be on Broadway someday! In fact, I'm going to be on Broadway and then make an album like this that everyone will listen to! You'll have to say you knew me when."

"Hey!" My sister suddenly turned the volume all the way down on the stereo, silencing Bette. "I just had an incredible idea. Just guess what is an hour and a half train ride away?" She plunged ahead, too excited to wait for my guess. *"Broadway!* Do you want to go see a real Broadway show?"

My mouth dropped. "Are you serious? Could we really go see a Broadway show?"

The next day we boarded a Conrail train bound for Manhattan. I was breathless with excitement as my sister explained that we would window shop on Fifth Avenue, eat tacos in Greenwich Village, and then wait in line at TKTS, a half-price ticket booth in the middle of Times Square. "We'll just wait in line and pick out whatever show looks best." I didn't care what show we saw. All it had to be was Broadway. The day was amazing. I'd seen Manhattan in movies, but nothing could prepare me for the sky-high buildings, the flurry of people, and the rush of the subway. I felt like the blood was coursing through my veins at three times its normal speed. I was hooked. The highlight of the trip was Times Square. A neon homage to my favorite thing, Broadway, I felt right at home and very far from the misery at Anderson Middle School. After we secured tickets to *Barnum* with Jim Dale and Glenn Close, we walked around Times Square eating a huge, slightly burned soft pretzel. "When I'm on Broadway, I'm going to eat a soft pretzel every day," I announced to Susan and Tony. "And I will always sign autographs for my fans at the stage door." We made our way to the St. James Theater on Forty-fourth street, where *Barnum* was playing. As we took our seats in the balcony, I poured over the actor's biographies in my playbill. Who were these people? How did they make it on Broadway? Had they all been actors since they were children? Did they all grow up in New York City? And the most important question of all: What would I put in my playbill biography when I was on Broadway? Before I could complete the thank-you section of my imaginary bio, the lights dimmed and the show started. Just like years before at *Oliver* I started to cry, and I didn't stop until it was over. It was beautiful—the lights, the music, the acting. I couldn't explain my reaction to anyone; it was beyond words, stuck in a nonverbal feeling place that could only be summed up as *desire*. My love affair with Broadway had officially begun.

Rejuvenated from my trip to Yale and Broadway, I took a long, hard look at my life. Was more of the same what I wanted? As all the other eighth-graders geared up to make the big move across the street to Anderson High School, I realized I was dreading high school. I looked around at my classmates—some of whom had been calling me names since first grade—and I decided to make a drastic change. I would go to a new school where I didn't know anyone. I chose Ursuline Academy, an all-girls Catholic school twenty-five miles from my house. The brochure talked about what Ursuline Academy had—a college-prep curriculum, a great music department, a small teacher-student ratio, a drama club, a desire to help young girls become leaders—but all I could think about was what it didn't have: no Madison, no Trisha, no name-calling, no boys.

I couldn't wait.

act two

"When you have a dream,
you've got to grab it and never let go."

—*Carol Burnett*

chapter 6
bells are ringing

After my messy Anderson years, I wanted everything at Ursuline to be perfect.

I spent the summer after eighth grade baby-sitting my little cousin and dreaming about becoming a Catholic schoolgirl. My sister, Susan, who had also gone to Ursuline, was home from college for the summer. She prepped me for my new role as an Ursuline girl by taking me to get my uniform. I pumped her for information as we headed into the dressing room at McAlpin's.

"What if I can't make friends?"

"Ursuline is great." Susan handed me a black watch plaid skirt. "They are going to love you."

"I don't know." I buttoned up the itchy wool skirt. "What about the course work? It sounds hard."

"You have to be in the glee club." Susan unfolded a hunter green Ursuline sweatshirt. "It's *the* thing, and everyone loves it. You'll be getting all of the solos in no time."

"I hope so." I took the soft sweatshirt and pulled it on over my head. "But what about the real school work? It was easy for you. You're the smart one."

"I hate it when you say that. You're smarter than you think you are." The academic of the family, Susan had aced her Ursuline years and gotten into Yale. She was famous among the faculty at Ursuline for being one of the first students accepted into an Ivy League college. "You just have to study."

"Easy for you to say." I'd scored low on the entrance exam, but thanks to my sister's stellar academic performance, they'd let me in anyway. "I'm no good at studying."

Susan laughed. "That's because you haven't had any practice. If you just sit down and do it, you'll be fine."

I hoped Susan was right. After my messy Anderson years, I wanted everything at Ursuline to be perfect.

Right off the bat, I loved the campus. Ursuline Academy's building was constructed in the 1970s, a time when the Catholic Church was attempting to modernize its image, so it was not your typical all-girls Catholic high school filled with ruler-wielding nuns, Virgin Mary statues, cold stone walls, and bleeding Jesus. On the contrary, like Ayer Elementary, it was designed with "open classrooms" and cozy wall-to-wall carpet. The faculty embodied this warm, nurturing atmosphere by taking great pride in the school.

At freshman orientation, the principal, Shirley Speaks, addressed all of us new Ursuline girls.

"Here at Ursuline Academy, our mission is to nurture young women spiritually and academically. We're preparing you to do great things in the world."

Yes, I sat up in my chair. *That's me! I want to do great things.* I'd heard some of the other girls complain about the so-called disadvantages of a girls' school. No boys? They didn't like me anyway. Uniforms? I'd always wanted to wear the same clothes as everyone else. Miles from home? I wanted to get as far away from Anderson Middle School as I could get.

---

bells are ringing

Determined to do great things, I wasted no time in finding the faculty member who could help me the most—the music teacher, Judith A. Brown.

Miss Brown taught voice lessons, and I desperately wanted to take them. But the curriculum packet clearly stated that there were no voice lessons for students under the age of sixteen. There was no way I was waiting until I was sixteen, which would have meant December of my junior year. Fired up by Principal Speaks, I decided to take action immediately. I would try to talk my way in with Miss Brown. And if that didn't work, I would sing my way in.

Rumor had it that Miss Brown was strict and a little unapproachable, so I was nervous as I found my way to the music room. I was relieved to see that she looked like a pretty version of Sister Berthe, the nun in *The Sound of Music* who helps the von Trapps escape the Nazis by pulling the spark plugs out of their cars. Given my deep love of all things *SOM,* I was drawn to her immediately. She was unpacking sheet music from large cardboard boxes. With the confidence of Maria herself, I walked right up to Miss Brown.

"Hi. My name is Sharon Wheatley and I'm going to be a freshman this year. I was told I needed your signature to sign up for voice lessons." I whipped out the form with a flourish. "Will you sign this?"

Miss Brown hardly even glanced up from her work. "I don't teach girls until their voices have matured. Until then, you can sign up for glee club. That's available to everyone." Her smile was nice but firm, and she went back to unpacking her boxes.

"Miss Brown, I know what the policy is, but there must be exceptions. Some girls' voices mature faster. My voice has matured faster. I'm ready right now." In truth I knew nothing about the human voice, but I wanted to sing.

Miss Brown looked at me over the top of the box. "You think your voice has already matured?"

"Uh-huh. It has!" I said a quick prayer, figuring God was quick to answer an Ursuline girl's prayer. She stood up, and I noticed for the first time how tall she was. Her height and remarkable posture were intimidating, but I held my ground.

"How old are you?" she asked.

"I'm thirteen, but I don't sound like it."

"I'll be the judge of that. Let me hear you." To my surprise, she strode to the piano and sat down. "What songs do you know?"

I hadn't expected an impromptu audition. I was nervous but determined to prove that I had an exceptional and mature voice, a voice that broke all the rules. I decided to pull out my *Wow* song—it worked every time. "I can sing 'Edelweiss' from *The Sound of Music*."

"Okay, let me hear it." I waited for her to start playing, but she just sat and looked at me expectantly. "You brought music, didn't you?"

I shook my head.

"Then sing it by yourself. You don't need another instrument if you are truly a good singer."

Vowing to carry music with me at all times from that moment forward, I took a deep breath. It had been a long time since I had sung for anyone. Ignoring that familiar nervous feeling in my stomach, I started to sing. My voice didn't boom around in the choral room as much as it had in the gym years before for my *SOM* audition at Indian Hill, but I still thought it sounded pretty good. I waited for her reaction—for the *Wow*.

She looked at me for a long moment. I couldn't tell if I'd done well or poorly.

"Try it again, but this time, start on this note." She played a note that was much higher than the note I had started on in the first rendition. This time I didn't like how my voice sounded at all—kind of thin and weak.

"I liked the way I sounded before, when it was lower. I don't sing up high very well. Can I try it again, a little lower?"

Miss Brown shook her head. "The way you first sang that song probably felt good, but it's not singing, it's just bellowing. If you want me to be your teacher, you are going to have to learn to sing up here." She ran her finger up the highest register of the piano. "That's where your voice should be. There's a voice in there, but I don't want to hear that shouting again, understood?"

I nodded.

Miss Brown took the registration sheet out of my hand and signed it. "I expect you to be prepared and I expect you to practice. I like smart singers, so add music theory to your classes, and we'll get you started." She looked me in the eye. "Singing is not just for fun, Sharon. Remember that. Good singing takes work."

I walked out of the choral room with my signed permission slip in my pocket. I knew I should feel happy, but instead I felt unsure of myself. Until that moment, no one had ever said anything but "wow" when I sang. And here was Miss Brown, telling me that what I thought was singing wasn't singing at all. I was a little nervous, but I knew I was up for the challenge. I pulled out the slip signed with Judy Brown's perfect penmanship, and I couldn't help but smile. I'd done it! I was going to have voice lessons!

Later that night, I curled up in my bed with my new curriculum guide. After three years of a music-less existence at Anderson, I wanted the choral room to become my home away from home. I read through every single class Miss Brown taught: music theory, glee club and vocal ensemble, masters of the symphony, music history, introduction to opera, and theory and composition. I would take them all. I'd let Miss Brown train me like a racehorse for the next four years. Music would become my identity.

jekyll & hyde

Marla didn't fit with my new Ursuline persona, and I wanted to make this clear in no uncertain terms.

If I'd realized how long the bus ride to Ursuline was, I might have rethought my decision to go there. Each agonizing morning started at 7:05 and ended at 8:30 when we finally pulled into the parking lot.

I endured the first week of morning bus rides in a sleep-deprived fog of carsickness and total boredom. At first, I tried to do homework on the bus, but I stopped after my algebra teacher complained that she couldn't read my numbers. Reading nauseated me, looking out the window was boring, and as tired as I was, I couldn't sleep. All that was left was Marla Twine.

Marla Twine was the only other student from my class at Anderson to make the transition to Ursuline. Throughout middle school, I'd secretly called her Casper the Friendly Ghost. Short and squat, Marla had really white skin and the face of a seventy-year-old librarian.

On the first day of school at Ursuline, Marla spotted me in the cafeteria and sat down next to me, even though we'd never spoken before. She was absolutely, positively, the last person I wanted to talk to, ever. I'd gone to Ursuline to get away from Anderson, and Marla simply reminded me of it. Marla was using the "let's be friends since we don't know anyone else" approach, which I found unbearable. She reminisced about Anderson the entire time, asking about people we both knew, and acting like we'd left behind gobs of great friends. I tuned her out after a while.

"Did you hear that Madison Pepper moved to Hollywood?"

"What?" Even though we weren't friends anymore, I'd known her since the first grade and I was sad that I couldn't say goodbye.

"Hollywood. Isn't that so Madison?"

The fact that Marla Twine knew this before I did made it even worse. I'd never liked Marla, but now that she'd trumped me with her news of Madison Pepper, I hated her.

Undeterred, Marla tried to become the new Madison Pepper in my life. She saved seats for me in the cafeteria and on the bus as well. Every morning, I slumped down in my seat and put my backpack next to me, so the entire seat was occupied. But without fail, Marla magically appeared next to me, clutching her schoolbooks.

"Can I sit with you?" Marla would say in her small, soft voice. Everything about Marla was soft—with her white, pudgy appearance she reminded me of dough. If you stuck her in the oven she'd come out a toasty brown crescent roll.

"There are only six people on this entire bus. We can all have a seat to ourselves." I felt slightly guilty, but Marla didn't fit with my new Ursuline persona, and I wanted to make this clear in no uncertain terms.

"Okay." Marla settled into the seat directly across from mine, propping up her knees on the back of the seat in front of her. We looked like a matched set of dough-girl dolls in our uniform skirts. Her white granny panties peaked out from under her skirt; I didn't tell her that she should wear shorts under her skirt like everyone else, because I didn't want to be seen talking to her.

About a week into the school year, the oldest girl on the bus, a feisty junior named Grace, stood up in her seat. "This bus ride *blows*! I'm bored out of my mind. Let's play a game or something."

The rest of us popped up our heads from behind our seats to look at Grace.

"Okay! I'll play a game!" said Marla.

Grace looked her up and down. "Not *you*, fatty. What about the rest of you? You wanna do something?"

I wasn't sure what to do. I was just as fat as Marla, if not fatter. While the other girls switched seats to be closer to Grace, I stayed put, hiding my fatness. I didn't go unnoticed for long.

"What are you doing?" Grace yelled at me. "Homework or something? Come up here." I stood up in the aisle, bracing myself for the fat comment, but it never came.

"Well don't just stand there, you freak, come up here."

I walked up the aisle, careful not to look at Marla as I passed by her seat. I knew just how she felt, but I certainly wasn't going to defend her to a junior. One wrong move could turn the tides against me. The last thing I wanted was to be sent back with Marla.

"Is she a midget?"

"What?"

"Your fatty friend back there." Grace grinned at me. "Is she a midget?"

"Uh, I don't know. Maybe."

I hadn't ever teased someone before, and I felt torn between my sympathy for her and the fun, new feeling of being a part of the crowd.

"I think she's a midget." Grace turned to the other girls. "Midget, midget, midget!"

The girls joined in the chorus, and I did, too.

From that morning on, we tortured Marla. We commented endlessly on her short, puffy, white body. We laughed and pointed and teased.

I usually came up with the worst stuff—the stuff that made her cry. I knew just what to say, because it had all been said to me. I was always the first one to point and say, "Look, she's crying! You big baby! You big, fat crybaby!"

There was something intoxicating about becoming the "teaser" instead of the "teasee." No one teased me, and I thought it was because Marla got all the negative attention. I thrived on my new, powerful role. I couldn't stop. Even after Grace got her driver's license and abandoned the bus, I kept it up.

"Fatty," I mumbled as she passed me on the bus. "Tub of lard." I knew I could say anything, and she would pretend to ignore me. I knew her tricks because I had played them all. I knew it was wrong, but I couldn't stop myself. When I teased her, I was saying, "Look at *her*. Leave *me* alone."

School had been in session for a couple of months when I finally got my comeuppance. I was on my way to my locker before homeroom. Even from down the hall I could tell that my locker had been decorated. Thrilled, I quickened my step. My birthday was coming up, and I'd prayed that someone would decorate my locker with balloons and cards. Birthday lockers were an Ursuline tradition, and I felt so lucky to be a part of it.

But as I grew closer, I realized that the stuff on my locker wasn't birthday decorations at all. My locker had been duct-taped closed.

Duct tape covered every hinge, every crack, every seal. Even the lock itself had been wrapped with tape at least fifty times. The signs were not the pretty pastel happy birthday signs I'd hoped for. Instead, heavy ballpoint pen on notebook paper called out, *You are a fat ass* and *You suck*.

I turned to see if anyone had noticed my locker, and I was mortified to see half of the freshman class behind me, watching.

A lean, muscular girl named Lisa stepped up to me.

"You big piece of shit!" Lisa yelled. "You apologize for everything you've said to my friend on the bus, or I'm going to beat the crap out of you!"

That's when I noticed a very nervous Marla Twine standing next to her.

Lisa pushed forward, backing me up against my locker.

I was terrified. There was a heavy silence in the hallway—a collective holding of breath, while everyone waited to see what would happen next. I was too scared to look at Lisa, so I looked at Marla. She was even paler than usual.

"I'm sorry, Marla," I said. "I'm really sorry."

"Marla is my friend, and I'm warning you, Wheatley." Lisa put her arm around Marla. "I'll kick your ass if I ever hear you've said another bad thing about her. Get it? I'll kick your big fat ass."

They started to walk away.

"Have fun getting your locker open, Wheatley, you nasty bitch." Lisa laughed. Some other girls in the hall laughed, too, but most just finished packing up their stuff and left for class.

I struggled to keep it together as I pulled the tape off, but I couldn't. Everything she had said was true. If she had beaten the crap out of me, I'd have deserved that too. I couldn't believe that I had said all of those awful things, that I had purposely made another fat girl feel so terrible. And then I sat down with my back against my sticky locker door, and I started to cry. I deserved everything I got, and I knew it.

But my shame wasn't the only reason I was crying. I was jealous that Marla had a friend who would stand up for her like that. I was more jealous of that than I'd ever been of anything in my whole life. Why hadn't I ever made a friend who threatened the people who teased me? The best I'd ever had was Madison Pepper, and she didn't even try to defend me; she just didn't laugh when people called me names. She never would have taped someone's locker shut for me.

I knew I would never tease anyone again. What's more, I knew that I needed to make some friends—friends who would decorate my locker for my birthday and tape a locker shut if someone were mean to me. Real friends.

Myth: Cafeterias are for lunch. Truth: A high school cafeteria has very little to do with lunch, and everything to do with friends. At Anderson Prison, I dreaded lunchtime. At Ursuline, I knew my quest for friends would begin there. I had a plan.

At Ursuline, the modular schedule was built around a six-day rotation, named with letters: *A* day through *F* day. Mods were twenty-minute increments; classes were either two or three mods long, and scheduled randomly by a computer. So each student ate lunch in the cafeteria during her "free mod."

This meant I never knew who would be in the cafeteria at any given time, which left me with my lunch tray facing down an ever-changing roomful of strangers.

Most girls snacked rather than eating an entire lunch. Even if they brought their lunch from home, they'd eat half a sandwich during a morning free mod, and the other half during a later free mod. Or, they'd wolf down the sandwich by 9:45 A.M. because they hadn't eaten breakfast, and then spend their remaining free mods bumming money for the vending machine.

This provided me with the opportunity to find a permanent place at a popular table, meet new people, and make a little money all in one fell swoop. And I did it the best way I knew how—with food.

I told Mom it was all for charity. A bake sale—for which I must have brownies and Rice Krispie treats. I didn't tell her that I was the charity.

On my first day as a purveyor of baked goods, I staked out a centrally located table in the freshman section of the cafeteria and set up shop. I hung a multicolored sign that read: SHARON'S BAKE SALE: ALL ITEMS 25 CENTS. I helped myself to a brownie, sat down behind my table, and waited.

At first, I only got a couple of curious glances. I recognized a girl in my Latin class and waved, yelling the only two Latin words I could remember. *"Agricolae! Bellum!* Come over! Free treats for those suffering through Latin!"

She laughed and came over.

"They're good. I promise." I gave her a brownie and took another one for myself. "I made them in a tree with a small group of elves I borrowed from Mr. Keebler."

Within five minutes a line had formed. Thirty minutes and fifty students later I was completely sold out. I could not believe how brilliantly it had worked. While people were waiting in line, I made jokes, introduced myself, and asked people questions. I was thrilled at how friendly everyone was.

After a week, business was so good that I began to make double batches. I also expanded into gum—one piece for five cents. I had gone from the Anderson outcast to the Ursuline It Girl. I loved walking through the open hallways while people yelled out, "Hey, Sharon! Are you free mods eleven and twelve? I want a brownie!" I'd get notes in class: "Sharon, Can I buy a piece of gum?" I'd send back a piece of Juicy Fruit and a nickel would be rolled in my direction. My business was thriving, and I was always invited to sell my goods at all the tables in the cafeteria, since I gave free food to the people sitting at my "store." One girl even invited me to her birthday party and paid me to bake her a cookie cake.

Social perks aside, another perk to my business was the unlimited supply of quarters I earned. I had bags and bags of them. These quarters opened up a whole new world for me— the wonderful world of vending machines. While the rest of my classmates feasted on my baked treats, I methodically sampled the contents of the entire vending machine, starting with A1, going in order to GG7. My favorites were Snickers and barbecue Fritos washed down with a Coke.

Something about my baked goods made me easily approachable, even when there wasn't a brownie in sight. I didn't have to work as hard to make friends; they just came to me. One day I found a note on my desk in study hall.

Dear Cookie Girl, I noticed how good your business is, so I'm going to open a banana split cart as a competition. Watch out! Your archrival, Carolyn Häagen-Dazs.

Carolyn Kraft was a quiet, dark-haired girl who sat in the alto section of Glee Club. We'd never spoken, and I was surprised to hear from her. But the note made me laugh and I sent one back. *Dear Double Scoop, Only an amateur could believe ice cream could outsell my fine baked goods. Go back to the dairy farm you came from. Signed, Betty Crocker.*

Carolyn was unhappy at Ursuline, struggling to find a good friend at a school she hadn't wanted to attend. And even though I'd met lots of people during my bake sales, I hadn't found the one *real* friend I was looking for. We bonded immediately. Within a week of our note-passing session, I was spending the night at her house, which became a weekend ritual for the rest of high school. Unlike my friendships with Madison and Trisha, my friendship with Carolyn was even and two-sided. I felt as though I'd finally found the pot of gold at the end of the rainbow. Finally, I had a real, live best friend—a friend who always decorated my locker for my birthday and who was always there to talk when I had a bad day. Carolyn was the kind of friend who'd do anything for the people she loved. And even though she never had to prove it, I'm pretty sure that if the situation had called for it, she would even have duct-taped a locker or two in the name of friendship.

chapter 8

nunsense

Without boys to impress, we came to school dressed in our wrinkled uniform skirts and whatever solid-colored shirt was closest when we got out of bed.

Going to an all-girls school was wonderful. Without boys to impress, we came to school dressed in our wrinkled uniform skirts and whatever solid-colored shirt was closest when we got out of bed. Few of us wore makeup or curled our hair, resulting in a relaxed atmosphere free of the feline competition I'd experienced at Anderson. For most students, academics took priority over who was dating whom.

In most respects, my life at Ursuline was great. I loved my new school, I loved my new friends, and I loved my fabulous voice lessons. Finally, it seemed, I had what I always wanted. I should have been ecstatic. On the outside, I was Sharon—Little Miss Sunshine. But there was a dark side.

First: My eating was completely out of control. The wicked metabolic cocktail of puberty and vending machine buffets took its toll quickly. I'd never had Kit Kats and Snickers at my beck and call before, and I couldn't escape the allure of C2 or E7 at the machines. Any day now my new friends would notice that I was getting bigger by the minute and abandon me.

Second: My parents' marriage was falling apart. My father's swimming pool business was failing, and my parents constantly fought about it. My brother and sister were both away at college, so I was the lone audience for these financial wars. I tried to cheer them up as best I could by cracking jokes and staying out of their way, but I was so busy trying to be good, that I didn't tell them the truth. I was failing several classes.

Ursuline was tough, and I'd barely passed the entrance exam. I was so busy having fun in class—goofing off and passing notes—that I hardly ever paid attention. And when I did, I was still lost because I was so far behind.

At night, when I should have been doing my homework, I was gabbing on the phone to all my friends—a luxury I'd dreamed about for a long time. I managed to keep my grades up in some classes by copying Carolyn's homework at the last minute, but the classes she didn't take, I failed. I honestly thought my phone calls and notes were more important than school, since I'd never really had friends before. I wasn't about to interrupt my extensive social life with periodic tables and *A Tale of Two Cities*. With no parental input and a packed social calendar, I let everything slide until my teachers started mentioning academic probation. Because my parents were having financial problems, they hadn't paid my tuition, therefore, they hadn't received any of my report cards. They had no idea that I was outright failing Latin and algebra, and not doing much better in my other classes, and I wasn't planning on telling them.

Solution: Lie. I concocted grandiose schemes to distract people from how huge I was becoming and how terrible my grades were. The heavier I got, and the worse my grades got, the more desperate my lies became.

I skipped classes I didn't like, hiding out in the Ursuline Chapel. I loved the chapel. Quiet and carpeted, it was the perfect place to take a nap during algebra.

I stretched out on the floor of the chapel. Away from the chaos of my family, my grades, and the vending machines, I felt a peace that I had come to rely on. That's when it came to me: This peaceful feeling was God calling me to devote my life to Him. True, I wasn't religious in a perfect church attendance kind of way, but a good hymn could make me misty-eyed. Maybe that was another sign. God was really speaking to me!

Joining the convent would solve many of my biggest problems—my weight, my grades, my parents' fighting, even my lingering guilt over my relationship with Trisha Luce. As fat and ugly as I was, I figured I'd be celibate for the rest of my life anyway, so why not?

I loved the thought of wearing a habit, saying things like "Bless you, my child," and pulling out my guitar and singing "Climb Every Mountain" to make people feel better. My decision made, I prepared to announce my intention to join the convent to all of my new friends. I even told them that I'd already written a letter to the school nuns requesting permission to join.

Later that day, Carolyn and I were sitting in the cafeteria between classes, and I explained my calling to her in earnest. "I heard Him speak to me."

"Out loud?" Carolyn looked skeptical.

"No, in my head. He told me I'd be Sister Mary Sharon. Isn't that amazing?" Some girls at our table overheard me and looked at me in shock, which I interpreted as respect. "I'm at peace with it. It's what I'm supposed to do."

"I thought you wanted to be a singer."

"Nuns sing."

"Right. You know, nuns actually have to work." Carolyn had a way of cutting through my bullshit. "They don't just sit around and sing songs from *The Sound of Music* all day."

"I will pray over the matter." I stood up. "God will show me the way. I'm going to the chapel to pray."

Back in the deserted chapel, I once again stretched out on the carpeted floor. I unbuttoned my skirt, which grew tighter by the day. I looked up at the ceiling, and again I felt flush with peace and goodwill. I could see myself in the service of the Lord.

The chapel was warm from the sun through the skylight, and in the toasty quiet, I nodded off, dreaming of my new life at the convent.

When I woke up, Sister Mary Jane was standing over me. One of the most popular teachers at school, she was one of the few actual nuns who taught at Ursuline. Sister Mary Jane wasn't anything like the nuns in *The Sound of Music*; she didn't wear a habit or carry a ruler. Smart, easygoing, and athletic, the liberal Sister Mary Jane wore jeans. Looking at her, I vowed to wear a traditional habit—the black dress would be more slimming on me. But I would skip the headpiece, since I had such nice hair. And I'd top it off with just a touch of makeup—for natural glow.

I quickly buttoned up my uniform skirt and stood up. I figured I was busted for skipping algebra, but Sister Mary Jane didn't look angry.

"Carolyn tells me that you have been called to a life of service for the Lord."

Goddamn it, I thought. I should have kept my mouth shut. I'd gotten myself in over my head. Lying in church—to a nun!— would surely land me in the fiery pits of hell.

"I'm not sure it's an actual calling." I tried to look sincere, but confused. "It was more just like a thought from God, you know? I don't really know who started it. Him or me." Suddenly, algebra class wasn't looking so bad.

"By *Him*, I am assuming you are talking about God?" Sister Mary Jane looked at me through her large round glasses.

I nodded.

"Sharon, I think it's really cool that you want to be a nun, but becoming a nun isn't just about getting away from things. There are a lot of people like you, people who have self-esteem problems, who think that joining the religious life is a way out of the misery they are in. That's not what religious life is for. It's not an escape."

How could she possibly know that? How could she know I was trying to escape? How could she know I was miserable? What made her think I had self-esteem problems? "No, no, that's not *me!*" I laughed. "I mean, I can see that you might have a problem with that, but I don't have a self-esteem problem. I think I'm fantastic! I need to be a nun, that's all. How old do you have to be to sign up?"

She laughed. "Older than you." Sister Mary Jane sat down on the carpet Indian style and patted the floor for me to sit down too. She looked me right in the eye. "I heard you sing at the spring concert. You have a beautiful voice. Did you ever think God might be calling you to use your voice for worship?"

"What do you mean?"

"Why don't you sign up to sing for school Mass, Sharon? That way, you're using the instrument God gave you for some spiritual good. Just to tide you over, until you can sign up for the convent. Your voice can be a powerful instrument of peace and joy, just as much as a religious life.

"We'll be happy to have you once you are through high school and college, but no sooner. Understood?" She stood up and gave me a little wink. "Now, out of the chapel. I believe I hear God calling you back to class."

I'd never thought of my singing as a gift I was supposed to share with other people. I had always focused on what singing could do for me—not what I could give others. Maybe Sister Mary Jane was right.

I talked to Miss Brown and she agreed to let me join guitar club, which was the group responsible for singing at all of the school Masses. At first I was uncertain that I wanted to volunteer to sing in Mass. School Masses had always been the time when I could stealthily finish undone homework or catch a quick catnap, but now I would have to participate fully. I reluctantly attended the rehearsals and decided I'd try it once—before I decided to quit. My first Mass was November 1, the celebration of All Saints' Day. It was a Tuesday, and also a "casual dress day," which meant I'd have to squeeze into a pair of jeans that no longer fit since my vending machine bonanzas, and then, with my fat on full display, sing high notes. I had not sung a solo since grade school, the hymns were higher than I'd ever sung in public, and I had an algebra test I was going to bomb later in the day. All in all, All Saints' Day was making me a nervous wreck.

Because the chapel was too small to house the entire school, Masses were held in the gymnasium. Because the gym was so big, we sang into microphones. As I watched the entire student body and faculty quietly file into the gym, my nerves got the better of me and I had to turn to God for strength. "Hi, God? Uh, yeah, it's me, Sharon Wheatley, and I know I've been really terrible about going to church and paying attention when I'm there. And to be honest, I use your name in vain a lot, but I really promise I'll do better. Could you do me a favor and please help me not run out of this gym right now? I'm really nervous, and I'd like to do well, so could you, like, I don't know, send down a little Holy Spirit dust or something to give me some confidence? Thanks so much. Oh, and while I've got your attention, just a tiny reminder that I'd like to be on Broadway someday, and I'd also like to get thin. Okay, here goes. This one's for you!" With that, Miss Brown played the opening bars of "Glory and Praise," and I took a deep breath and sang.

Over the reverent silence of the congregation, my amplified voice enveloped the room, inviting people to join me in a jubilant song of prayer. I loved making eye contact with the other students, especially the nonmusical ones, encouraging them to sing. Ironically, singing at Mass became one of my favorite activities, and I sang every one until I graduated.

Sister Mary Jane helped me realize my voice could be shared with God and the faculty and the students. I'd breathe in the silence as I finished each song, feeling happy that I was part of a larger group than I had ever been before. At Mass, I sang without expectations of anything in return, especially applause. After that day in the chapel, I thought of Sister Mary Jane as my champion. I would have done anything for her. So when asked to write a term paper about prejudice for her Christian morality class, I wrote about weight. Usually, this was a very painful and private matter for me—a subject I never, ever discussed.

At the time I wrote "Prejudice Against Obesity," I weighed an all-time high of 230 pounds. I wrote it as an act of faith, believing I was safe with Sister Mary Jane. I felt like I was turning in my guts on a plate.

In the paper, I challenged the need to conform to America's obsession with a size-four figure. I dropped hints about my own feelings about being overweight throughout the paper:

Many people feel guilty if they are overweight.

Some teenagers are terrified to be overweight.

Overweight girls wonder, why would anyone date someone who is fat?

Secretly I hoped the paper would prompt Sister Mary Jane to approach me again, as she had in the chapel. I was sick of carrying around the emotional pain and hurt of so much weight, and I was ready to admit it—but only to Sister Mary Jane. She was the only one I could trust.

Sister Mary Jane gave me an A on the paper, but the payoff was bittersweet. Despite my good grade, she never approached me in person about it. She did write a note on my paper, and long after the glory of my A wore off, her comments stuck with me:

> *Sharon: I offer the following comments after reading your paper. I have to admit that I never thought of this issue before reading your paper and thus thank you for "opening my eyes" to another issue in morality. However, I think there is another side to the issue. . . . Is it immoral to be obese according to the Natural Law, which says we should take care of our bodies and not do anything to harm or destroy them? Doctors have said that to be overweight is bad for our health, so from that perspective, being overweight could be immoral. Just something to think about.*
> *Sister Mary Jane*

I felt as though I'd been hit on the side of the head with a frying pan. This was worse than the years of teasing. I couldn't believe that Sister Mary Jane, who had opened up a whole new world of singing to me, had now opened up a Pandora's box. My fat was more than gross—it was immoral. *I* was immoral. A nun said it, so it had to be true. Shocked and humiliated, I could barely look at her in class for the rest of the semester.

Joining the convent was now out of the question. For years, I'd comforted myself with the knowledge that, like Maria von Trapp, I always had God as a backup, just in case my singing career never materialized. I knew I wasn't perfect for the convent, but I thought my biggest obstacle would be something technical, like the fact that I didn't know all the prayers on the rosary, or even that I didn't like to go to church. But deep down, I thought that God would be the one who would always accept me for *me*, no matter what I looked like. But I was fat, and nobody liked fat. Not even God.

chapter 9

a chorus line

Without God as a backup plan, Broadway was my only option.

Without God as a backup plan, Broadway was my only option. So when the opportunity arose to visit the Great White Way as part of Ursuline's Community Learning Week, I was the first student to sign up for the trip.

The night before I left for New York, my dad and I had one of our late-night powwows in the kitchen. He was peeling potatoes to cook with a cottage ham the next day. It was one of the few meals of his that I truly hated, and I was glad I'd miss it. While he prepped the meal, he gave me a detailed description of his latest invention, a new security system comprised of pieces of our doorbell and our VCR. "Look here, see that image right there?"

I squinted at the fleeting black blob that was on the videotape.

"It's a fox! See that? I caught a fox on tape. Now, just imagine if it were a person! Do you have any idea how revolutionary this is? I'm telling you, honey, this is it. I'm gonna make a million with this!"

Once we'd exhausted his ideas, we moved on to me.

"Guess what?" I said. "I'm going to have a solo in the Christmas concert! Usually you have to be a senior to get a solo. Isn't that so great?" I danced around the kitchen. "How does that feel, Chuck Wheatley? To have a daughter who has a solo in the Christmas concert? And it's just the beginning! My crystal ball predicts big things, a career on Broadway, solo albums, a talk show." I ended with a big twirl. "I'll get discovered while I'm in New York! You're looking at the next big thing in show business right in front of you. I'm gonna make a million, then I'll buy you a Rolls Royce convertible."

When Dad was finished in the kitchen, he settled down with a piece of apple pie to watch *Some Like It Hot* on TV.

"Have you ever seen this?" he asked me. "It's a classic. Hell of a movie."

I grabbed a fudge pop and joined him. We watched for a while in silence.

"Marilyn Monroe is the sexiest woman who ever lived," Dad said. "Ever." He leaned in close and spoke softly. "It's a known fact, honey, that's what you have to look like to be a star." He pointed to the screen at Marilyn. "That's what success in show business looks like, Sharon, and if you don't look like that, then there's no room for you."

I felt the joy drain out of me. I understood what he was saying, and I hung my head in shame, embarrassed by my ridiculous crystal ball speech. The fudge pop in my hand felt like it weighed 100 pounds, and the chocolate soured on my tongue.

"I'm not saying this because I'm trying to make you feel bad. I'm saying this because I don't want you to get hurt. You know that I think you are talented. In fact, I think you can out-sing any kid I've ever heard, but I have to be realistic with you. You have to lose that weight if you want to be a success, because that is what success looks like." He pointed at Marilyn with his fork. "Sexy sells, and fat isn't sexy."

His words ricocheted inside me and as hard as I tried not to, I began to cry. I knew he was right. I was nothing but a big, fat fraud. I tried to wipe my tears away, but he caught my hand.

"Hey, now. I'm not trying to hurt your feelings. I didn't mean to upset you."

I nodded my head to say I knew that, but I was afraid to speak. I took a series of deep breaths and calmed myself, blowing my nose on the napkin he'd passed me.

Dad usually yelled at me about my weight; this new, soft-spoken approach was even more upsetting somehow. Dad felt it, too; he set his plate aside without finishing his pie.

For a long time, there was only the sound of the TV. The pain hanging in the air between us was excruciating. I wanted to make up and get past it. "I'm sorry, Dad. I didn't mean to get upset." I got up from the couch and threw away my fudge pop. "I know you're right, and I'm going to work on it. I promise. I'll go on a diet. Okay? I will."

I wanted to go to my room, but I needed to clear the air before I left. "Don't worry, Dad. I'm okay. It's just that I should go to bed. I've got my big trip tomorrow."

"That's right, your trip to the Big Apple." The energy had gone out of his voice.

"Yep. While I'm there I'm going to spend all of your money!"

He smiled at me, and I gave him a quick kiss on the forehead as I left the room. "Good night, Chuckles."

Up in my room I let New York's bright lights push my dad's opinion of my weight out of my head. He's wrong, I told myself as I finished packing. What does he know?

The next morning, I hesitated before boarding the bus. None of my friends were going; I didn't know any of my sister travelers. But, as one of the few people on the bus who had ever been to the Big Apple, I ended up the leader before we'd even left the parking lot.

As I considered myself a New York City expert, I enthusiastically elected myself tour guide. As the bus rolled away from Cincinnati, I passed out leftover Halloween candy to my naive travel mates and I told them what to expect.

"Okay. First of all, there are tons and tons of people. Most of them are going to try to mug you, so you have to hold on to your purse, and it might even be smart to put your money in your shoe." I delivered this information as casually as I could, as if I had been there zillions of times. I unwrapped another piece of bazooka to add to the four others already in my mouth. The more candy we had, the louder we got. "Oh my God! And there are totally hookers all over the place! They wear these shirts with their boobs out to here!"

I kept it up until Miss Brown stepped in. "Girls, it is 3:37 in the morning. I want it quiet back here. I want you all to sleep, and Sharon, if I hear one more peep out of you, I'll confiscate that candy. Go to sleep."

I tried to be quiet—we all did—but the thought of being in New York City for a week of Broadway shows, hotels, and restaurants, with no parents, worked on us all like NoDoz.

The trip flew by in a haze of happiness for me. We stayed at the Edison Hotel in the heart of Times Square. We screamed when the water came out of the faucet brown, we ate New York bagels and New York cheesecake, we leaned out of our hotel windows to take pictures of the XXX movie theater across the street. Best of all were the shows. We saw *A Chorus Line*, one of my personal favorites, and *The Pirates of Penzance*. I loved it so much, it almost hurt.

Afterward, as part of the school package, we got to go backstage. As we all lined up to meet the stars of the show, most of the girls made a big, giggly racket over Robby Benson and Kevin Kline, the handsome leading actors in the show. I didn't join in; their immaturity embarrassed me. I wanted to separate myself from the whole group.

To me, backstage was a holy temple. I wanted to give it the respect it deserved. Even though I'd been the foremost jokester the whole trip, suddenly I was the solemn one. I was the only person there who was serious about musical theater as a profession, and seeing it right in front of me made me realize how much I wanted it.

Throughout the entire backstage experience, I was uncharacteristically quiet. I didn't ask for autographs. Instead, I hung back, observing. I watched the wardrobe people, the wig people, and the stage crew packing up for the night. I watched the lighting guy flip off the house lights, and I shuddered as the backstage went dark. I breathed in the dusty, woody smell of the backstage, and memorized it. I didn't know when I would be in the backstage of a Broadway house again, but I prayed that the next time I was there, my name would be on the dressing-room door. It was the one of the many times during high school that I wished I could fast-forward to my adult life, because I knew it was going to be great. Being in the theater both thrilled and saddened me; I was thrilled for what the future would hold but sad that I had to wait for it.

Miss Brown had planned our days down to the minute so we could experience all of the culture New York had to offer. On the last day we took a trip to the Metropolitan Opera, which included a tour of the opulent building with its famous chandeliers and lobby. The tour guide was a meticulously groomed older man, and he barely spoke above a whisper during our tour, as if we were in a house of God. His hushed tones annoyed me at first; this was a theater, not a monastery. I was bored by the opera, and throughout the tour, I kept cracking jokes to the girls around me. At one point we were so loud, the tour guide stopped speaking and glared at us.

The tour ended on the upper tier of the balcony so we could look at the chandeliers up close. We weren't allowed into the balcony, but instead we stood in a doorway, looking up. I wandered away from the group and found another open doorway. I checked to see if anyone were watching, then slid into one of the red velvet seats in the back. The chandeliers were off, so the house was dark. The only light came from a single bulb on the stage, which was so far away I had to squint to see it. I felt someone walk up behind me and stand in the darkened doorway. It was Miss Brown.

"Beautiful, isn't it?"

I stood up, afraid she was upset I'd wandered from the group.

"You know, Sharon, you could sing on that stage one day if you worked hard enough. I must say it's exciting for a teacher to have a student with your potential."

It was too dark to see her face, and I was glad. I knew how much she loved the opera, and how much of a compliment this was. Miss Brown didn't give compliments easily. I was so surprised that I wasn't sure what to say, especially since I didn't share her love of opera at all. I thought it was for old people.

"Okay now, get yourself back with the group, young lady." Miss Brown snapped back to her normal self, but her tone was still affectionate. "Enough of these daydreams."

The tour ended, as all good tours should, in the gift shop. I wandered over to the enormous posters of the famous singers who had performed at the Met: Luciano Pavarotti, Placido Domingo, Joan Sutherland, and Beverly Sills. I stood there looking at them for a long time. "Isn't she the most ravishing creature you've ever seen?" Our fussy tour guide appeared beside me, gesturing to Beverly Sills. His tone was reverent. "She is such a beauty, such a prima donna, with a voice like an angel."

I actually thought she looked kind of ridiculous, all dressed up in a big puffy gown with flowers in her hair. I was about to say so, but the tour guide gushed on.

"Here she is as Violetta in *La Traviata*. Do you know *La Traviata?*"

I shook my head.

"Oh, you must listen to it. It is a classic. It will make you weep! My biggest regret in life is that I never heard her sing it live, although I did fly to San Diego to see one of her final performances in Menotti's *La Loca*. It took me weeks to recover. *Bella! Bella!*"

His intensity embarrassed me, but I asked him what *bella* meant.

"*Bella* is Italian for beautiful," he answered, "and *bella* she is. Just look at her, the face, the eyes, the mouth, all so regal. Beverly Sills is a true American diva. We are so lucky to live in her lifetime."

It was time to leave. I thanked our tour guide, and noticed how handsome he must have been once. I imagined him as a very handsome young man infatuated with Beverly Sills. I glanced at her picture one more time. She must have been at least a size 18, the same size I was. I asked him once more, "You really, really think she's beautiful?"

"Not just beautiful, my dear." He put his hand over his heart and gazed longingly at the poster. "She's ravishing."

The word *ravishing* stuck with me all the way to the bus, all the way through New Jersey, Pennsylvania, and Ohio. For most of the ride home, I pressed my forehead against the cold glass and gazed out the window, watching the farms fly by. Ravishing. *Ravishing.*

I thought about what the performers we'd seen in the musicals looked like. Naturally everyone in *A Chorus Line* was thin, because it was a dance show. *Dancers have to be thin,* I told myself as I'd watched it. *That's not the kind of show I'll be in. I'll do a show like* The Pirates of Penzance. *Singers don't have to be stick-thin like dancers do.* But even the singers in *The Pirates of Penzance* were tiny. The only overweight actors I'd seen on Broadway were the older character actors, who were at least fifty and weren't attractive at all. I had not seen one person on a Broadway stage who looked like me during my entire trip. Not one.

I flashed back to the upsetting conversation I'd had with my father about Marilyn Monroe. Maybe he was right.

I leaned my forehead against the cold bus window and thought about thin dancers and tiny chorus girls and the glamorous world of show business. Would I really be shut out if I didn't lose weight? I closed my eyes and tried to fast-forward to my adult life. Would I be on Broadway some day? Did I have to be thin to do it? What would happen to me if I weren't thin?

I didn't think I could ever be Marilyn Monroe, but I knew in my heart that I had enough talent and drive to be *someone.* I thought about the Metropolitan Opera tour guide, Miss Brown's surprising comments, and Beverly Sills. And suddenly, a plan came together in my head. As the bus pulled into Ursuline's parking lot, I pushed Broadway out of my head, jumped off the bus, and threw myself into the only option I had left: opera.

I decided to be *ravishing.*

Not long after the New York trip, reality hit. Being ravishing was a lot of work. It meant convincing the world that I loved opera.

Lies were not unknown to me. I lied about big things and little things alike, ranging from "My assignment isn't done because my great-aunt had a heart attack at our house last night" to "I like to drink a cocktail or two every night before bed to unwind." I lied to get out of trouble, I lied to get attention, I lied just to see if I could get away with it.

But I lied about opera to justify my size. My love for opera was my lie; my fat was my truth. I lied in order to escape that truth.

Who would believe the new opera-singer me? Everyone knew I'd been obsessed with musical theater since I was eight; I didn't believe I could pull this off. My newfound passion for opera was so contrived in those first few months that the entire dream would have come crashing down had even one person challenged it. But no one did.

Convincing people that I was "off" musical theater and "into" opera turned out far simpler than I anticipated. Part of me wished someone would call me on it—"Hey, Wheatley, give me a break. You hate opera; you're just doing this because you are getting so fat."

But one by one, the people closest to me bought my story. In fact, my friends and family were relieved, as it gave them an easy answer to the burning question: "Why is Sharon fat? Oh! She's going to be an opera singer!"

I should have felt good about this, because it meant my lie was working. But instead, I felt very much alone; no one seemed to know me at all.

Despite everyone's ready willingness to believe, adopting my new opera persona was hard work. I'd never needed to convince anyone that I was a future Broadway performer. My god-given pedigree was bubbly, animated, and dramatic. I was always the first to cry at a party or a sappy movie, always the best happy birthday singer—I was a natural ham and a natural musical theater performer.

But opera singers were different from most people and very different from me. Serious and studious, most had an old-fashioned quality about them—a result of losing themselves to an art form that had seen its heyday some 200 years earlier. They willingly learned several foreign languages. I was sure they'd never skipped around in overalls and flip-flops humming tunes from *Hello, Dolly!* as I had.

Miss Brown was instrumental in my transformation. When I told her I wanted to sing opera, she was thrilled; she'd been waiting for an enthusiastic student like me to come along. Like *The Karate Kid* learning ancient lessons from a master, I relied on Miss Brown's guidance, thoroughly surrendering myself to her wisdom. She told me to immerse myself in opera, and I listened to it at the expense of everything else.

Once I declared my desire to become an opera singer, my relationship with Miss Brown became very special. My new appreciation thrilled her; she entered me in competitions, added classes to the curriculum for me, and told me about good college programs. With Miss Brown at the piano, I was on my way to ravishing.

Sometimes I wasn't sure I could go through with it; I was falling deeper and deeper into something that, in my heart,

I knew I didn't like. I prayed that it would grow on me. Still, I made a big show of my new career choice, diving into it with a loud and obvious splash. I checked operas out of the library and carried them with me wherever I went, even though I couldn't pronounce any of the titles. I wore a scarf wrapped around my neck to protect my voice for extra operatic glamour. All to convince myself as much as everyone else that I was a future prima donna.

I suffered through *HMS Pinafore* and *The Merry Widow*, and despaired that I would ever learn to like, much less love, this art form; then I remembered the fussy tour guide from the Met, and I checked out the Beverly Sills recording of *La Traviata*.

"You like opera?" The librarian looked at me skeptically. "I do. I just adore it," I said, launching into my standard opera diatribe. In public, I was usually self-conscious about my weight, especially around strangers. I was convinced that they were thinking about how I looked, so I tried to work opera into the conversation as often as I could. It was amazing how people's attitudes changed.

"That's wonderful!" The librarian embraced my exotic diva persona with Midwestern enthusiasm. "I don't think I've ever met a future opera star before!"

I smiled and adjusted the scarf around my throat for effect.

"I don't know what it is, but you just seem like an opera singer." She handed me my stack of books and looked at my name on my library card. "Sharon Wheatley. I'm going to remember that name. The next Jessye Norman!"

I wondered if the librarian realized that the "air" I had that made me seem like an opera singer was nothing more than my "fat." I thanked her, feeling her eyes on me as I walked away. As my mom and I drove home, I flipped through the books and drew comfort from the pictures of the overweight women. I looked up Jessye Norman. Wow, she was big. In the opera world, I was downright skinny. I wondered if I should show the pictures to my mom when we got home, just to prove that I was skinny in some part of the universe, but I decided against it. Bringing up the subject of weight with my mother was never a good idea.

When I got home, I popped in the recording, lit a candle, turned off the lights, and lay down on my bed. I wanted the music to fill me like the Holy Spirit.

I was prepared to hate it, as I had all the other opera I'd heard up to this point in my life. But the overture to *La Traviata* drew me in. It was simple, beautiful, evocative. I listened to the entirety of side one, then listened to it again while trying to sing along with the score. It still wasn't as good as *Annie*, but I had to be realistic. Like it or not, I had a much better shot of being cast as Violetta than as some ten-year-old, red-haired orphan. I heard my dad's words in my head: *Sexy sells and fat isn't sexy.* I decided to test his theory.

I took off my clothes and looked at myself very shrewdly in the mirror. Even when I wanted to stop looking, even when I loathed what I saw, I forced myself to look. I turned sideways and I looked. I looked at my butt and hips. Everywhere I looked, every angle was the same. Big rolls of fat stood between my Broadway dreams and me. I made myself sing "Tomorrow" from *Annie* while watching myself in the mirror, just so I could see how ridiculous I looked. I tried out a few high notes, with my best opera voice. Even without the fluffy costumes and orchestra, even with my untrained voice, it was believable. It was no stretch to imagine myself as an opera singer, to see myself as Joan Sutherland or Beverly Sills. I didn't know that I would ever love opera the way the tour guide at the Met or Miss Brown loved it, but I could like it enough. That was all I needed, to like it enough.

chapter 10

the threepenny opera

Even future opera stars have to do math.

By April of my sophomore year, I was flunking out of school. The school sent a letter informing me and my family that I was officially on academic probation—which I promptly intercepted from the mailbox before my parents could see it.

I knew I needed to study hard; academic probation scared me enough to try. I'd never had to try very hard at Anderson to receive the Bs and Cs that kept my parents off my back. I started actually doing my homework—and discovered that Ursuline was hard, harder than I'd imagined. I was so incredibly behind that I didn't see how I could possibly catch up. Flunking out—and being sent back to Anderson—became a very real possibility.

My probation required that I see a guidance counselor twice a week to discuss my study habits. The office was in a large van in the school parking lot. I stood outside the van, reluctant to go inside. I'd never been to a counselor before, and didn't know what to expect. It couldn't be good.

"Come on in," said Mrs. Dettenwanger, a nice-looking woman with curly hair and a warm smile. "You can sit wherever you're comfortable." She sat on a chair next to a small desk attached to the side of the van. I chose the driver's seat. Elevated about a foot, the seat allowed me to spin around to face any direction.

Once I got comfortable, I informed her that I didn't need to see her. "I don't need to be here," I told her as I spun around, uniform skirt flying. "I'm not dumb, it's just that I don't have a lot of time for regular school work. I have to spend all my time on my music classes because I'm going to be an opera singer." My plan was to play up my musical ambitions. Ursuline wouldn't dare flunk out a future star.

"Even future opera stars have to do math." Apparently Mrs. Dettenwanger wasn't going to let me off that easily. "Otherwise, how will you count up all your money?" She had a point. We were both quiet for a moment. I dug down into my enormous quilted purse and pulled out a king-size Snickers bar. Mrs. Dettenwanger crossed her long legs and watched me as I unwrapped it. I swung my legs and looked around while I took big bites in the heavy silence.

"Is that your entire lunch?"

"Yeah." I swung my legs harder.

"It doesn't seem like a very healthy lunch. Did you consider having a sandwich instead?"

"Haven't you heard? 'Snickers really satisfies you.'" I said, quoting the commercial.

Mrs. Dettenwanger laughed. "Very funny." She grew serious again. "Do you eat a lot of candy?"

"Aren't you supposed to teach me how to take notes or something?"

"We'll get to that. I just thought you might like to talk about your weight."

Over the past year, my weight had skyrocketed, past 200 pounds, 220, and higher—to the point where I'd stopped weighing myself on my parents' scale covered with the furry yellow carpet. The only time I'd ever talked about my weight was that essay I'd written for Sister Mary Jane—and I certainly didn't want any more lectures on my immoral weight gain. So I maintained my code of silence on the subject, and expected others to as well.

The bigger I got, the more people talked about my weight behind my back and ignored it to my face. I appreciated that my aunts and uncles, grandparents, friends, and teachers avoided the painful topic. Instead, the talk focused on my more positive features—good hair, nice earrings, cute shoes, great voice. As my weight climbed, my family actively encouraged my opera dreams. No one knew that I really didn't like opera, or that I still listened to *Annie* and *The Sound of Music* when I was alone. My Christmas presents all focused on my new career path—a Metropolitan Opera key chain, the scores from the *Mikado* and *La Traviata*, a new scarf to wrap around my throat to protect my voice. It made sense to everyone. I could sing really well and I was fat. Opera was my perfect match.

Everyone believed I was happy, and I wanted to keep it that way. Now this Mrs. Dettenwanger was stirring up trouble. I wanted to jump up and yell, "Didn't you get the memo, lady? No one brings up my fat, no matter how big I am!" I didn't yell or jump up; instead, I felt the familiar lift out of my body—as if my body were saying to my brain, *See ya later, alligator. You're on your own.*

I shoved the Snickers back in my purse.

"I don't want to talk about my weight," I said in an uncharacteristic monotone. "There's nothing to talk about. I'm going to be an opera singer and I need the extra weight to sing better." I gave her a big smile. "That's all. It's for my singing."

"I don't understand how all that extra weight could actually help you sing." Mrs. Dettenwanger looked perplexed. "I'm talking simply physiologically. It doesn't make sense."

"It has to do with the size of my diaphragm." I tried to stay calm, impersonating my music teacher Miss Brown, throwing around musical terms that I'd heard her use in my voice lessons. "The diaphragm is a singer's most important air supply, and the bigger it is, the better a singer you are." At the look of disbelief on Mrs. Dettenwanger's face, I panicked. The words rushed out. "In the opera world I'm actually quite petite, and my current sound reflects that. Do you see what I mean? I actually have to eat this candy to become a better singer!" Sweat dripped down my back, landing on the waistband of my too-tight uniform skirt. My pulse raced, and I couldn't seem to stop talking. "And Beverly Sills is bigger than me, and Jessye Norman is bigger than me, and Joan Sutherland is bigger—"

"Sharon, I didn't mean to upset you," said Mrs. Dettenwanger, interrupting my frantic list of singing fat ladies with a compassionate look and the calm voice of reason. "If you don't want to talk about this, we don't have to."

"I don't want to talk about it." I took a deep breath, and it felt like the first breath I'd taken in several minutes.

We sat quietly for a moment, and I wiped the beads of sweat off my face with a tissue. I felt both relieved and somehow— unsatisfied. I considered telling her how I really felt about my weight, how horrible it was, instead of pretending it was necessary for my singing, but I couldn't. The words just wouldn't come out. I looked at Mrs. Dettenwanger, and thought, *I wish I could. I really wish I could tell you how I'm feeling right now.*

"Okay, then let's talk about your grades." Mrs. Dettenwanger uncrossed her legs and leaned forward, pulling notes out of my file. "I have a note from your geometry teacher saying that you rarely turn in your assignments. I have a note from your biology teacher saying that you haven't passed a quiz this quarter." Mrs. Dettenwanger delivered this news in a direct, yet caring way, like a sledgehammer protected with bubble wrap. "What's going on? Why aren't you doing your work? Every one of your teachers thinks you have the ability, but you just don't seem to apply yourself."

I hated the words *ability* and *apply*, which were inevitably used against me. I tried a counteroffensive. "Do you have any reports from Miss Brown in that file? She'd say nice things about me."

Miss Brown's approval meant everything to me. I worked at a frenetic pace for her, often at the expense of my other classes. I'd spend hours on my music homework, but minutes on biology and geometry. I couldn't draw a simple isosceles triangle, but I could dissect Schubert's Unfinished Symphony in the key of G, measure by measure, on graph paper.

"Sharon, this isn't a performing arts school," pointed out Mrs. Dettenwanger. "Here at Ursuline, you have to do well in all of your classes. How else are you going to get into a good conservatory?"

She was right about that, so I didn't say anything.

"I'm a big fan of your singing, Sharon," Mrs. Dettenwanger said, "but there's more to getting an education than music." She rose to her feet. "I'm here to help you do just that. Our time is up for now, but we'll continue to meet twice a week."

Over time, I began to look forward to my trips to Mrs. Dettenwanger's van. Once I understood that everything I said to her was "confidential," I started to spill my guts about everything but my weight. Mrs. Dettenwanger realized my problems began at home, and she kept the conversations about grades to a minimum after that first visit. She still checked in with me and talked about the reports from my teachers, but we whittled it down to the first five minutes or so. The next thirty-five minutes were reserved for my day-to-day familial dramas. "I can't stand my parents," I told Mrs. Dettenwanger. "Seriously. They fight over the dumbest stuff."

"The dumbest stuff?" Mrs. Dettenwanger asked in her concerned, therapeutic voice.

I loved that voice; I drew comfort from it—comfort I needed given the escalating war at home.

Their ongoing battles about money grew more ferocious, and for me, more depressing. On the weekends that I didn't spend at Carolyn's house, I hid out in my room, listening to my parents go at it. I told Mrs. Dettenwanger everything as it happened—when our heating oil ran out, when our credit cards got rejected, when my father's swimming-pool business failed.

This emphasis on my situation at home during our sessions lulled me into a false sense of security. So when Mrs. Dettenwanger sat me down a few months into our counseling sessions, I was not prepared for the worst.

"You are still not performing as well as you need to," she told me. "Everyone is concerned. Your teachers have been calling me. Your friends have approached me. If you do not improve your grades, you'll have to leave Ursuline."

"They can't kick me out!" I dismissed this notion out of hand. "This school needs me. Who else will sing for Mass? Who will sing the solos in the concerts?" I figured they'd keep me at Ursuline just because they liked me, no matter what my grades were.

"Sharon, you are important to this school." Mrs. Dettenwanger sighed. "But I don't think you are hearing me. I need you to listen to me very closely." She leaned forward, her dark eyes locking on mine. "They will flunk you if you don't turn your grades around *right now*."

The truth hit me, and it hurt. I could hardly breathe. I felt as if I were going to pass out.

"You have to see it from my point of view," said Mrs. Dettenwanger, her voice softer now. "Here sits this wonderfully talented, smart—"

I made a face.

"Yes, Sharon, you are smart, no matter what you want to believe. You are a smart, funny, charming girl with everything going for you. In spite of this, you are failing out of school." She leaned back in her chair again, her compassionate face drawn. "And I know you don't want me to mention your weight, but your weight is dangerously high and that's a concern too. Weight is a shield, Sharon, and you can't hide behind a shield forever."

It struck me that she was upset, too, and that realization made it real. *I was flunking out.* My world was crashing down around me.

"You can't flunk me out of this school." All of the feelings I'd been burying for so long just let loose, and I started to sob. "I won't make it if I'm sent back to Anderson. I'm not kidding. I won't do it. I'll run away first!" I knew I sounded dramatic, but I kept going. "And what about my parents? They don't care. They just fight all the time and get on my case about my weight and my grades and my room being a mess and being on the phone all the time. I'm sick of it. The one good thing I have in my life is this school, and if I can't go here, I'm gone. I'm serious. I'll run away."

"Sharon." Mrs. Dettenwanger regarded me with such sympathy that it hurt. "No one at this school wants you to flunk out. Not one person, especially me. You don't have to run away, and you don't have to go back to Anderson; you just have to study.

I've been talking to your teachers, and I think I've narrowed down exactly what you need to do."

With Mrs. Dettenwanger's help, I became incredibly focused. We compared my current grades with the grades I needed to pass the classes. With "heifer" and "whale" in the back of my mind, the decision was easy. I could only imagine what new names the kids at Anderson would call me when they saw me at this weight. This prospect was horrific enough to keep me off the phone, away from the TV, and into my books.

My only distraction during this time was one I'd never anticipated and wasn't even sure I wanted—a boy. His name was Jeremy. He was the son of Jeanie Schwarz, one of my mother's coworkers. My mother dealt with our family's financial woes in her usual pragmatic manner—she got a job. A long-time volunteer at Channel 48, the local PBS station, she jumped at the chance to work there full-time. They offered her the job, and she took it.

I was thrilled. I loved having a working mom because it gave me unlimited time in the kitchen after school. It had always been much easier to sneak food when my dad was home than when my mom was home, given his penchant for watching TV with the volume turned all the way up. Even though I was glad to have her out of the kitchen, I liked to visit Mom at Channel 48. Since she was away from my dad and making money, she was usually in a good mood, and we got along much better. I dropped by as often as I could—and it was there that I renewed my acquaintance with Jeremy.

Jeanie Schwarz and Mom had been friends since I was in grade school, so I knew her well. She had two sons, and Jeremy, the oldest, was close to my age. He liked to hang out at Channel 48, too. Jeremy was a nice kid and, like me, had a big weight problem. I'd never thought of him as anything but a friend, so

I was surprised when Mom and Jeanie's coworkers started to tease us about being a couple. I figured it was just because we were both fifteen and they thought it was so cute.

Encouraged, Jeremy started to flirt with me. I liked the attention, but I wasn't sure how I felt about him. So when he asked me to go to the movies with him, I put him off until I could get a second opinion.

I passed a note to Carolyn in biology class.

> *Dear C.*
> *Jeremy asked me to go to the movies and I'm not sure if I should go because I don't think I like him like that and I don't want to lead him on. What should I do??*
> *Sharon*

A few minutes later a note landed on my desk with a plop.

> *Dear Miss Academic Probation,*
> *You should be paying attention rather than passing notes, but . . . one question. How are you ever going to know if you like him if you don't go out with him? Isn't that what a date is for?*

She had a point, so I called Jeremy and agreed to the date. In my opinion, there was absolutely no spark between us; but as overweight as I was, boys weren't exactly knocking down my door. I'd never been on a date before and beggars couldn't be choosers. I wondered if he felt the same way about me.

The night of our date, Jeremy's mom drove us to the movies. After an awkward who's-going-to-sit-where moment, Jeremy and I ended up together in the backseat.

"You two just relax, and let me chauffeur you!" Mrs. Schwarz called from the front seat. Embarrassed, I slunk down in the beige leather seat to avoid her enthusiastic glances in the rearview mirror. I just knew as soon as she got home, she was going to call my mom and report our every action, so I was determined to give her nothing to talk about. Jeremy must have been on the same wavelength, because we sat in stony silence until we got to the theater.

"That was awkward," I mumbled as the car drove off.

"Totally."

We loaded up at the snack bar with the cash our parents had given us. One of the plusses about going out with an overweight kid was that I didn't have to watch what I ate. We carried our stash to our seats, and Jeremy showed me how he liked to pour his M&Ms right into the popcorn.

"Try it!" he said, thrusting the big butter-drenched tub under my nose. "You'll love it. It's salty and sweet."

He was right. It was salty and sweet, and when I had reached my hands into the tub, our fingers brushed for a moment and I had a little flicker of affection for him. *We could get along,* I thought.

We settled in to watch the movie—a horror flick. During the scary parts, the girl in front of me screamed and snuggled with her boyfriend. I watched her, fascinated. I wasn't very good at being a girlie-girl, and I thought that's probably what Jeremy wanted me to be, so I took my cues from the girl in front of me, as she obviously had more experience than I did. When she screamed, I screamed. When she hid her eyes, I hid my eyes. Ridiculous, but it worked.

Soon Jeremy was holding my hand. It was my first time holding hands. It was fun at first, but then our flabby palms began to sweat. I was embarrassed, but I was afraid to move. By the time the credits rolled, we were wiping our palms on our pants. Relieved to see the taillights of my mom's car in the parking lot, I quickly jumped into the front seat. We dropped off Jeremy, and we said an awkward goodbye.

"How did it go?" asked my mother.

"Okay." I didn't know what to say, especially knowing that whatever I did say would undoubtedly be repeated to Jeremy's mother. "Uh, I don't know if I like him or not."

"Take your time," Mom said. "It's not like you have to make up your mind today."

It really bothered me that I wasn't attracted to Jeremy, and I worried that it was because he was overweight. It seemed like a terrible double standard, and I was ashamed of myself.

Jeremy started calling regularly, and before I knew it, we had a "thing" going. I even called him my boyfriend around school. I liked the way "my boyfriend" sounded. Not to mention that if there's one way to get clout at an all-girls school, it's by having a boyfriend. *They'll never know what he looks like*, I consoled myself.

Then, one day in the cafeteria my friend Gloria came up with a brilliant idea. "Sharon! You need to have a pool party at the end of the year so we can all see your big fancy pool and your boyfriend. How about it?"

I laughed. "If I don't flunk out, I'll have a huge pool party to celebrate. We'll invite everybody, okay?"

Having my friends meet Jeremy was not the worst thing that could happen.

The worst thing that could happen was already happening— despite my best efforts, I was still failing biology. I'd managed to pull up my grades in every other subject, but unless I passed biology, I'd get kicked out of school.

Mrs. Dettenwanger crunched the numbers, and she told me that I'd have to ace the biology exam to avoid expulsion. My grade was currently an F. The only thing standing between Anderson High School and me was a 92 on an exam in a subject for which I had absolutely no aptitude, and I had only seventy-two hours to prepare.

I didn't even know where to start. So, I turned to Carolyn. Unnerved at the thought of losing her best friend, she was determined to help me pass. She designed a grueling study schedule for me.

I was a most willing student—but after the first in-depth tutorial it was clear that there was no way I was going to learn an entire year of biology in one weekend.

"What am I going to do?'

Carolyn looked at me. "You know, I have a lot to lose here, too. I can't have my best friend flunk out of school; it just can't happen. I'll wither and die." She grinned at me. "We'll think of something."

That night, Carolyn and I worked out a plan to get me through biology. All I'm going to say is that it worked—and that I owed her one. I passed biology.

chapter 11
big

Every step I took was a squishy walking reminder, like a pedometer clicking:
Fat. Fat. Fat.

I packed up my locker at the end of the year, relieved that I'd be filling another locker nearby in the fall. But I still wasn't happy. I had another, bigger problem, and it was only getting worse. I was huge.

I avoided mirrors like a vampire, but when I absolutely had to look, I barely recognized the girl gazing back. My face was puffy and distorted, plopped on top of an accordion of several chins. My clothes were out-of-date and ugly, with big elastic waistbands to fit around my enormous stomach. Every step I took was a squishy walking reminder, like a pedometer clicking: *Fat. Fat. Fat.*

I never had anything to wear. I suffered through event after event—weddings and other special family occasions—in dresses akin to pup tents. I wore black all the time, hoping it made me look thin, but knowing it couldn't possibly make me look thin enough. I "accessorized," hoping to pull people's eyes "away from my problem areas" like the magazines said. The truth was, necklaces weren't made big enough to hide my "problem areas."

When I had a particularly bad "body day," I would hide out in my room, light candles, and turn on the most depressing music I could find. For most teenage girls, depressing music might mean sappy love songs, but for me it meant the final movement of Tchaikovsky's "Pathetique" Symphony no. 6 in B Minor. I would turn it up until the walls shook with the booming of the strings and throw myself down on my bed.

Now that summer was here, I had all the more reason for my pathetic despair. I'd promised my friends a pool party if I didn't flunk out of school—and now I was expected to have one. Worse, at this swim celebration I was expected to introduce my "boyfriend" Jeremy to my friends. My first boy/girl party—and I'd be wearing a bathing suit the size of a circus tent. Not to mention that I didn't even know if I actually liked Jeremy enough to go out with him again, let alone try to flirt with him while my friends watched. A date in a bathing suit—I'd rather have a root canal.

In the end, I decided that *having* a boy at the party was better than *not* having a boy at the party, so I called Jeremy and asked him. Excited, he accepted right away.

My girlfriends were excited as well. There were rounds of phone calls about who was wearing what kind of bathing suit—two-piece or one-piece—and what cover-up to wear over it. I participated enthusiastically in the conversations, describing my suit and advising on waterproof makeup, all the while dreading the party. I hated that I had this huge monstrosity of a body, while my friends were all so cute and trim. For a 230-pound fifteen-year-old girl with a maybe-boyfriend, a pool party was, in a word, hell.

The day before the party, I bit the bullet. I tried on the bathing suit that my mom had bought me a few months earlier, hoping that it would miraculously look fantastic and sexy. An expensive suit, we'd bought it because the tags promised an "extra-slimming" guarantee. If the suit didn't make you look ten pounds slimmer, you got your money back.

I slipped it on, and it felt strange. I had to tug to get it up, so I walked over to the mirror to see if there was a twist in the straps or something that was making it fit wrong. My bedroom mirror didn't lie. There was nothing wrong with the suit except that it wasn't even remotely slimming because it didn't fit—at all. I'd eaten my way out of my slimming swimming suit. The straps cut into my shoulders, the bottom stuck in unthinkable places every time I took a step.

What would I tell my mother? The truth was out of the question. The truth was, in a food, potato skins. I'd taken to making them every time my parents went out, which was several times a week. I hated being left alone, and food was an easy comfort. I would bake three potatoes, cut them in half, and scoop most of the insides into a bowl. On top of the halved potatoes, I would add bacon and cheese, and put them back into the oven to brown. I'd grabbed the waiting bowl and make mashed potatoes with cream, butter, and salt to eat while the potato skins cooked. A delicious routine: Finish the mashed potatoes, pull out the skins, top them with sour cream, *voilà*.

To the salty wonder of potato skins I added the sweetness of Nestlé Toll House Morsels. I'd discovered bags and bags of them in the garage freezer and soon was adding half batches of chocolate chip cookies to my evening snack fests. I was cooking so much that the house smelled like a diner by the time my parents came home. Afraid they'd find me out, I burned a single slice of American cheese in a skillet each night after I cooked. The smell of burned cheese obliterated everything else.

"Sorry about the smell," I'd tell my parents. "I was trying to make a grilled cheese sandwich while you were gone, and I burned it."

The effects of these late-night potato skin/chocolate chip festivals, well hidden by my school uniform, were on full and not-so-fabulous display in my suit.

Hoping the suit would stretch out, I decided to take a dip in the pool. I wrapped myself in the biggest beach towel I could find and hustled out the back door without being seen. I paused at the screen door and breathed in the summer air. The opening of our pool was the official beginning of summer.

Standing at the edge of the water, I scanned the windows that overlooked the backyard to see if anyone was watching. The coast was clear. I dropped my towel, adjusted my suit, and inched my way into the icy water.

My mother chose that moment to prune the rose bushes by the pool. As she rounded the corner to the backyard, I heard her—and plunged headlong into the freezing water to hide my new, super-size body.

Trapped, I tried to splash around as if I were having a great time. Mom walked to the edge of the pool, slid off her sandals, and stuck her toes in. She recoiled. "I don't know how you are in there! It's freezing!"

I was starting to lose feeling in my feet, but I decided I'd rather risk hypothermia than let her see me in my too-small suit.

"Honey, you are starting to turn blue! Get out of there."

"I'm not cold."

"You are freezing. Come out." She picked up my towel and held it open for me at the top of the steps. I slowly swam over to the stairs and climbed out. I don't know which was worse, the cold or the dread.

"Sharon, your bathing suit is so tight!" She moved my top strap. "You have big red marks from your straps! Doesn't this hurt?" She fussed around with the straps a little, looking alarmed. "Sharon, this bathing suit fit you a few months ago. How in the world could it be this tight?"

"Um, I think it shrunk," I lied, bracing myself for the lecture.

Instead, she started to cry. "Sharon, I don't know what to do for you. I don't know how to help you. I'm worried for your health."

In that moment, I saw myself through her eyes, a big, gross, dieting failure, and I knew it must be terrible for her to have me as a daughter. She was so thin and pretty, and she must hate going out places with me.

"I don't want to look like this either, you know." Something snapped inside of me. "I'll never be skinny like you; I just won't." I wasn't hurt or embarrassed or guilty anymore. I was angry. "I know you and Dad think I'm fat. Dad told me. He said he didn't want to use that word, but he had to for my own good. He said that you were upset about it and that he didn't like me upsetting you." All those years of comments at the dinner table, the awful low-calorie lunches, the desserts I had to skip. "I don't have your discipline. I'm more like Dad. I can't help it. I might just look this way for the rest of my life!" I looked at the pool and thought about all the pool parties I'd had to host since childhood. Birthdays and Fourth of July swim parties with family and friends. And me, fatty fatty two by four, in a bathing suit, front and center. "I don't want to have this stupid party. I don't want to have to wear a bathing suit again, ever!"

I grabbed my towel, wrapped it around myself, and ran to my room in tears. I was angry with everyone, and everything, especially my stupid body. Mostly, I was angry that I couldn't stop eating. Even in my distress over the suit, my stomach rumbled with hunger. I lit a candle and turned on my best friend Tchaikovsky as loud as I could.

---

big

When I emerged from my room hours later, my mom was waiting for me.

"I'm sorry," I said. And I was sorry. I'd never exploded at my mother like that. I usually considered my mom too fragile to handle my emotions, so I sheltered her from them as best I could. I saved the good stuff for Mrs. Dettenwanger.

"I feel terrible."

"Me, too. I didn't mean what I said. I'm really sorry, Mom."

My mom brightened up. "Hey, I think I've got a little room on my Visa. What do you say, let's go get you a new bathing suit for the party? And if you want, we'll have Mexican for dinner."

"Okay." Mexican sounded good. I promised myself I would eat something small to make my mom happy.

We went to the mall, and we each got a bathing suit. Mom got a two-piece with a wraparound skirt, and I bought an expensive turquoise one-piece with wooden beads on the straps. At the fast-food Mexican place, I limited myself to one hard-shell taco, as a peace offering. It made me feel a little better.

The party was surprisingly fun. All my girlfriends came, and my mom made tons of great food. I wore my new turquoise bathing suit, with a large oxford cloth shirt over it for the majority of the party. Very few boys showed up, but Jeremy came.

I was shy about introducing him at first. I wasn't sure what my friends would think of us, but no one seemed to notice our joint tonnage. My friends accepted Jeremy right away, and I relaxed.

Jeremy was very attentive. He followed me around a lot, which unnerved me at first. I was busy playing hostess most of the night, but as the party wore down to a close, I finally sat down next to him on a double swing. We held hands as I talked to my friends. I felt as if I were playing the part of a girl used to having a boyfriend, rather than actually liking it. Part of me missed the camaraderie of the girls-only group. Adding boys to the mix changed everything. I was no good at playing the giggly, flirty girl.

Parents started to show up to pick up my guests, Mrs. Schwarz among them. "My mom's here," Jeremy said. "I have to go."

I was relieved. I was glad he came, and I had a good time, but flirting was hard work. I'd hit my quotient of cute comebacks and conversation starters.

He stood there, waiting. I wondered if he were expecting a kiss. I hadn't ever kissed a boy before. Maybe it wasn't such a bad idea, but I just couldn't do it in front of all of my friends and our parents. I decided to hug him goodbye instead. As I leaned in to hug him, he whispered in my ear. "I can sneak over later on my moped if you want."

My stomach did a flip-flop. This was going to be more than a good-night kiss. I was fifteen, why not? "Umm. Okay." I giggled. "Call me when you get home."

When the taillights from his mother's car disappeared down the road, I ran and told Carolyn.

"He's going to ride over here on his moped?" For some reason she thought this was hilarious. "It's so Romeo and Juliet!"

"Oh, yeah. We look just like Romeo and Juliet."

"No one's ever ridden a moped to my house in the middle of the night. You *have* to call me as soon as he leaves."

Everyone left, and I waited for Jeremy. I watched for him out of my bedroom window, which faced the street. I listened to my mom go to bed, then my dad, and wondered who was still awake at his house. As I waited for him, I wondered what he would do when he arrived. I thought of Trisha Luce and the boys in the woods. *How far would he expect me to go? How far was I willing to go?*

---

big

It was around two in the morning when the little light of his moped appeared. I turned off the security alarm and ran outside to meet him. I was excited and nervous; I'd never snuck out before—that was my brother's domain. And I knew from Buzzy's stories that boys didn't ride four miles on their mopeds at two in the morning to talk.

"Hi."

He looked nervous, too. "Hi."

Jeremy parked his moped in a small parking lot we had in the front of the house where my dad parked the company pickup truck. The smell of pine was thick in the summer night air.

Jeremy didn't waste time. He kissed me, and it was a very soft, wet kiss. Our teeth clinked together. I don't know what I was expecting, but this grossed me out.

"Sorry," he muttered.

As we kissed, I was acutely aware that Jeremy might be the only boy who'd ever be attracted to me. The thought made me incredibly sad, but I decided to try to enjoy the moment, since I might spend the rest of my life a fat, ugly spinster reminiscing about the one night I'd had next to the pickup truck with Jeremy Schwarz.

Once we got past the clicking teeth, things went pretty well. But I kept hearing these voices in my head: *You'd better just go for it, if he wants to. This might be your last opportunity. You're lucky he's here, and you'd better put out if you want him to come back.* I felt his hands going up my shirt and down my pants, and I didn't object. It wasn't romantic and it wasn't passionate. In fact, it was nothing like I thought it would be, but the voices kept urging me on.

Things were progressing to the "let's take our clothes off" stage, when I had a moment of clarity. Unfortunately for Jeremy, my moment of clarity came just as he put my hand in his very excited lap. Something about feeling it, which was undoubtedly incredibly pleasurable for him, served as a wake-up call for me.

I don't know where the words came from, but suddenly they were in my head: *I'm not this person.* The words were so strong that I said them out loud. It felt good.

"What's the matter?" Jeremy looked nervous, like I was going to report him to the principal. "I'm sorry, did I go too far?"

"No. It's not your fault." I thought it was sweet that he was willing to take the blame. "I thought I was this kind of a girl, but I'm just not." I flashed back to Trisha. I hadn't wanted to be this kind of a girl then, either.

"What kind of a girl?" Jeremy looked confused.

"The kind of a girl who lets a guy go all the way, just so she knows what it's like. I'm just not that girl. I'd rather wait."

"We don't have to go all the way, Sharon." Jeremy responded well, despite where most of the blood in his body was currently pooling. "We can just fool around. Or just hang out. Whatever you want."

"I think it's better if you just go home. I'm really sorry."

"Are you sure?"

"Yeah. But I think it's really nice that you came all the way over." I gave him a little kiss good night and watched him pull out of the driveway.

Later Carolyn laughed at my story and called me a chicken. I didn't feel an ounce of regret, and life went on, boy-less, as it had before Jeremy. Except inside, I knew something was different.

The rest of the summer flew by, and the words played themselves over and over in my head: *I'm not that person.* I wasn't sure what it meant, but that was okay. All I needed to know was that it was true.

chapter 12
starting here, starting now

"I'll have a chef salad, vinaigrette dressing on the side, and a hot tea."

My defining moment came with the utterance of a simple sentence: "I'll have a chef salad, vinaigrette dressing on the side, and a hot tea."

"Are you feeling sick?" Aunt Nancy looked at me from across the table at the café where we were dining with my family. "No," I said, feigning ignorance. "Why?"

"Nothing." Nancy picked up her fork and tried to act as nonchalant as I was. "I just noticed you ordered a salad, that's all."

I smiled at her and shrugged my shoulders. What I wanted to say was, drop it before anyone else notices. I'd been so miserable about my weight that I'd decided—just on a whim—to try a low-cal dinner to see if I could bear a diet. I wasn't committing to anything, so I didn't want it to become a topic for discussion yet. Especially since I was considering calling the waitress over and changing my order to the tutti-frutti waffles.

The decision to order a salad was small, but it was motivated by several small events, all of which led me to one major question: Is this who I want to be?

The first incident involved my sister's fiancé, Tony. An artist fresh out of Yale's art school, he asked me to model for him. It was a muggy day in late July, and I agreed as long as I could stay in my bathing suit and lie on a beach chair. Translation: I'll do it as long as it takes absolutely no effort on my part.

I flopped down on my stomach to take a nap, and when I woke up, Tony was putting the finishing touches on the painting. I hopped up and begged to see it. At first, I didn't understand what I was looking at. Tony was an abstract painter, so I held onto the small hope that the thing I saw in the painting was not me. But slowly the truth came into focus: What looked like a blurry Shamu-like object propped up on the beach chair was actually me, in my extra-large, supposed-to-be-slimming black bathing suit with white stripes on the sides.

I felt betrayed. I loved Tony like a flesh-and-blood brother, and he painted me as a whale. Tony is a kind soul, and I knew that he'd never hurt me intentionally, but the reality of that abstract painting was too much. It was the first time I had ever seen myself through someone else's eyes, and I was mortified.

Maybe Tony had painted me bigger than I was, but in my heart I knew that wasn't true. His eye was unforgiving if accurate, and I was appalled at the hugeness of me. Still, the image fascinated me—but as much as I longed to storm off in a cloud of self-pity, I couldn't. I was riveted by my raw doughiness, my arms, my legs, my butt, all so much bigger than any of the worst renditions I'd made in my head.

"Is this really what I look like?"

Tony's answer was honest. "Sharon, I painted what I saw. I didn't mean to hurt you."

For a couple of weeks, that painting ranked as the worst moment of my life; then I went back-to-school shopping with my mother.

Mom and I had recently found a way around humiliating dressing-room moments. When we went to the mall together, she gave me her credit card, and I shopped, tried on clothes, and made purchases alone. We'd meet up later for lunch, and I'd show her what I'd bought, minus any tags that included the size.

A perfect scheme—until the day her credit card was rejected.

"I'm sorry, miss," the clerk said to me over my pile of clothing. "There is a problem with your card."

Not surprising, since these days my parents were only paying the essential bills. I told the lady to hold on to my clothes, and I'd go find my mom and get a different card.

"I'm sorry, ma'am, but I'm going to have to make a call." She smiled disingenuously at me as she picked up the phone. "If you just wait right here, I'll contact the manager."

I eavesdropped on her conversation. "This is Doris in the plus-size department. I have a bit of a situation here. Uh-huh. A customer is attempting to use a card that's been rejected. She says it's her mother's card." There was a pause as she listened, and then she said in a low voice, "Well, she's a teenager, and she's grossly obese."

Grossly obese. Grossly obese. Grossly obese. The words hit me like a scud missile. What was happening? I wasn't grossly obese! I resisted the urge to yank the phone out of her hand and hit her with it. How could a total stranger describe me in such a mean, thoughtless way? Grossly obese was 400 pounds. Grossly obese was someone who was so huge he couldn't get out of a chair without help. Grossly obese was having to be lifted by a crane out of your apartment. I was not grossly obese; I was Sharon

Wheatley, a fifteen-year-old with a slight weight problem—a future opera singer. I ran out of the store and sat on a bench in the main part of the mall, waiting for my heart to stop racing.

What if she were right? What if I were grossly obese? I remembered Kathy, the assistant manager from the cupcake aisle of the Stale Store. Was I really like her? I quickly made a mental list:

Fact. I was shopping in the plus-size department, and the smallest sizes didn't fit me anymore. I was now midway through the plus-size department and was eating my way into the XXX-larges.

Fact. Tony had painted me as Shamu the killer whale.

Fact. A total stranger had just described me as grossly obese.

Sitting there on the bench, I had a moment of clarity similar to the one I'd had with Jeremy. Inside me, that familiar little voice was begging me to justify my fat. But this time I ignored it. Instead, I asked myself, *Is this who I want to be? Do I want to be the girl in Tony's painting, the girl described as grossly obese by a total stranger? Am I her?* The answer rang so loudly in my head that it almost hurt. *No. I do not want to be that person. I am not that person.*

The truth was cathartic. This was my moment to attempt to turn the tides of fate. Or, in my case, the tides of weight. Like an alcoholic checking into rehab, I'd hit bottom.

That's why I ordered that fateful chef salad. The beauty of growing up around an Olympic dieter is that no matter how much I'd tried over the years to block out my mother's suggestions of fruit over French fries, a lot of it had seeped in. I knew what to eat to lose weight because it was the food my mother had offered me for years. "Honey, why not have a salad instead of a burger?" "If you leave off the gravy, you'll save hundreds of calories!" "How about a peach?" My mother, right or wrong, had filled my head with so many low-calorie options that the day of the chef salad, I knew what to order, with dressing on the side. The hot tea was my own addition; I liked the sound of it.

Even when I ordered the salad, I didn't know if I could diet longer than the meal itself. I picked through the lettuce, trying to ignore the tantalizing smell of the restaurant's greasy kitchen. I lusted after my aunt's patty melt, and coveted my brother's pancakes. As I nibbled my way through greens and lean meat, I was already thinking about the chips I'd seen on the top shelf of the pantry at home.

But I made it through that night and the next and the next, making on-the-spot decisions each time I encountered unhealthy food. *Is it worth it?* I asked myself over and over, especially when I had the urge to sneak food. *Why are you sneaking this? If you don't want to eat it in front of other people, should you eat it at all?*

As I started losing weight, I kept it to myself. After so many years of listening to everyone else's opinions on my weight gain, I was unwilling to invite other people's opinions on my weight loss. I'm sure my parents noticed, especially since my meals had changed so drastically, and I'd started to work out in my sister's old room multiple times a week. There's no way to miss it when a 200-plus-pound person jumps rope right over your head. But if they talked about it, they never said a word to me. I think we were all afraid of jinxing it.

After a couple of months, I'd lost enough weight that I began publicly admitting I was dieting.

Every time I ran into someone, I heard, "Sharon! My God! You look fantastic! How much weight have you lost?" I loved it. The questions and accolades increased as my dress size decreased. "It's astounding! Tell me. How did you do it? I want every detail!" I'd never had compliments about my body, and I drank them in. I loved the attention, the pride, the relief. As I went to sleep at night, I replayed the compliments to myself, my diet version of counting sheep.

Thanksgiving was my first family holiday as the new, smaller me. I'd lost about thirty pounds by that point, and the difference was most apparent in my face and upper body. My weight loss was a hot topic throughout the entire meal. Talking about my diet helped keep me on track as I struggled with the vast amount of food on the table. I didn't want one day of stuffing and gravy to ruin my progress. I counted calories, and I spent a lot of the meal adding up the totals.

"The turkey alone isn't such a bad thing. I'm okay if I stick to that. It's the side dishes that will kill me." I watched my trim brother shovel mashed potatoes on his plate. "Like that. See Buzz's mashed potatoes? A portion that size has 360 calories—oh wait, are you adding gravy? That adds a lot of fat, bringing the total to 580. . . ."

At one point in the meal, I glanced down to my mother at the end of the table and noticed that we had the same foods on our plates. She saw what I was doing and winked at me.

All my life I'd longed for the kind of mom whom I could talk to about my weight. Not in a "How many calories are in this taco?" kind of way, but really talk to her.

When I was younger, I wanted to go out for double scoops of ice cream with my mom and fess up to all the teasing at school. But I never shared this with my mother, ever. I was afraid that if I admitted how miserable my fat made my life, my mom wouldn't want to *talk* about it; she would want to *fix* it. And I knew from experience that fixing it meant something drastic. And now, I was trying to fix it. Her way.

I looked down the food-laden Thanksgiving table at my mother. Even though we bickered like all teenage daughters and mothers, I now had a new appreciation for her willpower. I winked back.

That night, my dad came to talk to me. "Honey, I gotta tell you, I was impressed with you today. It's not easy to stick to a diet with all that food around. You did a hell of a job. I sure couldn't do it, kid!"

"It felt pretty good." I laughed. "I mean, I really appreciate everybody's enthusiasm. Sometimes it's weird though, like when people I don't even know talk to me about it at school. One of the seniors actually brought her salad plate over to me and asked me to add up how many calories she was eating! Isn't that a riot?"

My dad looked at me intensely. "I want you to understand something here, Sharon. You're a role model, whether you realize it or not. You're managing to do something that a lot of people can't do. You've got life by the tail right now. Your weight is going down, your grades are coming up, and a lot of people are going to want to know how you've done it." His acknowledgment—about both my weight loss and school—made me feel wonderful.

Fixing healthy food, exercising, and losing weight took up a lot of time, and it had forced me to organize other parts of my life, including school.

"Did you know I got on the honor roll this quarter?" I did not mention that I'd just flunked an anthropology test. I hated anthropology. I hated anything with *-ology* or *-ometry* at the end of the word.

My dad's eyes started to twinkle—the same twinkle he got when he came up with a new invention. "I think you should start to write down everything you're doing."

"Like a journal?"

"Maybe a journal, maybe something bigger. Make it something you can hand people when they ask how you've done it."

"Dad, I can't advise people when I haven't finished what I started."

"Well, then it will serve two purposes, won't it? Not only will you be motivating people, but you'll also continue to motivate yourself. You'll be holding yourself accountable to finishing what you started. Listen, I'm on to something here. This is a great idea." His voice rose with excitement. "Who knows? This could really go places. You could turn this into a book and make millions!"

All of my father's ideas were about a way to make millions. "I could write a little explanation of what I'm doing, and then copy it and hand it out at Christmas."

"Hell, yes! That's a great idea!

"And I could make tapes of all the music I use for exercise."

"You'll be the next Jane Fonda. I love it!"

Jane Fonda, I thought, thrilled. Not quite Marilyn Monroe, but close enough.

I started writing that night. Since I had come through Thanksgiving with such flying colors, I decided to focus on holiday eating. I was surprised how easily the words poured out: If you have incredible, uncontrollable urges on the holidays, I do not suggest muzzling your mouth or wiring your jaw shut. Everyone expects you to kick your diet on holidays just like they do, then, BAM—you find yourself guzzling cookies just because it's Groundhog Day. This will never do! Give yourself a present this holiday season. A happy you!

I filled pages and pages with what I'd learned, how I did it, and who I wanted to become by losing weight. I asked my dad to turn off the late-night movie he was watching and read what I'd written.

"I think it's fantastic." He closed the notebook and looked at me. "You've got something big here, kid. Keep going."

As my junior year progressed, things kept getting better. I was running on a kind of adrenaline I'd never experienced before, and everything I touched seemed to go my way. I began to discover who I really was. One of the first things on my newly revamped to-do list was to join the drama club and audition for their spring production of *Our Town*. I was still studying opera with Miss Brown, but I decided to risk it anyway. Now that I was down to a size 16, I thought I might have a shot.

I decided to audition for the role of Emily, who was the young female lead of the show. I was the right age to play her, but since every auditionee was a female teenager, the competition was fierce. The director, Kathy Wade, asked each of us to prepare a selection from the play, and then we read for her, one by one. In my audition, Ms. Wade asked me to read many parts, including two older women and even one of the boy parts. She was very encouraging.

"Good, Sharon. You have natural acting ability. Why haven't you auditioned for shows before now?"

I didn't know what to say, so I just smiled and thanked her for the compliment. Later that night I replayed the moment in my head while I was trying to fall asleep. Ms. Wade was going to post the cast list before homeroom in the morning, and I was a nervous wreck, incapable of sleep.

On the one hand, it was great to feel appreciated, but I thought back to my audition for *The Sound of Music* when I wowed the director, but was sent home anyway. I had a gut feeling Ms. Wade wasn't going to cast me as Emily, but I didn't know what else I could do in the play. My fear was that I was going to end up playing a fat-girl part, one of the old ladies. I really didn't want to play an old woman, especially since I'd worked so hard to improve myself over the past months. I didn't want to have to hide the new me behind a bunch of old lady makeup and a wig. Around four o'clock in the morning, I realized I was being incredibly negative. I'd never done a play in my life and I'd be lucky to get cast at all. I decided that if Ms. Wade cast me, I would accept any role; what I needed more than anything was experience.

The next morning, I ran to the cafeteria door where Ms. Wade had posted the cast list. My heart leapt when I saw my name right at the top of the list.

Stage Manager—Sharon Wheatley

Stage manager? I didn't want to be the stupid stage manager. Stage managers weren't even onstage! They sat backstage and called light cues or some other thing that I had zero interest in and for which I had zero ability. I walked away from the list humiliated, with tears in my eyes. I wasn't ever going to be pretty enough to be onstage. Why even try? I was kidding myself. Right in the middle of my pity party I ran smack into Ms. Wade.

She seemed thrilled to see me. "Hey! Here's my leading lady! Congratulations, Sharon!" I was confused. Leading lady? What was she talking about? Then it dawned on me: there was some role in *Our Town* called the Stage Manager. I'd noticed it when I was blowing through the play looking for all the Emily scenes.

"Stage Manager? You mean I'm playing the role of the Stage Manager? I thought you meant that I was on the backstage crew!"

I hoped I'd earn a small role in *Our Town*, but I never expected to land the leading role—the Stage Manager. A huge role usually played by a man well into his sixties, the Stage Manager had monologues that ran two and three pages long. I was thrilled. I wanted to pinch myself. It was the first play I'd ever done, and they gave me the leading part!

Our Town was a turning point for me. Many of my friends were in the cast, including Carolyn, and we started to go out with the male cast members recruited from the nearby all-boys high school. I learned a lot of invaluable things during the run of *Our Town*, especially how to memorize huge chunks of dialogue. But the best thing was a boy named Gary.

A sweet guy with freckles and red hair, Gary was adorable, and—even better—he thought I was pretty great, too. Playing the lead in the show gave me confidence, and for the first time in my life, I felt as though I could flirt without looking like a total idiot. We flirted all through rehearsals and I was having a great time.

It all started on Valentine's Day. I came out from rehearsal, and there sat a real live romantic Valentine's Day card, propped up on the steering wheel of my blue Volkswagen Bug. *To The Stage Manager*, the envelope read. I ripped it open, hoping it was from Gary. Inside in neat block letters it read, *To a girl with a lot of talent. Be My Valentine, Gary.* I'd never received a Valentine from a boy before, and it made me laugh and cry with delight. Something so simple—a valentine on Valentine's Day—was a huge moment for me. I felt so *normal*.

We started a real, honest to goodness relationship, just like in all the teen movies. We went to football games at his school, dances at my high school, and we went on drives in his pride and joy—a restored 1952 Ford. I liked his car too, especially because it had a huge bench seat in the front where we could make out in my driveway at the end of our dates. One night, we were busy in the front seat of his car when there was a knock on the passenger side window. We couldn't see through the steamy windows, but I panicked, certain it was my father.

I quickly rearranged my clothes and rolled down the window.

"Sharon? Oh man. I'm so sorry!" My brother's shocked face filled the window frame. I quickly got out and shut the door.

"*Buzzy!* What are you doing? I thought you were Dad," I whispered, hoping we wouldn't wake up my parents. Buzzy was attending a local college, Xavier University, and he'd moved home to save the expense of rooming on campus.

He loved exotic cars and was busy examining Gary's restoration job. "Is this Gary's car? It's a beauty!"

"*Buzz.* We were a little *busy*, ya know? How about a little privacy?" I hissed at him.

Buzz snapped to attention. "Hey, you're right. Sorry. I didn't know anyone was in there, and the car was blocking my way in the driveway." He took a peek back in the window. "So is this the guy I've been hearing so much about?"

"Can we talk about this later?" I was not about to get into some big conversation with my brother while Gary waited for me in the car.

Buzz was agreeable. "Yeah, sure. You get back to doing whatever you're doing." He gave me a little wink. "Good for you, lil' sis. I'm proud of you. This is just what you need—a nice Catholic boy to get you pregnant in high school."

"*Buzzy!*"

"I'm kidding. Well, actually, do you want a condom?"

"*Buzzy!* Stop it!" I wanted to kill him. I prayed that Gary couldn't hear us through the window.

"Oh, come on. This is normal, Sharon. Just have fun!" Buzz hopped back into his car, drove in the grass around Gary's car, and dashed in the door of the house without a look back. I watched him go inside as my heart filled with joy. My brother thought I was normal!

And normal was what I most wanted to be. My goal: to be so normal-looking that no one would even think twice about my weight if they passed me in the mall. Normal meant buying clothes from the Gap, getting on a roller coaster without looking at the maximum weight, sitting on a folding bamboo chair without worrying about it breaking, and most important—looking good in a bathing suit. Normal, I realized, even meant breaking up with Gary a few months later when I realized that he was more into me than I was into him. After nine months of dieting and exercising, I was on my way to a normal body. Dieting was easier since I'd gotten my driver's license. If someone had told me a year earlier that I'd be using my car to pick up healthy groceries, I'd have thought they were crazy. But, it was true. I was on my way to thin. I was in the zone.

In fact, I was in the zone about a lot of things. I was studying, and continuing my nightly weight journals. I'd been elected vice president of the drama club, and my most recent achievement had received citywide attention. I'd been published in the newspaper.

A few weeks before, the *Cincinnati Enquirer* had run a huge feature in the Sunday magazine talking about how overweight teenagers were destined to grow up to become overweight adults. It was a multipage article complete with glossy color photographs of overweight kids my age eating crappy food, captioned with depressing statistics. I'd been furious when I'd read it, and fired off the following letter, which was published at the top of the editorial page, complete with the headline:

Who says fat kids can't lose weight?

To The Editor: This letter is in response to the article "Slimming the Obese Child." I found many of the ideas expressed in the article to be misleading and sometimes offensive.

I know what it's like to be a "fat" child. I am 16 years old and I was always extremely overweight. I was constantly teased by my peers and often found it difficult to make friends, typical of fat kids, according to your article. That was pointed out many times, I noticed. To date, I have lost 54 very painful pounds, with a goal of 26 more. I know that I can take the weight off and keep it off.

Naturally, I was drawn to your article immediately. After all, the issue of what to do for fat children is not dealt with often. From looking at the pictures included and the title, I was under the false assumption that the article would offer helpful hints for overweight kids. Instead, I found what I considered a very negative attitude.

The authors of the article used examples of children who had lost weight—by far the most optimistic part of the article. But then they ruined the successful atmosphere by going on to explain how it was virtually impossible to lose weight as a child. They explained that no one was willing to help children; and that if by some miracle a child lost weight, the chances are 85%–90% that the child would gain it back.

Children must be motivated to lose weight, but the motivation must come from within (not from parents, doctors, etc.) in order for them to keep the weight off. No one can force a child to lose weight, but once the self-motivation starts, the child must be taken seriously. I lost weight, and I am not a special case.

Children can lose weight if they want to, but not if they believe the negative impression left by your article. You might as well have offered the fat kid a huge ice cream cone. With your attitude, we fatties who can't lose weight might as well weigh 400 pounds.

I did it! And I sincerely believe that anyone can lose weight with a little support from family and friends.

My letter struck a chord with a lot of people. I started to get letters from kids and parents, people I knew and people I didn't. I was astounded by the amount of attention I got. I had no idea that so many people felt the way I did. Kids wrote me, and they all asked me the same thing: *Sharon, I read your letter in the paper and I was very inspired by your story. How did you lose so much weight?*

After the flood of letters I received from kids like me, I realized there needed to be a book written by someone their own age, someone who had dealt with all the same frustrations. So, I took my dad's advice: *If you can't utilize, improvise!* I couldn't find a good, motivating diet book to recommend to teenagers, so I decided to write it myself. I decided to spend the summer turning my journals into a book called *Look at Me! A Teenage Guide to Weight Loss.*

chapter 13
crazy for you

I assumed it was because he had annoying habits like tickling people and sampling dishes right out of the serving bowls during Christmas parties.

I spent my summer evenings working on my book, and my days baby-sitting my eight-year-old cousin Jennifer for Aunt Nancy. Jennifer was the little sister I'd always wanted. We spent our afternoons taking excursions in my VW Bug. One such excursion was a visit to my great-great-uncle, Uncle Ralph.

"He's funny, you'll see." I promised Jennifer that she'd like him. "He's really old, but he's goofy. We don't have to stay long, I just want to say hi, and then we'll take off, okay?"

I had a soft spot for Uncle Ralph because the rest of the family ignored him. No one talked about why they didn't like him but—I assumed it was because he had annoying habits like tickling people and sampling dishes right out of the serving bowls during Christmas parties.

I frequently defended him to my family. I'd really gotten to know him during my freshman year at Ursuline. My mom had organized a carpool; my drop-off point was my great-grandmother Ga's house, where she and Uncle Ralph, her brother, lived together. I absolutely loved going to Ga's. She cooked me wonderfully unhealthful dinners of fried chicken, pork chops, and potato pancakes, all soaked in grease and cooked in an ancient cast-iron frying pan. During those long winter afternoons waiting for my mom to pick me up, I'd alternate between sitting in her warm kitchen and watching her cook, and keeping Uncle Ralph company. He was a funny old guy with big glasses and an even bigger nose. At eighty-four, he still had a mischievous nature. After dinner, we'd watch game shows and try to outsmart each other. I hadn't seen Uncle Ralph since Ga died, and he was happy to hear from me when I called to say Jennifer and I were coming over. Uncle Ralph was even happier to see me than I'd expected. After I introduced him to Jennifer, he hugged me repeatedly.

"Oh, you sure know how to make an old man wait! I've sure missed you, you little devil. Let me look at you!"

I backed away and did a spin so he could see me. I'd probably lost seventy pounds since the last time we'd seen each other at Ga's funeral, and he couldn't get over it.

"Oh boy, look at you! Sis would be so proud of you!" He choked up a bit. "Oh, I miss her so much, honey. I get so lonely here without her. I spend all my days in this house by myself, and my son works such long hours."

I hated the thought of Uncle Ralph spending long days alone, and I felt guilty that I hadn't seen him sooner. "Hey, we're going to change all that, okay? Now that I have a car and I know where you live, I'll come by all the time."

"You promise?" His face brightened like a kid's on Christmas morning. "Just like the old days?"

"What can I give you lovely ladies to drink?" He winked at me, popping open a can of Red, White, and Blue beer. "I know what you want. You want a beer!"

"You're awful." I laughed. "I'm not going to drink a beer, and you know it. Don't go trying to give me a beer in front of Jennifer!"

Jennifer had taken a seat at the chrome kitchen table near the window.

"Just ignore him. He's always trying to get me to have a drink. He's been trying to get me to drink something called a highball since I was your age! I don't ever take it; he just likes to tease me."

"Oh don't you fib now. You would have had some if you hadn't been worried about what your great-grandmother would do if she found out."

"That's not true!" I feigned shock. "I'm a good girl!"

We laughed some more and he handed me a little glass bottle of Coke—the kind I loved when I was younger. I took it to be polite; now that I was on my diet and just pounds away from hitting my goal weight, I didn't drink anything with sugar in it. I took a few sips and watched Jennifer admire her little bottle.

Uncle Ralph didn't sit down, so I sat on a tall stool near the pantry so I was near him. "I've sure missed you, you little devil." He took a deep drink of his beer. "You sure know how to make an old man wait."

I had a deep longing for Ga right then. Seeing Uncle Ralph really drove home that she was gone. I realized that it had been Ga who'd kept the conversations going among the three of us when she was alive; I'd never been around Uncle Ralph without her. "I miss Ga," I said, wondering if he missed her in the same way I did.

"Me, too," Uncle Ralph said. "But it sure is good to see you. Come here and give your old uncle a hug." He put his beer can down on the counter and came over to me. I stood up, feeling uncomfortable. *Geez, did he always hug me this much?*

Before I had the chance to think of anything else, he was hugging me. Hard. So hard that he pushed me against the doorframe of the pantry. Alarmed, I wasn't sure what he was doing. I wanted to push away from him, but the voice in my head kept saying, *Don't push away. That will hurt his feelings. He's just happy to see you. He's missed you.*

I felt his mouth very near my right ear. His breathing was thick. I felt his hardness press against my hipbone, and I got scared. *Something's wrong.*

I felt the emotion drain out of me; I felt absolutely nothing. It was as if every part of me had shut down, and I was left standing as empty as a shell, staring at the air vent on the wall over the kitchen window, powerless to stop him. Then, he ran his aged, rough hands up my shirt, fumbling to get beneath my bra. Eventually, he succeeded. All the while, the voice in my head was saying, *Sharon, take it easy here. This isn't what you think. He's an old man. He loves you. There's nothing bad about this.*

He pushed me harder against the doorframe, and I kept my eyes on that air vent. It was very dirty.

His breaths became quiet moans as his hands found their way down my yellow running shorts and under the stretchy waistband of my underpants, which were too big as a result of my weight loss. As his fingers scratched their way around, the very calm voice in my head said, *You should probably get away from him, but you'll have to be careful because he's a very old man. If you push him, he might fall. You'll have to wait for the right moment.*

My eyes drifted away from the air vent and suddenly Jennifer came into view. I was so caught up in what Uncle Ralph was doing to me, that I'd forgotten she was even there. She was standing next to the table, holding her Coke bottle, her eyes as big as saucers.

Seeing her snapped me back to action. I gently but firmly pushed Uncle Ralph away. "Stop it."

He wouldn't. I pushed harder. "I mean it! Stop it!" I broke away from him, grabbed Jennifer, and pushed her ahead of me. "Go to the front door—run!"

Jennifer bolted, and I followed right behind her. We were trying to cross the busy street to my car as Uncle Ralph ran out the front door.

"Wait! Oh God, wait! I'm sorry, honey, I went a little too far. Come on, come back inside!"

I ignored his yells as I dashed across the street and into my car. Breathless, I started the car and pulled out. As we screeched away, I saw Uncle Ralph crumble into a sobbing heap on the front porch. I was terrified he was going to die of a heat attack right there, and if he did, how I was going to explain it to his son.

I noticed the time on the clock I'd glued to my dashboard— 3:20. We'd only been in Uncle Ralph's house for fifteen minutes. I asked Jennifer if she was okay.

"What was he doing to you?"

Oh, God, I thought. *I don't know how to answer her. I need help. Where can we go?* I kept driving, wanting to put as much distance as I could between me and Uncle Ralph. I knew he didn't drive and couldn't follow us, but I sped away anyway. The farther we got from his house, the worse I felt, as what had happened sunk in. I struggled with the clutch and gearshift because my legs were shaking. I knew I wasn't going to make it home, which was at least a half-hour away. I needed someplace safe and nearby to calm down. I went to the first place I could think of—Grandma's. We ran up the concrete steps to the front door, and I could see her through the screen, vacuuming. I knocked on the door, hard.

"Heavens to mergatroid, you scared me!" She turned off the vacuum and came to the door.

"Grandma, . . . we . . . I. . . ." I didn't know what to say. "Something happened, something bad." My grandma and I had never been particularly close. She always heavily favored my sister, seeing me as overly dramatic and too sensitive. I wondered if I could count on her to believe me.

"What's happened? Are you hurt?" She looked confused.

For a moment, I regretted coming to her house at all. I wasn't sure how to describe what had happened, and I didn't know if she'd even know who I was talking about, because Uncle Ralph wasn't on her side of the family.

"No. It's not like that. It's different. We were just at Uncle Ralph's house. Do you know him?" As I stood in her doorway, looking for the right words, I started to shake so hard that I had to lean against the doorframe for support.

"Yes. I know who he is. What happened?"

"We were just there and he. . . ." I paused, stumped. I didn't want to go into graphic detail, since Jennifer was soaking in every word like a sponge.

"He . . . well, I, uh, guess he tried to take off my clothes. And Jennifer saw the whole thing, and I didn't know where to go, so I came here." I prayed that she would understand that I wasn't being overly dramatic. I needed her to tell me what to do.

We stood in the doorway and several uncomfortable moments of silence passed. Grandma neither responded nor invited us in. She seemed lost in thought.

Finally, I spoke again. "I don't know what to say to Jennifer."

"Honey, I don't think I can help you with that."

I looked at her, and she looked at me. Was everyone in my family crazy? How could she do this? Didn't she believe me? How could she choose this moment to desert me? I didn't know what else to say, so I grabbed Jennifer and we left.

Even though I was confused and angry, I'd calmed down enough to drive home. Jennifer sang along with the radio, acting as though nothing had happened. I replayed the incident in my mind, including my grandmother's reaction. What did it all mean? Whom should I tell? What would happen to Uncle Ralph if I told my parents? And then I started to doubt myself. Grandma must have thought it was no big deal, and that's why she acted like that. Maybe she was right.

By the time we pulled into my driveway, Aunt Nancy was home from work. As she and Jennifer were getting ready to leave, I pulled her aside. "Nancy, something happened today, and I feel like I should tell you because Jennifer might ask you questions." Nancy turned white. Jennifer was her entire world.

I felt a rush of guilt. What if I had scarred Jennifer for life? It was my fault. I'd taken her there and I'd let him do that to me. I could have gotten away sooner; I'd let it go on too long. Then, another thought hit me. *What if this really were no big deal?* Jennifer seemed fine—she'd just eaten twelve Ritz crackers with cream cheese and chased the cat all over the house. Actually, as I thought about it, I decided she couldn't have seen a thing, because Uncle Ralph's body blocked what he was doing the whole time.

I looked at Nancy and sadly realized that even though I wanted to tell her, I shouldn't. The whole thing was too weird and confusing. If she believed me, then I risked her getting mad at Grandma for not helping us, or worse, she might get mad at me for taking Jennifer over to Uncle Ralph's in the first place.

The worst-case scenarios though were what if I told Nancy, the person who'd always listened to me, and she didn't believe me? Or what if she agreed with Grandma? What if she thought I was making a big deal out of nothing? I could take rejection from Grandma, but I couldn't take it from Aunt Nancy.

"It was nothing," I said, but I could tell Nancy didn't believe me. "Seriously, Uncle Ralph got a little excited to see me, and it might have confused Jennifer—that's all. I just thought you should know. You know, in case she brings it up."

"What does that mean? What happened?"

"Nothing!" I was embarrassed. "He hugged me for a really long time, and then he was really upset when I left." I looked at Nancy, sorry I'd brought it up. "It's fine, really. I'm sorry I brought it up. You know me, always making mountains out of molehills!" I laughed.

"Are you sure? Are you telling me everything?" Fortunately, Jennifer chose that moment to jump back into the pool, and that distracted Nancy. I wanted out of this conversation. I wanted to get in the shower. I wanted to get away.

After everyone left, I went up to my room. My Snoopy phone rang, and it startled me. I slowly walked over to Snoopy, happy to have his friendly dog face in the room, and picked the receiver off his outstretched paw. I heard crying on the other end, and then his voice.

"Honey, Sharon? Are you there?" It was Uncle Ralph.

My first instinct was to slam down the phone so hard that Snoopy's arm would break off, but I didn't. When I heard his pathetic crying, my pity for him overrode my desire to break my phone.

"Honey, I'm so sorry. I'm so sorry." His voice had never sounded so old. "Please come back and I'll make things right."

"I will never, ever come back." I was so angry and so hurt that he'd done this, but I still felt scared for him. I worried that he was so upset and so old that he was going to die of a heart attack. He was crying so hard he could barely speak. All I could hear from his end of the phone was a string of jumbled apologies and sobs. I tried to stay angry, but his cries wore me down. Next time I spoke, I wasn't as convincing. "Do you hear me? I will never come back." His sobs frightened me. I listened to him for a minute, feeling sorry for someone and wondering if that someone was him or me.

"Promise me you'll come back. Tell me you still love me, Sharon. Ga would want that; she would want you to forgive me."

Mentioning Ga broke me to pieces inside. He wasn't allowed to talk about her.

"Don't call here again!" I slammed down the phone with such force that I surprised myself. I hadn't ever defended myself to anyone like that before. I took a couple of deep breaths before I stripped off my shirt, shorts, bra, and underwear and shoved them deep into my garbage can. I was sad as I stuffed my yellow-and-blue shirt into the trash. That had been my favorite shirt.

As I scrubbed him off me in the shower, I thought about what had happened, and what it all meant. The whole thing had probably only lasted two minutes, tops. I thought about the catastrophes people suffered through: the Holocaust, rape, a child's death. I decided that on the big scale, this was minor—a mere two minutes of confusion, which were not life-threatening or life-altering. Perhaps I deserved some part of the blame, too. I should have stopped him. He was an old man and I was a sixteen-year-old girl. If I'd wanted to get away, I should have. That's what people would say if I told them, and they'd be right.

The worst part of it, I decided, was that Uncle Ralph was the first person who'd touched my new, thinner, size-eight body. Even my make-out sessions with my former boyfriend, Gary, had happened months ago, when I was barely out of plus sizes and still shaky with my body confidence. I had wanted the right to choose the first person to feel my newly thin sixteen-year-old body, instead of someone choosing me without my consent. A cute boy, not an old man with cracking skin and age spots.

For the next few days, I tried to make myself feel better, but all I did was sleep. Uncle Ralph called seven and eight times a day, begging me to come back, and that made it even harder to escape. So even though it was the middle of August, I pulled out the only thing that seemed comforting—my flannel nightgown, the one with the penguins dressed as Santa Claus. I unplugged my Snoopy phone, told my parents I had the stomach flu, and got in bed.

A few days later, I had to come out of my cocoon for the wedding of a close family friend, where I'd been asked to sing *Ave Maria*. Somehow I managed to get up, get dressed, and sing at the wedding. At the reception, my parents and I were seated at a table with long-time friends of our family; it felt good to be around people I knew I could trust. My parents' friends had a daughter who was a little older than my sister, and I'd always liked her. Maybe it was because she reminded me so much of Susan, but I stuck close to her, never letting her out of my sight. I still hadn't told anyone what had happened with Uncle Ralph, and I decided that if I had an opportunity, I would tell her my secret, and ask her what I should do. She was a nurse in a nursing home, so I thought she might have a solution about how to handle Uncle Ralph.

I had my chance after the cake cutting, while everyone was dancing. We ended up at the table alone. I launched into my story, knowing it was an awkward time to talk about something so personal, but it was now or never.

"I guess I'm worried that I'm needlessly punishing him," I explained. "He sounds so upset and sorry. Maybe I'm just making a big deal out of nothing. What do you think?"

"Sharon, he's just a dirty old man," she said. "I see them every day. They're always grabbing at me and the other staff. You have to just give him a smack and tell him to keep his hands to himself. Don't worry about it. He's just lonely, and he doesn't know how to show it. Go forgive him and give him a little company; that's all he wants." She laughed. "He's just a frail old man and you're a strong young girl. I'll bet you could take him out if you needed to."

Her words fueled my guilty conscience, and one Sunday after two months of crying phone calls from him, I finally agreed to see him again.

"I'm not coming if you're home alone," I told him. "I'll only come if you swear your son is going to be there."

Uncle Ralph swore to that, and I arrived wearing many layers of clothing: a blouse, a sweater, a blazer, and a winter coat. When I got there, he was alone, explaining that his son had been called into work.

Immediately popping open a beer, he offered me one, and then begged for a hug.

"I swear I'll behave," he said.

But he didn't. He grabbed me to "hug me," but within seconds his hands dug under my many layers. This time I was ready for him. I pushed him away and rushed to the door.

"You blew it." I flung open the door. "I wanted to believe you, but I was an idiot to come back. Don't ever call me, *ever*, understand? This is the end of it!"

---

crazy for you

I slammed the door behind me and left. This time his cries didn't bother me much at all. I was too busy crying myself. I pounded the steering wheel with my fists the whole way home. "You are such a *jerk!*" I told myself over and over again. *"You are so stupid."*

About a week later, a card came for me in the mail. I recognized Uncle Ralph's shaky handwriting right away. I rushed up to my room and shut the door. I couldn't breathe. My mouth went dry when I saw the smiling Ziggy face on the card; it seemed so out of place. I opened the card and a blue slip fell out. It was a check for $50. I read the card full of apologies and promises, then shoved it in a drawer and left it. I vowed that I would never use that money.

About six months later, Carolyn and I were planning a trip to the mall. I was low on cash and remembered Uncle Ralph's $50 check. I pulled it out of the back of my drawer. *He owes me new clothes*, I thought, remembering the clothes I'd thrown away that day. I flipped the check over and signed my name on it in big sweeping letters. I cashed the check and spent it, letting a little of what had happened in the kitchen that day go with it.

My other grandmother, Meema, finally told me the truth. Meema and I were very close, and I was at her apartment for one of our usual late nights, when the subject of Uncle Ralph came up.

"Why don't you like him?" I asked her.

Meema liked everyone. Uncle Ralph was the only person I'd ever heard her say a mean word about. "Well, honey, he was never right. He was always in some kind of trouble."

This was brand-new information to me. "What kind of trouble?"

"Oh, he drank, and he chased young girls. Ga was afraid of what he'd do, so she never left my sister and me alone with him."

Suddenly everything came together. I flashed back to my afternoons at Ga's years before. Every time she left the room, Uncle Ralph started a tickle fight, shushing my giggles. I'd never understood why Ga always showed up in the doorway to break it up or yelled in from the kitchen to ask what we were doing. Now I understood. Uncle Ralph had a history of liking young girls, and Ga didn't want to leave me alone with him. The realization made me sad. I wished I'd known this earlier. I would never have gone to his house, or if I had, I would have taken an adult with me. I certainly wouldn't have taken Jennifer.

Why do families keep secrets like this? And then I realized that I was keeping the secret, too, and that I needed to do something about it. I took a deep breath, and I said it. "Something happened. . . . "

I told Meema the whole thing. She paced around the room, faster than I thought she should be moving.

"That bastard!" Meema usually talked about Renaissance paintings and fairies in acorn hats, so to hear a swear word come out of her mouth was jarring, but a confirmation that I was right to tell her.

As far as I know, Uncle Ralph spent the rest of his life alone. He died in a nursing home at the age of 100. I've always wondered what his nurses there thought of my great-great-uncle. Was he known as the dirty old man down the hall?

chapter 14
carousel

"Sharon? Is that you?" Her jaw dropped.
"That's unbelievable! You look so
different. I didn't even recognize you!"

After the summer of Uncle Ralph, I was relieved to get back
to school. The school year kicked off in a surprising way when
one of my favorite teachers didn't recognize me. On the first
day of senior year, my homeroom teacher, Ms. Wade, called
attendance. When she got to my name, I answered, and then
she stopped and looked around the room. "Sharon Wheatley,
are you here?"

"Right here!" I raised my hand to get her attention.

"Sharon? Is that you?" Her jaw dropped. "That's unbelievable!
You look so different. I didn't even recognize you!"

I'd lost a lot more weight due to a late-summer job at
Kings Island, a local amusement park. I'd been assigned to
the "ecology" department and given a job as a "litter-gitter";
translated it means I swept trash for nine hours a day, roaming
the amusement park with a broom in one hand and a pan in the
other. There were a lot of rules about sweeping, and the biggest
rule was that you were not allowed to stop walking. It was my

first "real" job and I absolutely hated it, but I'd dropped a ton of weight and gotten a nice tan, so I'd stuck with it.

I knew I looked a little different, but I was surprised at Ms. Wade's reaction. She had directed *Our Town* the year before, and I thought she knew me extremely well. I couldn't believe my looks had changed so much that she didn't recognize me. I happily assessed myself in the bathroom mirror later on that day, wondering what looked so different.

I'd changed my appearance on purpose. My raging desire to be a "normal" teenager hit a frenzied pace after the afternoon in Uncle Ralph's kitchen. Before school started, I swore to myself that I wasn't going to let his wandering hands ruin the spectacular senior year I had planned, so I pushed what had happened far from my mind and distracted myself with a total makeover.

I decided that the new me should look mature and stylish. I cut off the long, curly locks I'd had since I was a child and dyed my hair red. I loved my new haircut. I loved how grown-up and in control it made me feel. Between my extreme weight loss and my haircut, I finally resembled a normal, healthy, modern sixteen-year-old girl.

My friends and I started to spend a lot more time with guys, but I never really had another boyfriend. From September to April of my senior year, I did four full-length plays and musicals, and among the casts I met guys who became my friends for years. The boys who were drawn to theater were cute and sensitive and had a fantastic sense of humor. I didn't really feel up to dating anyone, but I did want to spend time with guys and flirt just like my friends, and these boys didn't seem interested in dating me, which was perfect. Nothing turned me off faster than a boy who wanted to take off my clothes, so I avoided that kind of guy at all costs. Free of sexual pressure, my senior year was all about hanging out with my theater friends, where I felt safe and loved.

Unfortunately, things were still bad at home. My parents fought on a daily basis, and I was sick of getting caught in the crossfire. I started visiting Mrs. Dettenwanger again and spilling my guts about my parents' fights over money. Their fighting grew worse, and I escaped to Carolyn's house on weekends as a matter of course now.

So when the local media came to call about the book I'd been working on, I was ready to be distracted. With my sister's help, I'd mailed *Look at Me! A Teenage Guide to Weight Loss* to all of the major publishing houses, and I'd received some great responses.

A reporter from the *Cincinnati Post* called; she'd heard through the grapevine that I had a book on the brink of being published and she wanted to do a story about me. At the same time, I was interviewed by the local midday news and soon my story was everywhere.

The newspaper article came out in mid-March, and I was interviewed on TV a few days later. The response was overwhelming—as with the letter to the editor I'd written the year before, times ten. Fan mail filled my mailbox, and my Snoopy phone rang off the hook. A mini-celebrity, I was recognized a few times when I went out. I reveled in the spotlight—even though sometimes it seemed so strange that this publicity was about me as a writer and a dieter, rather than as a singer. I wanted to end every conversation with a song, just so people knew what my real talent was.

But there was a downside to my book fame. Most people who contacted me wanted to know where they could buy a copy, and I hated having to explain that they couldn't. I felt like a fraud. As a consolation, I'd copy a stack of pages and send that off, with a note of apology. "Sorry it's not published yet! I'm working on it! Good luck!"

As much as it bothered me, the lack of a publisher didn't seem to stop groups from inviting me to speak. I was invited to local youth groups and to Cincinnati's Children's Hospital Obesity Clinic. I couldn't believe how many overweight teenagers had heard my story and wanted to talk to me. One night I got a phone call from a young girl who introduced herself as Cindy Powers, Julie Powers's little sister.

"Yeah, I remember you." Julie was a girl I'd become "friends" with in seventh and eighth grades at Anderson Middle School. A beautiful, tall, thin cheerleader, Julie had always run hot and cold toward me, depending on whether her friends were around. Her boyfriend, Chris, was the one who drew the whales all over my yearbook back in the eighth grade. I hadn't talked to her—or even thought about her—in nearly four years. And I barely knew her little sister. "Why are you calling?"

"Julie asked me to call for her," Cindy said. "She's too embarrassed."

"Why? What does she have to be embarrassed about?"

"Julie's gained a whole bunch of weight," Cindy paused. "She was wondering if she could have a copy of your book."

I almost laughed out loud. But as much as I wanted to gloat, I just couldn't bring myself to do it.

"Sure." I sent her a copy of my book, just as I did everyone else.

There was a dark side to all the publicity, though. Even though I was doling out weight loss advice left and right, juggling my life kept me so busy that my diet and exercise started to slip.

To save time, I started driving through to get my meals instead of packing them ahead of time. I never went so far as to order

French fries, but I frequently agreed when they asked if I wanted cheese on a chicken sandwich, and sometimes I'd get a small yogurt hot fudge sundae (hold the nuts, light on the fudge) as a dessert.

It was just enough—a bite of a cookie here, a handful of potato chips there—that my clothes started to get tight. I kept it a complete secret, praying no one would notice. Despite all of the attention, I was sick and tired of everyone talking about my book and my diet all of the time. It made me feel as though I only mattered to people when I was thin. I didn't want to be known for being thin; I wanted to be known for my singing. On top of that, I was terrified that I'd get fat again before my book was even published. I was scared that I was going to let myself and all of my fans down.

As senior year progressed, my life became a circus act of spinning plates. I was constantly running, trying to keep all my plates spinning, but as hard as I ran, I couldn't seem to keep up, and the plates constantly came crashing down.

On the one hand, I seemed to be the It Girl. My book was getting a lot of attention, I was thin, Miss Brown had me singing all over the city, and I was cast in every show I auditioned for—from *Bye, Bye, Birdie* to *The Diary of Anne Frank*. I was part of a large group of friends I adored, and a singing career seemed within my grasp.

On the other hand, one by one, everything I thought I could count on fell apart. Overloaded with difficult classes, including three AP classes, I fell behind. My opera voice wasn't "maturing" the way I felt it should. No publisher had accepted my book, and my parents' battles reached fever pitch. In spite of all the work I'd done to get myself together, things were spiraling out of my control.

College application time loomed, and I wasn't sure what to do about school. I'd studied classical music with Miss Brown for four years, and I had professed my love of opera so strongly that I was too embarrassed to turn my back on it now. I couldn't admit to her that I wanted to study musical theater. I rationalized my desires away by telling myself that I didn't know anything about musical theater programs and it was too late in the application process to start now. Ignoring the little nagging voice in my head that kept asking if I were good enough to be an opera singer, I applied to all the top music conservatories in the country.

When I started to research schools and send away for college applications, I was shocked to discover that I was going to have to *apply* like everyone else. I thought admission was all based on musical talent; I'd sing one song and be accepted. I never realized that music schools actually looked at grades and test scores, too. I was in trouble. Another plate dropped.

Oberlin was my dream school. Stranded in the cornfields of northern Ohio, Oberlin had a fantastic five-year undergraduate opera program. The other conservatories I applied to were very small; Oberlin was the only school with a music department integrated into the normal college curriculum, so it seemed to offer the best of both worlds—a collegiate atmosphere as well as a small, well-regarded music school. I filled out my application with high hopes, included a copy of my teenage diet book to dazzle them (and detract from my horrific grades), and showed up for my audition eager to get a scholarship. Both of my parents had made the trip to Oberlin with me so they could see the school I'd fallen so in love with. Dad joked that the school would turn me into a communist because of the extremely liberal political posters around campus, which of course made me like it even more. I'd picked out which dorm I wanted to live in and I'd even bought a sweatshirt. It had not even crossed my mind that they might not accept me.

My audition was on the stage of the conservatory's main theater, and I sang the aria "Non so più cosa son" from *The Marriage of Figaro*. I knew there were girls who could out-sing me, so I'd chosen this aria to show off my acting ability. Miss Brown had made me write out the English translation so I'd understand that the character was wildly in love. Infusing my singing with the passion of a young Italian lover, I performed the energetic aria with gusto, running all over the stage. Certain that this combination of singing and acting would win them over, I added lots of arm gestures, and at one point, I almost broke down in tears. When I finished, I waited for the "Wow" from the faculty running the audition. No one said anything. Instead, one of the faculty members approached the stage. "Sharon, can I talk to you for a minute?"

"Absolutely!" Surely she was going to tell me I was the best singer they'd ever seen.

"Well, first I wanted to say that you did a really nice job acting the aria. We don't usually see that from a singer your age."

"Thanks!"

"We were just looking at your transcript, and I noticed that your grades aren't very good. You know Oberlin has a very strenuous academic curriculum. I was just wondering—actually we were all wondering—" she gestured to the other faculty members who were busying themselves with paperwork—"if you knew that Cincinnati has one of the finest conservatories in the world?"

I knew. Many people had asked if I was going to apply to CCM, the University of Cincinnati's College-Conservatory of Music. I'd turned my nose up at it, not willing to go to college in my hometown. I wanted out. I didn't want Cincinnati; I wanted Oberlin.

"I want to go to Oberlin." I told the smiling faculty member. "It's my dream school."

"Cincinnati has an excellent musical theater program, and it's a state school with lower academic expectations and a more reasonable tuition. You'd be lucky to go there."

"I want to go here." I couldn't figure out why she was saying this. "Everyone knows that I want to go here!" I could see Dad's face through the glass doors at the back of the theater, watching this entire conversation. I wanted to deliver good news to him. I needed to prove that I could make it in show business. I needed to prove that I was so ravishing that I could get a big fat scholarship to this school.

"I don't think this is going to work out for you. We need stronger grades, and if I'm being perfectly honest, I don't think you seem like a good match for our opera program. You seem better suited to musical theater." She gave me a sympathetic smile. "Why don't you try applying there?"

Oberlin was not the only school that rejected me. Eastman and New England Conservatory sent letters as well. I was accepted to the Boston Conservatory, but there was no scholarship available, so I couldn't afford to go.

As all my friends celebrated their acceptances to college, I sulked at the irony of the situation. I was the only person I knew who'd known what I wanted to do since I was five years old—and I was the only one who was squarely rejected. My grades were barely good enough to get me accepted into a community college, let alone some of the top schools I'd approached.

By the end of senior year, I was starring in every concert and had lead roles in two different schools' spring productions, but I didn't have a college to attend. All of the voice lessons with Miss Brown, the vocal competitions, the AP music classes hadn't meant a thing. I'd been rejected. To add insult to injury, the book I'd been writing, pushing, and publicizing for over a year was rejected by every major publishing house. I was failing at everything—but still getting fan letters.

Right before graduation, I assessed my life. I felt as though there were loose ends everywhere, and I had a lot of questions. Did I want to be an opera singer? Did I want to be an author? Did I want to be known as a diet guru? Could my parents, whose financial problems were worse than ever, afford to send me to college at all? When I managed to quiet the jumble in my brain and stop spinning plates for a minute, the answer was right in front of my face. I needed to take a year off, to see if there was any future for my book, and to apply to a good musical theater school in the fall.

Spinning plate, caught.

chapter 15

unsinkable molly brown

To make matters worse, my best friend became the mall food court.

My year off was miserable. While I was living at home, working at the mall, and listening to my parents fight, my friends sent me letters from college regaling me with the great times I was missing.

To make matters worse, my best friend became the mall food court. I lost my commitment to my diet, slowly adding back food that I'd sworn off for almost two years. I gained back thirty of the seventy-five pounds I'd lost, pushing back up to a size 14. Feeling terrible about myself, I sank deeper into depression. How had I lost my way?

I'd had some interest in my book, but nothing came of it. I managed to get a literary agent, who sent my book to every major publishing house. One company seemed very interested, but ultimately I decided that the changes they wanted to make were too extreme. They wanted to bring in a doctor to coauthor the book, while I served as inspiration to America's teenagers. I wanted the book to be good, but I hated their idea; I thought the doctor's diet was too rigid for a teenage audience. As it bounced from publisher to publisher, I watched the heart go out of my book, and I took the only option I felt I had left—I pulled the plug on the whole thing.

Once I abandoned the book, I felt like a huge weight had been lifted off my shoulders. The pressure I'd been under to publish my book and my strict diet to keep my weight down had held onto me like a vise grip. Petrified that I'd shoot back up to 200-plus pounds before it got published, I'd become obsessed and unhealthy by skipping meals as a punishment for dietary and exercise lapses. Skipping meals never worked because I'd get so hungry that I'd overeat later. At my worst, I stooped to an all-time low and tried to gag myself to throw up unwanted food. I couldn't seem to make it work, so next I tried drinking a combination of hot water, mustard, and salt, which I'd heard would make you puke for sure. After two cups, I had a terrible stomachache, but everything stayed down. Frustrated, I purchased a small bottle of syrup of ipecac to carry around in my purse. All I knew about it was that it was used to make babies throw up if they ingested poison, and I figured it was a good thing to have on hand. It seemed more drastic and dangerous than just sticking your fingers down your throat, so I carried it around in a secret compartment in my purse for a few weeks, not certain I wanted to try it.

One night, I had a craving for Mexican food, specifically a "grande" bean and cheese burrito. This had been a favorite of mine in my fat days, and I decided to drive through and grab one on my way home from work. *I'll only eat half,* I promised myself. After I ordered, I drove up to the window to pay. As the cashier counted out my change, the car filled with the familiar Mexican smells, and my mouth began to water. I was sick of dieting and denying myself. I was starving and I wanted to chow on my favorite food. I remembered the unopened bottle and thought, *They give it to babies. How bad can it be?* I ordered extra sour cream, a side of nachos, and a churro. I knew there was a way I could eat like this every day and not gain weight. I pulled over to the side of the parking lot, opened the small bottle, and downed the sticky, sweet syrup. Then, I plowed through my Mexican feast, savoring every drippy, fatty, caloric bite as I drove down a winding country road to my house. *I could get into this,* I thought, as I wiped the sour cream from my mouth and took a long drink from my non-diet Coke. About halfway home, I suddenly felt violently ill. I'd had plenty of stomach flus in my life, but I'd never had nausea hit me in such a debilitating way before. I barely got the car pulled over as I retched out the car door, sweating and grunting out my "grande" dinner.

When it was over, I sat in my car on the dark country road for a long time thinking about what I had done. Scared and shaking, I thought, *Geez, Sharon. Is* this *who you want to become? A person who throws up to stay thin just because you wrote some stupid book? Don't be an idiot.*

I didn't want to be that person, and I didn't want to be the teenage diet guru of America. I wanted to be a singer. Case closed.

Despite my depression and weight gain, my parents' marriage was getting back on track. They sold our big house in the woods and bought a smaller, more affordable home—a move that salvaged my parents' marriage. Still, I was more than ready to leave home and devote myself to the study of music. I applied, auditioned, and was accepted to both the opera program and the prestigious musical theater program at the University of Cincinnati's College-Conservatory of Music. Once I finally admitted that musical theater had always been my first love and that I'd been waiting for this acceptance my whole life, the decision was easy. I turned down the opera program, threw myself into musical theater, and never looked back.

Immersing myself in UC's program was like entering heaven after a long penance in opera purgatory. At orientation, I looked around in glee. Four years of musical theater training! Next stop, Broadway! I couldn't wait to get on my way. Somebody had to be a musical theater star, why not me?

The first day of class was a major wake-up call.

One of the professors got up to speak. "Ladies and gentlemen, please look to the student to your left." We did. "Now please look to the student to your right." We did. Then, he dropped the bomb. "Due to the highly competitive nature of this program, one of the students you just looked at will be cut from the program by next year. Half of you will fail before you are sophomores, leaving only the most talented, the most resilient, and the hardest working. Attempting a career in show business is extremely competitive and this program, the best musical theater program in the country, is designed to reflect that. Good luck."

As he described it, every good theater school was like boot camp. We were expected to work harder than we had ever worked in our lives. While other college students were out drinking beer and going to football games, we would be building sets, attending rehearsals, learning music, and making costumes. We would start at 8 A.M. and finish at 11 P.M. We wouldn't even get weekends off.

I wasn't scared. Certain that I would make the cut to sophomore year, I looked around, scoping out the competition like a lion searching for the weakest gazelle. I noticed that some of my classmates were doing the same.

We began with a diagnostic to help the faculty assess where we were, and what we needed to work on. We were asked to sing two contrasting songs and then stay for critiques, and we were to perform in alphabetical order by last name.

As a *W*, I watched almost all of my twenty-six classmates perform before it was finally my turn. My confidence faltered as they made their way down the alphabet. I couldn't believe how talented they all were; this was a completely different league from the people I'd worked with before. By the time my name was called, I had two scenarios playing in my head: I finished to wild applause, or to an escort to the nearest exit. Either way, I'd become so nervous, it felt like I was on the verge of a heart attack.

I gave my music to the pianist and walked to the spot to sing. I faced my new classmates and the faculty, wondering if I looked as nauseous as I felt. I was wearing my best outfit; a flattering green dress and matching shoes. Mom had splurged on it for my high school graduation Mass and even though it didn't fit quite as well as it had, I still felt good in it. I had a great tan from my job at my father's latest business venture, a tanning salon, and my hair was long and back to its normal dark brown. Despite my weight troubles, I thought I looked pretty good. I prayed my makeup still looked fresh and that the skirt hid my shaking legs as I began.

I sang a song from *Once upon a Mattress* and the Gershwin classic "Someone to Watch over Me." Pleased with my performance, I thought I'd qualified as one of the best singers in the class. I watched the faculty scribble on their notepads. I hoped their notes included *Great voice! Amazing talent! Fun shoes!*

I was ready for my "Wow."

After the auditions were over, the critiques began. One by one, again in alphabetical order, the professors dressed us down, in detail, in front of the entire class. Brutal, the blasting lasted for hours. *Bad habits, clueless,* and similar insults were hurled out as the auditions wore on, and the critiques became highly personal. They told one kid that he was so badly dressed that he should give his clothes to charity; they decimated the girl next to me for what they called her pathetic Barbra Streisand impersonation.

Panicked now, I became extremely aware of my weight; I could feel my body swell as I sat in my chair. The rolls in my stomach pushed out of my pantyhose. My legs were so fat that I had to hook my foot under the chair rung in front of me to keep them crossed. I was fat again. *When had this happened?*

I looked around the room to confirm the worst. Even if I had kept off *all* the weight I'd lost in high school, I still would have been the fattest one in the room. When I was first accepted into the program, I thought that acceptance meant acceptance of my looks as well. But hearing them critique everyone down to their hair color, I realized that my weight was a huge target. With a jolt, I realized their notepads were more likely to read *Unacceptably huge ass* and *Blimpy* instead of *Cute shoes.*

"Miss Wheatley. Where are you?" called Virginia, the acting teacher. She was the only woman on the faculty, and she was no shrinking violet.

I raised my hand.

"Oh yes, how could I miss all that makeup?"

I sat up, pencil at the ready.

"Miss Wheatley, do you have any idea what you were singing about?"

I didn't understand the question, and racked my brain for an intelligent response, hoping something clever could save me. "Uh. Well . . . I. . . ."

"I didn't think so." She stopped me cold. "Let me tell you what I saw today. I saw a girl who has a great big singing voice without any acting ability, whatsoever. Your songs, while probably perfectly musically executed, left me totally cold. You have to tell the story! You have to develop a character! You cannot just stand and sing, thinking about how beautiful your voice sounds, which is all you were doing today. You cannot be a funnel for a voice. My dear, you have a lot of work ahead of you."

She gestured to the other faculty members as if it were their fault I was there. "How am I supposed to make an actress out of a girl whose worst experience up to now is that she broke a nail on prom night? She has absolutely nothing to draw upon."

From that day on, my goal in life was to please Virginia. Not easy, as she was given to black-or-white thinking. If she loved you, she gushed. If she didn't, watch out.

Desperate for her approval, I worked as hard as I could in her class. She liked actresses who cried, and I *longed* to cry for her. I was willing to sob in a heap on the floor if that was what it took. In class, I'd try to conjure up images of my parents' fights, Uncle Ralph, the teasing I'd endured, anything to become an actress in her eyes. *"Emote!"* she yelled at me, over and over again.

And I would freeze, over and over again.

This was not good. Our first "boards" were coming up. There were two boards each year, and if we failed two of them in a row, we were kicked out.

These auditions were the single most stressful element of a CCM musical theater education. CCM had a very high flunk-out rate, sometimes graduating as few as eight from an original class of twenty-six. The musical equivalent of a Roman gladiator contest, boards attracted a crowd, which watched with a mixture of fear and anticipation. For the performers, the tension was unbearable. It was not uncommon for people to freeze up and have to start again; even the "stars" of the program often crumbled onstage or walked off altogether.

For my first board in January, I decided to pull out all the stops. I was so worried that I was going to fail, and I'd spent my whole life overcoming every obstacle to get here. Now I had to face every obstacle to stay. I chose a little-known Jerry Herman song called "Time Heals Everything." To help me "emote," I chose the most painful relationship in my life: Uncle Ralph.

The day of the board, I walked around with a picture of him and the Ziggy card he'd sent me. I waited to look at the picture until right before I stepped onstage, hoping the emotional shock would work for me. I envisioned myself collapsing at the end, heaving with tears, while Virginia jumped up from her seat, declaring me a fabulous actress.

It didn't happen that way. I took one look at that picture, my brain left my body, and I went onstage with nothing. Zippo. My singing—as in the actual quality of the tone that I was producing out of my mouth—was fine. The problem was that it wasn't making any kind of emotional connection. My great acting piece was reduced to the dramatic equivalent of singing the telephone book out loud. I was terrible, and Virginia agreed. "Miss Wheatley, that was terrible," she confirmed.

I flunked the board. Even though I knew I hadn't done well, the moment when the temporary head of the program declared "Wheatley—*Fail*" in front of all of my classmates I was just about as shocked as I have ever felt. How could they fail me? Couldn't they pass me based on my *potential*? Didn't they realize that I, Sharon Wheatley, was going places?

At least I was in good company. I wasn't the only talented student they'd failed. They failed all but three students, and even those had "passed with reservations." After the board critiques, my classmates abandoned campus to get plastered and make fun of the faculty who'd just failed us, but I couldn't. I wanted to hide under my covers. I couldn't face life with a "fail" hanging over my head.

They told us it was a "wake-up call" so we would all work harder. Terrified, I did work harder. All of my easy confidence from the first day of school was gone. I knew that if I couldn't get past Virginia's belief that I'd never had a bad day in my life, I was doomed. I had to learn to cry at the drop of a hat. That seemed to be the key to Virginia's heart.

Without Virginia on my side, I was as good as gone. I didn't know where to turn; in my desperation I found myself in the Catholic church just up the street from my dorm. If there was ever a time for Divine Intervention, this was it.

I got down on my knees. "Dear God. Sharon Wheatley here. Remember me? I was going to be a nun? Please help me! Make me a better actress! Help me cry for Virginia! I'll do anything!" As I prayed in that empty church, tears of frustration and panic streamed down my face.

I shook my head. What was the point of crying in an empty church where no one could see me? I needed these tears in acting class, in front of Virginia where they'd be useful—not here alone with God. That's when it hit me. I always cried when I was praying. Why not figure out a way to pray *during* my board? Brilliant!

By my next board, I was ready. I hunted around and found a song called "By My Side" from the musical *Godspell*. I sang it for my second board, tears streaming down my face, and passed with flying colors. I was crying out of *fear* instead of a more appropriate emotion, but since it solidified my place in the program, so be it. I don't think God minded.

I made it to sophomore year, where the critiques continued. Part of surviving an intense program like this was inviting and anticipating comments about every aspect of your self at any given moment. I'd spent my entire life trying to avoid comments about my personal appearance, and now, somehow, I'd ended up in the middle of a makeover reality show.

There were many compliments handed out to me at CCM, but it, like all theater programs, focused on making you ready for the harsh world of Broadway, so the negative comments reigned. Comments like "Miss Wheatley, that shirt makes you look pregnant" or "Miss Wheatley, your hair looks like it's been dragged through the bushes" were part of the daily routine. I wanted to succeed, so I took notes. While other college students were taking notes on the periodic table, I was scribbling down "Look into changing hair color to red. Redheads are funnier."

Or, "Remember, I'll have a disadvantage as a comedienne because I have no distinguishing feature (such as a large nose, or being really tall and thin or short and fat)." My personal favorite, and the most common comment I received: "I am too 'pretty' to be funny, and I will not have a place in the business when I get to New York. Right now I look like a fat ingénue, and no one hires fat girls to sing love songs."

For my junior boards, I sang a love song ("Unusual Way" from *Nine*) and a comedy song ("I Can Cook Too" from *On the Town*). I'd worked hard on my acting and I felt I'd done well; still, most of the reviews were lukewarm. I was disappointed, but it was better than "fail."

Virginia was next. I was never prepared for Virginia's comments; in my entire time at UC, she always surprised me with her sharp assessments of my work.

"Miss Wheatley." Virginia put down her clipboard and removed her reading glasses so she could see me. "Oh yes. How could I miss all that pink!"

My stomach lurched. I'd chosen a light pink suit, with a tight-fitting jacket to show off my waist, and a long, full, pink skirt with an underskirt of lace. The outfit was a little dressy for a board since most of the girls wore a simple floral skirt and T-shirt, but I'd decided to wear it anyway, because I felt more theatrical in it.

"Sharon, what were you thinking? I don't understand." Virginia looked to her fellow faculty members for help. "How does this happen? I am actually furious with you right now. *How* could you pick those songs and not expect me to be furious?"

I had no idea what was wrong—besides the pink.

"Sharon, I am *tired* of watching you attempt to sing love songs." Virginia shook her head. "You will *never* be hired to sing love songs. You will *never* be hired to sing sexy songs. Ever. Have you looked in a mirror lately? I'll tell you what I saw when I was watching you today. You are huge. You looked like a . . . a. . . ." She struggled to find the right words as the rest of the room went quiet. Suddenly, everyone was very interested in the carpet pattern, but I knew they were all listening. I saw the light bulb go off in Virginia's head, and I braced myself.

"You look like a big pink pillar." Virginia continued her diatribe, but I'd already switched her off in my head. Miraculously, in the moment that Virginia was trying to break me *down*, I had a break*through*. Virginia *thought* she knew me, but she didn't. She had formed a snap judgment about who I was—a simple Midwestern girl who wanted to sing love songs and look pretty—and she didn't like it. She was judging me the same way that the kids used to judge me on the playground, and I was falling for it all over again.

unsinkable molly brown

I'd started to believe that I was a bad actress because Virginia said so. I believed that I couldn't fall in love onstage because Virginia said so. Now I was supposed to believe I was a big pink pillar because Virginia said so. It was the exact same thing I'd done as a girl. I'd believed I was fat and ugly because others said so.

It was easy to give the negative comments more replay time than the positive comments. Even though the professor before Virginia told me that I'd done a great job, the compliment was nearly lost on me—I was trapped in Virginia's mean-spiritedness.

But why should I replay Virginia's comments? Why give her so much power? Why believe her? I really had no idea why Virginia didn't like overweight Midwestern girls. Maybe she'd been one herself. The point was that I wasn't a "big pink pillar." I wasn't a "funnel for a voice with no acting ability." I wasn't "too fat to sing a love song." That was *her opinion*, and *her opinion* was clouded by a lot of things that didn't have anything to do with me.

I was going to Broadway—and no one, not even Virginia, was going to stop me.

act three

"Always be a first-rate version of
yourself, instead of a second-rate
version of somebody else."

—*Judy Garland*

chapter 16
the pajama game

I fell in love with loads of handsome, sensitive men, and one by one, I brought them out of the closet.

When I started my senior year of college, I was still a virgin. My friends called me Hester Prynne—only with a "scarlet V."

I didn't plan it that way. But as a musical theater major, my choices were slim: gay boys or future gay boys. During my time at CCM, I fell in love with loads of handsome, sensitive men, and one by one, I brought them out of the closet.

As a result, I earned the nickname "the keeper of the keys" or "last stop on the straight boy express."

"Is there something you want to tell me?" I'd invariably ask. "You know, it's perfectly okay if you want to date men. I won't judge you."

For particularly stubborn cases, I'd refer to my own past. "I really understand more than you think. I was kind of gay once. I had a girlfriend in eighth grade."

That got them talking every time. Soon we'd be crying together, knee-deep in a confession that usually began, "You know, Sharon, if there was one woman in this entire world that

I could see myself with, it would be you. The thing is, I get so confused sometimes about what I want. There's this guy. . . ."

I usually stopped listening soon after that. How had this happened to me so many times? Although a lot of these guys are still my friends, each of them broke my heart in college. While other girls my age were rushing sororities and beating off various frat guys, I spent my college years snuggling, having heart-to-heart talks, and wondering why my boyfriend knew more about musical theater and hair products than I did. Gay men are attentive, loving, and well versed on such important topics as what shoes to wear on a date. To top it off, they always smell fantastic and sexy. I had a great time with them, and even though I cried myself to sleep many times, I never fell asleep crying because I'd had a one-night stand with a drunk frat guy.

My encounters with straight men were another story. Gay men were safe. They weren't going to touch me. No matter how much I begged or pleaded, I simply didn't have the right parts to excite *their* parts.

Straight boys, on the other hand, were unpredictable and horny. I felt pretty certain that I could—at any time—lose my virginity to a stranger, but I wanted a boyfriend, not a quick lay. I only met straight guys in bars, and college boys in bars aren't looking for girlfriends; they're looking for hookups. I never had a problem finding a guy who wanted to hook up, especially since you barely had to flirt—or even speak—to find them. They were willing to go home with just about anybody. Too impersonal and scary for me, I simply skipped the bar scene in college—until Maryday came along.

Maryday was my best friend and roommate in college. We met sophomore year when I was hanging out with gay men and she was flirting with every man in sight. The new graduate student in the drama program landing all the sexpot roles,

Maryday had long red hair that attracted a lot of attention, especially from men. Always dressed to kill in trendy outfits and well-applied makeup, she liked to look good.

The first time I saw her was in a rehearsal for a show. She wore a big navy blue bow in her hair, which matched her navy blue outfit, and she asked a million personal questions before she even knew anyone's last name. On breaks she frequently talked about sex, which made me both nervous and intrigued. I wasn't ever attracted to Maryday, I just liked that she sparked a side of me that had lain dormant for a few years. I knew hiding somewhere underneath my overalls and campy sense of humor there was a sexual person, but it scared me.

Maryday and I became fast friends during the run of the show, and we found an apartment together the following school year. Maryday became my dating coach, a job she took very seriously. She took one look at my anemic love life with gay men and made it her personal mission to find me a straight guy. She started by planning a night on the town. "We are going to a bar that a gay man would never set foot in. I'm going to show you what normal girls do on a Saturday night. Get dressed in something provocative and meet me in the living room." She disappeared into her room to begin her transformation. I stood in front of my closet searching for the right thing to wear. Somehow all of my clothes looked like enemies.

I finally settled on my standard uniform—a black turtleneck, overalls, and cowboy boots. I dressed it up with dangly jewelry, smoky makeup, and a squirt of Maryday's perfume, called "Passion." I thought I looked pretty good. Maryday, dressed to kill in a slinky black dress and high-heeled boots, disagreed. She flopped down on the couch and lit a long cigarette.

"You cannot wear that ridiculous outfit. You look like an urban hiker. Get back in there and put on something *provocative*, Sharon." She drew out the word to make her point.

"Overalls are very 'provocative,' didn't you know?" I began a bad impersonation of a striptease in my overalls to prove my point. "It'll drive the boys wild, wondering what's underneath them."

Maryday laughed. "Yeah, I'd believe that if we were going to a bar full of farmers." She looked me over, perplexed. "I don't understand this whole little-girl thing you've got going on."

"I'm not trying to dress like a little girl. I just suck at being sexy."

"It's not rocket science." Maryday pointed toward my room. "Put on something black, and *low-cut*! You've got great boobs, so show them off!"

A half hour later I emerged in a flowing velvet skirt Maryday found in the back of my closet and a V-cut sweater of Maryday's that was skintight and offered an eyeful of cleavage.

"Much better!' Maryday said. "But stand up straight. If you've got it, flaunt it!"

"I look ridiculous and I'm going to make an ass out of myself." I felt like I was walking around in some other, confident girl's clothes.

"You look great. But you need to learn how to flirt."

Maryday was patient with me, explaining that great flirting was nothing more than great acting.

"Take on a role, Sharon. Pretend you're someone else. Someone sexy!" I struck a stupid Betty Boop pose and Maryday laughed.

"Make it romantic if you need to. That's what I do. When I walk into a bar, I pretend I'm a queen looking for a chivalrous knight to ignite my passion. The guy doesn't need to know what you're doing. Toss your hair around. Just try it!"

Maryday took me to several bars over the school year to practice "my act"—not the all-boys gay bars I'd been to but real live bars. One night we went to a dive just off campus. We walked in, dressed to the hilt, cleavage on full display. Our nice clothes and shining hair looked totally out of place among the frat guys playing pool and drinking pitchers of cheap beer. Maryday knew we'd be overdressed, and that's what she wanted, since the point of the evening was to draw attention.

"Follow me," she whispered over her shoulder, once we were in the door.

I trotted after her like a puppy, mimicking the flick of her hair and her casual laugh, not wanting to lose her in the crowd. We both ordered cosmopolitans and sipped them while we watched the guys shoot pool. Within minutes, Maryday managed to get us into a game of pool with two reasonably attractive guys. I knew which guy Maryday would claim for herself, the tall one with the big nose. That left the dark-haired one for me. He wasn't bad looking, but not really great looking either.

"I'm Jeff."

"Uh, Sharon." I flashed a Maryday smile at Jeff, whom I'd already labeled "the straight guy" in my mind.

Friendly in a "Am I going to go home with you?" kind of a way, Jeff and I got to know each other as we played pool.

"So, what are you studying?" I asked him.

"Business."

Boring, I thought. "That's fascinating!" I said instead.

"Nah, it's boring. What about you? What's your major?" he asked after he took his shot.

"Musical theater."

He looked confused. "What's that? Are you, like, an actress or something?"

"Yes." I wondered if he'd like that. Either people thought acting was cool, or that actresses were flaky.

He looked at me with admiration. "That's very cool." Relieved, I relaxed and tried to have fun with this creature commonly known as a straight man.

Jeff grew more attractive to me as the pool game progressed and my bloodstream absorbed the alcohol. About an hour into our game, Maryday and I went to the bathroom to check in. She liked her guy a lot and wondered what I thought of mine.

"He has ugly shoes."

Maryday primped in the mirror. "Then don't look at his shoes."

"I suck at playing pool," I said, wondering if she was ready to go home yet.

"Sharon, who cares if you are good at playing pool!" She laughed at me. "That isn't what this is about! Trust me, all they care about is the view they get when we lean over to shoot."

"Oh my God!" I hadn't thought of that, and I instinctively covered my cleavage with my hand. I assessed myself in the mirror next to Maryday's beautiful body. "I look fat."

"You do not look fat." Maryday responded like a coach talking to a boxer between rounds. "You look beautiful and curvy and everything a real man wants in a woman. Come on, we're going back out there." She pushed me out the door and back into the smoky bar. "This guy is into you. Just relax."

I did relax, although it took me two more cosmos to do it. Soon it was just the two of us playing pool, since Maryday and her big-nose guy were making out in the corner. I guessed they'd be leaving the bar any minute. I wanted to kiss this guy in a bar too. I wanted to feel loose and collegiate. I wanted to flirt.

I brushed past him several times as I made my shots, giggling each time. My flirting was improving, and he was taking the bait. A few shots later, I asked for his help with a shot I didn't really need help with, and he ferociously kissed me instead. *Wow. This one's straight for sure.* He picked me up and placed me on the pool table.

"Can I come over to your place?"

I wanted him to, but I was nervous. I purposely thought about all my gay boyfriends and our frustrating "snuggling" evenings. I wanted a straight guy who was strong enough to lift me onto a pool table. I ignored my flipping stomach, choosing to focus on my stimulated libido instead, and agreed. "Let's go."

We left the bar and headed to my apartment. The long walk was awkward since we weren't playing pool or kissing, which was all we had in common. The winter wind sobered me up a little, and by the time I got him back to my apartment I suffered some serious second thoughts. "Uh, let me slip into something more comfortable." I ran for the bathroom and locked the door behind me. *There is a straight guy out there in my apartment, and he is waiting for me to emerge from the bathroom in lingerie and have sex with him. Oh shit.*

I sat down on the toilet and took a few deep breaths. I didn't know if I wanted this. I felt ridiculous. I was twenty-two years old and still a virgin. I didn't know *anyone* who was still a virgin at twenty-two—not even my mother. She'd had my sister by then, which she pointed out to me all the time. She'd even given me condoms about a year earlier with the hope that I would find a straight guy and use them.

I wanted to lose my virginity. I had a willing participant in the other room, a decent-looking male who was capable of getting and maintaining an erection in the presence of a female, even an overweight female, which was a rare occurrence in my life. I decided to go out there and see what would happen with a straight guy. I didn't think I wanted to have sex with him— I didn't even know his last name—but I wasn't going to rule anything out. I would leave deep conversations and cuddling to the gay boys. This time, I'd go with animal attraction first, and sort out the details later.

I was ready to walk back out when I realized I hadn't slipped into anything more comfortable. A pair of footed zip-up Mickey Mouse pajamas Maryday had made for me for Christmas was on a hook in the bathroom, so I put it on over my skirt, tights, shirt, and sweater, and zipped it all the way up. I knew it wasn't what he was expecting, but I was a nervous wreck and I needed a lot of clothes between him and me for a while. When I walked out, the straight guy stood up from the couch and took in my outfit.

"Cute." He grabbed me and kissed me. We kissed our way into my bedroom, where he had a good time slowly and sexily unzipping my footed pajamas. As he did it I imagined laughing about this moment with Maryday later.

"Hey," Jeff whispered in my ear, "what's with all the clothes?"

Fighting not to run out of the room to the nearest gay bar, I managed a fake giggle. "I'm just trying to make you work for it!"

That seemed to pacify him, and we continued. He took off my pajamas, my skirt, my shirt, his shirt, and his pants. I was self-conscious, so I was glad the room was almost pitch-black. Actually, judging from his reactions, I could have been a three-hundred-pound orangutan for all he cared. Thinking about how this guy really didn't know a thing about me and didn't care distracted me. It was all about the hookup, not the girl.

---

the pajama game

Stop thinking! I told myself. This was officially the farthest I'd ever gone with anyone. Over and over I told myself to relax, enjoy it, and take deep breaths. The problem was I couldn't stop thinking about Uncle Ralph. This had happened with the few guys I'd made out with in college, and it seemed to be the same thing every time. I'd be fine, making out, having fun, and then they'd push against me and I'd hear their heavy breathing. That sound panicked me—and I'd flee. I'd panic.

I wanted tonight to be different. I pushed the past out of my head, reminding myself it was no big deal. *You are making something out of nothing. It's not like he raped you. It lasted for two minutes, and it was four years ago. Get over it!* I opened my eyes and found a spot in the corner of the room where the paint had dripped, and I focused on it, wondering how I'd never seen it before. I wasn't feeling anything anymore; I just kept looking at the spot. Jeff took his underwear off. He was definitely a straight guy.

Breathing deeply, Jeff tried to spread my legs. "I have a condom."

We were seconds away from having sex. My heart started to pound.

"I'm sorry." I pushed him off me and stood up. "I'm so sorry, but you're going to have to leave. I just can't do this."

I frantically started to pick up his clothes, using them to mask my big, almost naked body from his view. "No way, we can't stop now." Jeff was clearly angry. "What's your problem? You were just as into this as I was!"

I felt like a freak. "I'm sorry. I really am, but I just can't do this. I've had things happen to me, I don't know, I'm just not really comfortable. It's not you, it's totally me." I started to cry. "I had an uncle, well, a great-uncle, he was really old, and he kind of screwed me up. I guess I'm not very good with guys."

Jeff stood up and hopped into his underwear. He walked over, and for a few seconds, I was terrified he wasn't going to ignore my "no." Instead, he took his clothes out of my hands and started to get dressed. I grabbed my purple terrycloth robe, hurried into it, and then sat on the edge of the bed, watching him and wondering what he thought of me—if he felt sorry for me or if he thought of me more as a person than he had a few hours ago. I wondered if he even remembered my name.

After he tied his shoes, we walked in silence to the front door.

"That sucks about your uncle. Sorry about that." Jeff started to go, and then turned around again. "Listen, you might want to think twice about going to a bar, picking somebody up and bringing him home. That usually means one thing to a guy, and you might end up hooking up with somebody who won't leave until he gets it. Ya know?"

This straight guy was really very sweet. "Hey, do you want my number? Maybe we can go out again sometime."

Jeff laughed. "Uh, no thanks. I don't really think I want to date you." He was still laughing as he walked away.

Of course he didn't want to date me. I was an idiot. I'd be single my whole life, outing gay man after gay man. That's what I deserved. I didn't deserve a straight guy. I went into the kitchen, pulled out Maryday's peanut butter–cup ice cream and ate every bit of it in the dark.

chapter 17
into the woods

Maybe it was the blueberries, the moose, or the craggy shores and dramatic surf, but I'd always wanted to go, so I decided to audition.

The end of my junior year was looming and I was facing a sticky Midwestern summer with no job when I encountered a simple white and green sign that read:

How would you like to live and work in Maine?
Quisisana, a summer music resort on Lake Kezar in the beautiful White Mountains of Maine is auditioning for its summer music staff. Singer auditions Saturday.

I'd never heard of Quisisana, but the word *Maine* caught my eye. Many people have a particular state they've always wanted to visit, and mine, for no explainable reason, has always been Maine. Maybe it was the blueberries, the moose, or the craggy shores and dramatic surf, but I'd always wanted to go, so I decided to audition. My friends wondered why I'd audition to go away to the middle of nowhere. The rather snobbish thinking was that we should only do "important" theater in the summer, jobs where we could "make connections" and further our careers in some way. Why would anyone want to work in the woods in Maine?

On the audition room door they'd posted pictures of Quisisana Resort. I looked them over as I waited my turn. I pored over the 4×6 snapshots, which revealed an alternate universe. Smiling, tanned faces greeted me in each picture, rowing canoes in a lake surrounded by mountains, holding a lobster next to a fire on a beach, performing in a rustic music hall that jutted out over the water. *Who are these people? It looks like an L.L. Bean ad.* I scanned the pictures once more, and I noticed that not one of the healthy, tan girls had on any makeup. Hmmm. I liked to wear makeup. A lot of it. Just as I decided that this crazy place in the woods was not for me, and started to leave, a man with nice eyes opened the door.

"Hi. Are you next?"

I could have easily said, "No, I'm waiting for a friend." Or "No, I was just checking out your crazy pictures," but I didn't. Instead, I walked through that door, auditioned, got hired, and went to Maine.

Quisisana, in Italian, means "a place where one heals one's self." A resort made up of small, comfortable cabins nestled in a wood of enormous pine trees flanking a beautiful lake, it's quiet, simple, and addictive. For this Midwestern girl, it was a huge adjustment, and I wrote things in my journal for the first few days, like *I haven't stopped since seven in the morning, and all I've done is pick up twigs and pine cones all day. I hope I get skinny here. It's freezing and the mosquitoes are disgusting. I got bit on my eyelid. Gross.*

Performing in the Quisisana music hall was a magical experience. The audiences were incredibly appreciative; no one noticed my weight. Still stinging from the scrutiny at CCM, I drank in the unconditional praise from the guests, who loved seeing their waiters and chambermaids belt out songs. By the time Quisisana closed for the summer, I returned to CCM a new person, more confident and mature, with a whole new "family" in Maine.

CCM was changing, too. The new head of the Musical Theater Program, Aubrey Berg, had begun slowly but surely improving the program by changing most of the cutthroat board policies. One of the best changes regarded the senior boards. During Aubrey's tenure, they became "farewell performances." Not graded, they more resembled cabaret acts than typical boards. We all had a great time writing our own shows and performing as "guests" in each other's boards. One of my classmates, Julia, asked me to perform in her board. At the rehearsals I noticed that Julia had acquired a pianist I'd never seen before. Cute, quiet, and (based on his clothes and shoe choices), clearly straight, he seemed suspiciously enthusiastic; I wondered if Julia's Southern girlish charm had anything to do with it. One day I pulled him aside after a rehearsal.

"Hey, Ron."

"Actually, my name is Rob."

I was embarrassed. I'd been working with the guy in rehearsals for a week. "Oh, sorry, Rob. Listen, I don't know what Julia is paying you to do this, but since you are new and apparently don't know much about the musical theater program, I wanted to give you some advice."

He laughed. "I'm not new. I've been playing classes all year."

"What classes?" I didn't know him, and I took all the classes.

"I play your classes, Sharon. I play for your acting class and your vocal coaching class."

I smugly corrected him. "No, that other guy with the beard and the glasses plays my classes."

"That's me. I shaved and put in my contacts."

I looked him over. "Hey, in my defense, you look really different. Actually, if you want my opinion, you look a lot better."

"I'm not really looking for opinions, but my mom said the same thing." Rob laughed. "So, what's your great advice?"

"I don't know what Julia's paying you, but I have a sneaking suspicion that it's just a batch of homemade chocolate chip cookies and a little flirty eye batting in your direction." I wished I could get things for free by flirting, but since I couldn't, I didn't want anyone else getting away with it. "She's famous for being cheap, and you should insist on being paid."

"Is that it?"

I nodded, proud that I'd been able to help this poor naive straight guy with the bright blue eyes and bad shoes. "You don't have to worry about me. I don't do anything I don't want to do. I'm happy to do it. Julia's been very nice to me, and I get to work with talented singers like you." He looked at his watch. "I've got to play a class. It's been nice talking to you, Sharon."

I watched him walk away. The entire conversation had backfired in my face. Even though he'd been nice, this confirmed it. Whenever I talked to straight guys, I always ended up feeling stupid.

Soon my life was consumed with my own senior board. My very good friend Jon and I decided to do a show together, and we spent months planning and rehearsing it. I hired a pianist and paid him with cash advances from the numerous credit cards I'd received in the mail.

Financially, I was a mess. My parents had completely run out of money, and I was paying for everything with credit cards. I took out a large student loan to get my tuition paid, and supplemented my other expenses like rent, utilities, and food with credit cards. In a very short period of time I had a drawer full of unpaid bills and my credit cards were being routinely rejected.

"Don't worry about it," I'd tell Jon. "Let's go out to dinner. I'll buy. I just got a new card in the mail!" I'd hold up a bright and shiny new card. "See, it's free!"

Sick of school, we spent the rest of our senior year blowing off classes and charging credit cards to the limit. The good news: Our board was a huge hit. The acclaim we received almost made up for the fact that I'd earned several "incompletes" in my classes. The bad news: I wouldn't graduate with my class on time.

I agonized over how to spend my summer. Jane had invited me back to Quisisana, but I'd also been cast in CCM's summer theater company, Hot Summer Nights. A well-paying job, it meant I could remain on campus and take some summer classes toward my degree. Staying in Cincinnati made more sense; I found an apartment with Maryday and Jon and called the Quisisana owner, Jane, to break the news. Jane was disappointed but nice on the phone. "If you want to come up and visit us, feel free to come at any time. You know you are always welcome."

Before we hung up, she added, "Do you know a guy named Rob Meffe? He applied to be our musical director and he said he knew you. Do you think he'd be good for the job?"

I knew I'd heard the name before, and then it hit me. Rob was the pianist who had played Julia's board. Rob would be fine for the job, but embarrassed as I was from our earlier conversation, I took it out on him. "No. I don't think he's right for Quisisana. He's not a Maine kind of guy."

Mayday, Jon, and I had a wonderful summer. So wonderful, in fact, that I ended up dropping all of my summer classes. At this point, I was a year away from graduating, and in debt up to my neck. I justified myself to Jon and Mayday. "I don't think I need to graduate. What I really need is to make money to pay off my bills. I heard about a theater conference in Atlanta called SETC, where all of the big theater groups go and audition for their winter seasons. We could all go together and share a cheap hotel room. Come on, it will be a blast. We'll become real working actors."

We all piled into the car and road tripped to Atlanta. The South Eastern Theater Conference was a huge, well-organized event. Every actor received two minutes to perform a song and a monologue, or two monologues in front of a huge audience of producers and directors. We all had papers with bold numbers taped to our chests, as if we might sprint off and run a marathon at any moment. I thought it was wonderful. Mayday hated it.

"It's a cattle auction." Mayday was uncharacteristically nervous. "How are we supposed to get noticed when there are so many people here?"

Mayday's mother was a professional actress, and Mayday had been performing professionally since she was a child. If anyone should feel confident about this audition, she should.

"What are you worried about?" I didn't understand her. "You are beautiful and you are the best actress I've ever met. They're all going to want you. You'll be playing Juliet or Blanche DuBois in some theater barn by Halloween."

Mayday managed a laugh. "I love your enthusiasm."

I was enthusiastic; I couldn't wait to perform my audition. Since I'd spent the summer playing a nun in *Nunsense*, and was still a virgin, I wrote a funny monologue about joining the convent because I was certain I'd never have sex. My monologue got a lot of laughs; when I segued into a song from *Evita* that began with the lyric "I'm their savior," I got even more laughs. It was my first professional audition and I knew I'd done well.

The theaters posted the numbers of the actors they wanted to see again, so for the next few minutes Maryday, Jon, and I squeezed through swarms of anxious actors and furiously scribbled down the room numbers of the theaters that requested to see us again.

After comparing notes, we went our separate ways and agreed to meet back in our hotel room for dinner. With seventeen callbacks, I had a busy night ahead of me. The callbacks were usually held in hotel rooms, where we repeated our original audition material and performed more songs. I had good feedback, particularly about the monologue I'd written, but I was disappointed to find out that most of these theaters paid very poorly. By the end of my night, I was exhausted and demoralized, but my spirits improved considerably when I read a posting on the door of my final callback.

> **This is a six-month-long national tour of *The Sound of Music*. Excellent pay. Lodging and travel provided. All actors must be excellent singers.**

Someone would actually pay me to be in *The Sound of Music*? I *had to, had to, had to* get this job. It was the answer to all my prayers. I could finally play Maria! I walked through the door ready to land my first big job—and the audition went well. So I had mixed emotions when a week later I got the call. I'd gotten the job, but I wasn't Maria. I wasn't even understudying Maria. They'd asked me to play a nun. Disappointed, I consoled myself with the fact that it was still a very prestigious, well-paid job—the best job available at the conference—and it offered me the opportunity to see the country as a real working actress. I talked to Aubrey Berg at CCM; we agreed that considering my financial position I should take the job even if it meant I wouldn't graduate. Jon had booked a different national tour, and Maryday had decided to work a corporate job in Cincinnati for a while. We said our goodbyes, and I packed my bags to hit the road.

The Sound of Music schedule was grueling because it was a nonunion tour, which means that we traveled by bus every day and performed in different theaters every night. As an example of our schedule, we once played twenty-one cities in Texas in twenty-one days without ever playing Houston, Dallas, Fort Worth, Austin, or El Paso. Although seeing the country was great, seeing it all from a bus window was frustrating. I seriously considered quitting, but I needed the money, so I found a "Maria von Trapp" solution. The kids in the show were touring with us (without their parents), so I entertained myself by playing with all of them. They were homesick and bored, and I was carsick and bored, so it was a perfect match. We whiled away our long travel days by telling stupid knock-knock jokes and playing with a Game Boy. The kids and I got along so well that eventually, in addition to my acting duties, I was hired as their chaperone and the assistant to the teacher who traveled with them. I loved the kids, and I consider it one of the most fulfilling jobs I've ever had.

As much as I may have acted like governess Maria with the kids, of course I was constantly disappointed that I wasn't playing Maria in the show. Instead I was typecast much more typically, given my size and my sex-life status, as Sister Margaretta.

One by one, people hooked up on tour. After a month it seemed like every single adult had hooked up with someone else, including my friend Kelli. I made jokes about it with her all the time. "I'm glad you're all banging away in your hotel rooms. Don't worry about me. If you need me, I'll be in the lobby playing hangman with the nine-year-olds." When she'd laugh, I'd continue, "Seriously, I'm so ugly and gross I couldn't get laid if I tried. Look at me!" I declared while dressed in my black-and-white habit from my head to my toes. "Who in the hell would be interested in a twenty-three-year-old virgin playing a nun? This is pathetic!"

Then I met Johnny, the company electrician. A throwback hippie who'd started smoking pot with his parents before he'd even hit high school, Johnny had long, curly hair, a sweet smile, and a laid-back quality that reminded me of my brother Buzzy. Johnny had a way of flirting with me that didn't scare me, probably because he was upfront that he was attracted to me, but he always left the first move up to me.

It started backstage in Waco, Texas. I saw Johnny on the loading dock on the way in the stage door and I said "hi" to him. He gave me a surprised look. "I wondered if you were ever going to speak to me."

At most I'd expected a "hi" back, so his retort caught me off guard. "What do you mean? We've talked before." I stammered.

"No we haven't. I had a bet going that you were going to ignore me for the entire tour."

I looked at him with sarcastic pity. "I'm sorry you lost the bet."

He gave me a wry smile. "I'm not."

I'd never had anyone behave that way around me; I figured it was just an impulse he'd regret later. But he persevered—and it became a game. I'd give the kids Hershey's Kisses to leave at his work station, then he'd send back a message with the girl who played Gretl. "Johnny said he thinks you are pretty."

I'd send her back. "You go tell Johnny that he shouldn't say that to a nun!"

For a couple of weeks, Johnny and I flirted in theaters across the desert southwest. Naturally, I was nervous. I liked him a lot, but I was damaged goods. "If I were you, I'd leave me alone," I would tell him. "I'm trouble."

"Yeah, you look like trouble, Sister," Johnny parried with a wicked smile. "I was just wondering. What do you have on underneath that habit?" He rubbed his hands together as fast as he could, as though he were excited just to be near me. I told him all the worst things about myself, rattling off my faults and hang-ups like a grocery list, but still he came back time and time again. By the time we were in Walla Walla, Washington, I told him flat out, "I'm fat and I hate how my body looks. You shouldn't be attracted to me." In Spokane I warned him, "I had a weird encounter with an old man, and I unexpectedly freak and throw people out of my room." In Boise I said, "Seriously, I seem to only date gay men. I'd find someone else if I were you. You don't want to be with me. I'm not good for you." The truth was, I liked Johnny, but I was scared of him and his strong attraction to me. Finally I revealed the real reason Johnny shouldn't want to date me. "Okay. I'll tell you the real reason you won't want to get involved with me. I'm a virgin. Isn't that pathetic?" I tried to laugh at myself. "Yep. I'm a twenty-three-year-old virgin." "Are you going to be a virgin forever?" For once Johnny was serious.

"Uh, no." My palms began to sweat. "I hope not. I just . . . I don't know. . . . I just want it to be the right guy, you know? I have to believe that he wants to be with *me*, not just any girl who'll take off her pants." I held my breath and waited for cute

Johnny to decide I was too problematic to pursue. I prayed he'd stick around.

"Well, let's just hang out," Johnny said. "We don't have to do anything you don't want to do. I'm not in any hurry."

Slowly but surely we started to fool around. And slowly but surely I grew more comfortable with him. Sometimes I would panic so much that I'd start to shake, and then he would just lie with me, holding me, telling me he loved me, waiting for me to calm down.

About six weeks later, we were in Canada doing a three-day weekend and staying in a nice hotel. After the show we were all having a drink in the hotel bar, when I quietly asked him, "Do you really love me?" I knew the answer to this, but I needed to hear it again.

Johnny smoothed my hair out of my face and looked me in the eyes. "I have never loved a girl the way I love you."

I smiled and delivered my big news. "Okay. I'm ready."

It took Johnny about three seconds to get us out of the bar, into the elevator, and into bed. I think he was ready, too. I've never regretted waiting for so long, because I waited until it was right. And boy, was it right.

Johnny and I spent a lot of time together over the next few months. Charming and romantic, Johnny almost made me forget that I was playing a celibate nun. He thought I was beautiful and sexy, and he told me that every chance he got. I thought he was sensitive and sweet, and everything I never thought I'd have. Johnny made it very clear that his intentions for our relationship were long term.

"I think you are the girl for me. We are so good together!" he'd say and rub his hands together.

Johnny's love changed me as a human being. I was so much happier with myself and my body than I ever thought imaginable. I loved him too, very much, but I wasn't as sure that the relationship could last because there was a problem, and it was a big one. I couldn't deal with his drug use. I'd made that clear from the beginning, so Johnny didn't get high in front of me. But I could always smell it on him, like a sweet, smoky cologne. My brother had had a drug problem while I was in high school, and I'd seen the bad side of drugs, the side that can tear families apart. Johnny said he did drugs to relax at the end of the day, and he swore that he only smoked pot—no hard drugs. From the beginning of our relationship, I had struggled to understand it, and together we made up some guidelines we could both live with. Not only did he agree never to get high in front of me, but he also promised he wouldn't do anything but smoke weed—no coke, ever. But one night, I walked in on him with a ten-dollar bill up his nose snorting a line of coke. I called Meema and told her what had happened. As a woman who had gone through an abusive marriage with an alcoholic who made lots of promises, her advice was swift and certain. "Dump him."

I did. Devastated, Johnny swore he'd change for me.

I had to be honest with him. "Johnny, I love you, but I think we are too different. There are a lot of people in the world who wouldn't care that you got high; they'd even get high with you. I'm just not that girl. I don't think you are some big drug addict. I don't want you to change for me, nor do I want to be the girl who made you quit. You'll end up hating me for it or sneaking around behind my back."

I promised myself that no amount of pleading or promising on Johnny's part would get me back after that. I knew what I wanted, and I also knew what I *didn't* want.

After six months on tour without a day off, I was exhausted. The tour was over and my relationship with Johnny had ended, so I decided to escape to Quisisana.

chapter 18
the boy friend

My first rehearsal was with the music director, Rob Meffe, the very same guy I'd told Jane not to hire the year before.

Emotionally and physically exhausted after the tour with *SOM*, I called the owner, Jane, and asked if I could come back for another summer. Her answer was generous and quick. "Yep. Come on up. We'd love to have you."

It was great timing; the lead in the musical *Anything Goes* had just left, so Jane asked me to step in. After spending the past six months in the back row dressed as a nun, I was happy to try something different, so I turned my little car in the direction of the pines and headed back to Quisisana. By the time I arrived, the staff had already been there for a week and rehearsals were well underway. I was worn out from the tour, depressed over breaking up with Johnny, and nervous at the thought of learning such a huge role so quickly. So instead of showing up fresh and prepared, I showed up stressed out and with laryngitis.

My first rehearsal was with the music director, Rob Meffe, the very same guy I'd told Jane not to hire the year before. I was sure he hated me. Terrified that once he heard my froggy voice he'd immediately give my part to someone else, I tried to apologize and charm him with a lot of dramatic pointing and waving.

"Don't worry about it." He was calm and sweet. "I know you can sing."

I felt immensely relieved.

"If you can't sing right now, let's at least try to get something done. I can just talk you through the music. Does that sound okay?"

I nodded my head wildly. Rob played through some songs, and we did a little work at the piano; then we moved to a lounge chair out near the lake. He brought his score with him, and I brought a legal pad and a pen, so I could "talk." Rob is a quiet guy, and I could tell that too much talking made him nervous. And because I'm so outgoing, it was hard for me to limit my conversation to a legal pad. But somehow it worked.

Of course, we got off the subject of the music very quickly and ended up talking—and writing—for a couple of hours. He told me that he had seen almost everything I'd ever performed in while he was at CCM, and I wrote, *You're a stalker!* He asked why I'd only dated gay men at CCM, and I wrote, *Why did you even notice who I was dating?*

The subject roamed from families to pets and, as the sun set over the mountains, our past relationships. I wrote about Johnny, and he told me about his recent devastating breakup. As we talked, I had an "aha!" moment. I thought, *This is the kind of guy my friends and family would want me to date.*

That night I made a decision. *Just try it,* I told myself. About a week later, my voice had recovered and rehearsals were in full swing. Rob and I had grown increasingly flirtatious, but he still hadn't worked up the nerve to ask me out.

Two nights before the show opened, I found Rob in the lodge. He looked adorable in an Irish fisherman's sweater, drinking a seltzer. I was sick of waiting for "the man" to make the first move, so I decided to move things along. I approached him and struck up a conversation.

"I think we are going to have a really good time tomorrow night," Rob said.

"Oh, we're going to have a good time tomorrow night? Where are we going?" I asked. I knew he was referring to opening night, which was the day after tomorrow. I could have corrected him, but I didn't.

Rob blushed. "Um, no—wait—I meant Monday night. We're going to have a good time on Monday night. You know—when we open the show."

I jumped in with both feet. "No, Rob. That's not what you said. You said we were going to have a good time tomorrow night. Which means you are obviously asking me out."

"You want to go out on a date with me?"

"Since you asked, I'd love to. I'll be baby-sitting in the cabin named Andante until six, so you can pick me up from there. See you then."

Before he had a chance to respond, I walked away, leaving quiet, handsome Rob in a daze of confusion.

I was nervous all day on Sunday. I'd never been this forward with a guy before, and I worried that he might not even show up. I sat on the porch of the cabin, wondering if I'd get my date or if I'd ruined my chances with Rob forever. At exactly six, I heard the crunch of pine needles. I looked up and saw Rob Meffe, ready for our date. He took me to a nearby marina for a romantic dinner, and he even paid. Very classy.

The rest of the summer was about Rob. We were totally different people but extremely compatible. He taught me new things, like hiking, and I talked him into buying a whole new wardrobe at the nearby outlets. After a while, we got to be such good friends that we worried we were going to ruin our friendship by dating. All summer long, we'd spend the night together and then swear that was the last time. We told each other, "Let's just be friends. I like you too much to date you! We are going to ruin this, and I don't want to lose you."

We even went so far as to break up at the end of the summer. Rob had a steady job at Notre Dame, and I was moving to New York in the fall; a long-distance relationship seemed futile. We ended the relationship on a friendly note, but I was still surprised at how much I missed him once I returned to Cincinnati to pack my stuff. About a week later Rob called.

"Sharon, my job at Notre Dame fell through, and I was thinking, how about if I move to New York?"

My heart started to pound with excitement. "Hmm. Are we going to be just friends?"

"That's not really what I had in mind. What did you have in mind?"

"I've been miserable without you," I admitted.

"Me, too."

Rob moved to New York the first of September and a few weeks later, my friend Jon and I rolled into Manhattan in our Ryder rental truck filled with our life's possessions. I'd planned to see Rob the night we arrived, but we'd run out of gas on the Pennsylvania Turnpike and we were hours behind schedule. I called Rob from the road to say I'd see him the next day. "We're not going to get in until two or three in the morning, so I'll call you tomorrow after we drop off the truck."

It was just after two in the morning when Jon and I saw the skyline of our new town. I bounced up and down on the springy rental truck seat. "There's the Empire State Building, and the World Trade Center, and *oh*, do you see her? There's the Statue of Liberty. 'Give me your tired, your poor, your huddled masses. . . .'" That's when it hit me. "She's the patron saint of actors! *We're* tired, poor, and coming in huddled masses. The Statue of Liberty is *our* symbol of hope. I think we should drive there immediately and place an offering at her feet." Jon pointed out that we'd have to be driving a boat to reach her since she's on an island in the middle of a harbor, but we made big plans to visit as soon as possible and place French fries at her feet (because she's French). We decided she needed a name, so we dubbed her "Margaret," and Margaret became my symbol for success in this scary new land, Manhattan.

When Jon and I finally pulled up to our new apartment around three that morning, a very sleepy, but smiling, Rob walked out of a diner to greet us. I jumped out of the truck and ran up to him. "What are you doing here? It's so late! You said you were going home!"

He pointed back to the empty diner he'd just emerged from. "Well, I couldn't leave my good friend Constantine all alone, now could I?" A very large Greek man waved to him through the window, and Rob pointed at me and mouthed, "Here she is!" Rob put his arms around me. "I wanted to be here to say welcome to your new life. I'm so glad you're here!"

Right there in the middle of this foreign city, I felt completely at home.

chapter 19

wonderful town

I have to immerse myself in the city that never sleeps!

Since I'd spent so many years fantasizing about my big move to New York City, I was sure I could predict my future there. I'd find somewhere to live, get a job waiting tables to make money, and go to auditions until I landed a big Broadway show. Simple. It wasn't until I arrived that I realized how wrong my plans were.

During my first months there, I learned four very important lessons:

Lesson One: Real estate. Even though Rob had found an affordable two-bedroom with a roommate in Queens, I wouldn't settle for that. "I am moving to New York City for the first time in my life, and I want to live in Manhattan. I have to immerse myself in the city that never sleeps!"

I'd grown up watching Manhattan in the movies—Woody Allen films, *The Goodbye Girl,* and *Fame*—and reading about New York in Judy Blume books full of words like "prewar co-ops" and "doorman building." I knew what I wanted, but as I scanned apartment listing after apartment listing in the *Sunday New York Times* real estate section, I realized there were no prewar-doorman-building apartments available for anything under ninety zillion dollars.

In the end, I shared a small one-bedroom apartment with Jon in the financial district. Our apartment had no kitchen, and the financial district had no grocery stores or cleaners, but we were in Manhattan and we could afford it—sort of.

Lesson Two: Manhattan is crazy expensive. I'd grown up in a house where there was no discipline about money, so I didn't even know how to begin to budget. Rob was a master at budgeting, and I tried to follow his advice about packing my lunch instead of eating out and taking the subway instead of cabs, but eating out and taxis were part of my fantasy New York life. I loved to order Chinese (the containers are so cute) or walk to the corner, raise my hand, and watch a yellow cab come screeching to a halt. I raced through the money I'd saved on tour, but I didn't worry about it. I'd get a show soon and have plenty of money. I was living my Manhattan dream!

Lesson Three: There are a lot of young, hopeful actors in New York. I'd heard this a million times, but *wow*. That's all I could think when I went to my first auditions in New York. *Wow.* There were a lot of talented people—and we all wanted the same job. We'd wait in line outside—in rain, sleet, snow, or tropical heat—for hours, sometimes arriving at five in the morning, to be seen for whatever Broadway show was auditioning that day, and only some of the actors were even seen. The only way to avoid these enormous lines was to have an agent; at the time I didn't have one, but I sure wanted one. I wanted out of those lines.

Today, most schools have "showcases" for graduating seniors each spring; students come to New York and audition for top casting directors and agents. This practice didn't exist when I came to New York. I had to get an agent the old-fashioned way—by mailing pictures and resumes over and over again until someone finally called. The whole system was miserable, and many of my colleagues quit the business and moved back home within a year.

I may have given up, too, but I had Rob, and his love for both me and New York City kept me sane. "Don't worry," he'd tell me after every deflating audition. "You'll get a job. Just keep trying." He was starting to break through in the music director world, and his successes encouraged me. *I can do this,* I'd tell myself as I fell asleep each night. *Someone will hire me at some point if I just stick it out.*

Lesson Four: The two words most actors hate—survival job. A survival job is the wretched job you have to take to pay your bills until someone famous discovers you and makes you famous. Ideally, a survival job is one you can leave on a moment's notice— that is, whenever Broadway calls you for a last-minute audition. A good survival job is very difficult to find, especially if you have no office skills or waitressing experience. And of course, I had neither. Eventually I called my friend Jane at Quisisana, and she called some families and got me a job doing the one thing I was really good at—baby-sitting.

I loved the kids, but the job still didn't pay me enough to stay in Manhattan. By February, I'd run out of money and moved into Rob's apartment in Queens, which was a little cramped, but very romantic.

Rob's first big purchase in New York was a piano. The decadent focal point of his otherwise spare living room, this shiny walnut Baldwin Studio upright was Rob's prize possession—and he played it from morning to night. In the mornings I would run down the street to get us cappuccinos and when I got back, Rob would play the "Cappuccino Song," a renamed Scott Joplin ragtime song that mimicked caffeine coursing through our veins. In my caffeinated euphoria I'd dance around in the living room and scream for him to play it again and again.

Rob and I were getting along better than ever, but there were some bumps in the road. Our biggest disagreements were about money. Rob would usually avoid confrontations at all costs, but my inability to budget pushed him over the edge. It started when I came home with a new winter coat. True, I got it on sale—but even so this glorious purple ski coat was far more expensive than I could afford. Still, I couldn't wait to show Rob, and I rushed through the multiple locks on our front door.

"Hey, Roberto, are you here? Come see me as a ski bunny!" I screamed down the long hallway. Rob emerged from his bedroom with a large manila envelope in his hand. His face fell when he saw me parading around the living room in my new purchase.

"Isn't it cute? I just got it at Macy's. Wait—let me give you the full effect. Close your eyes."

He did, and I pulled a long, striped ski cap with matching mittens out of the bag and put them on.

"Okay, now how do I look?" I swung my scarf around, making swishy ski noises to give the effect that I was swooping down the slopes.

Rob looked sullen. "It's cute."

He walked back into the bedroom and slightly pushed the door shut behind him. I followed him. Rob didn't like to talk about unpleasant things, preferring to work them out on his own. "What's eating you? Did I do something wrong?"

He kept his back to me and continued working. "No, I'm fine."

"You don't seem fine."

"This was sitting on the floor this morning, and I picked it up thinking it was mine." He held up one of several envelopes on the desk. "There are unopened bills in here from nine months ago. Most of the envelopes say 'final notice' and there are several from credit agencies. This is a default statement from your student loan. I don't get it, Sharon. How can you just ignore these?"

I was speechless. I usually had this conversation with my sister, who'd helped me out financially a few times over the years. Whenever she paid a bill for me she insisted on organizing my unpaid bills and teaching me how to budget. I always started out with the best intentions, trying to live on cheap ramen noodles and take the subway, but sooner or later I'd see an "apply for instant credit" sign and I'd jump on it. Like today at Macy's when I'd signed up for a new credit card to get 10 percent off my purchases. I'd figure out the money later.

Rob looked very serious. "Sharon, I want to be very clear with you. I love you and I think our relationship could go great places, but I'm not kidding when I say that if you don't become more fiscally responsible, it's over. I will not hesitate to break up with you if this pattern continues, and I will never be the person who lends you money to get you out of a bind. You have to pay all of this off." He threw the envelope on the bed.

I knew he meant every word, I knew he was right, and worst yet, I didn't know if I could fix it. I started to cry. "I don't know why I'm so bad with money. If I have a check or a credit card, it feels like free money. I know it's not. I tell myself that it's not, but still, I just spend it anyway, even though I'm broke. I'm so sorry. I'll take back my coat." I ripped the coat off of my body and threw it dramatically into the shopping bag.

Rob sat next to me and put his arm around me. "I know it's hard, and I also know you didn't really learn how to manage money, but that doesn't mean you have to repeat the patterns your parents had." I nodded and wiped my nose on the back of my hand. Rob handed me a tissue and continued. "I'll tell you what. I'm really good with money. If you want me to, I'll help you budget and figure out how to pay back your bills. The deal is, though, you have to make all of the money. I won't pay a dime of it."

"Really? You'd do that for me?"

"Of course. The thing is, we're never going to have a job that has any kind of financial stability. That means we have to be more careful about how we spend our money. We'll never be like other people, Sharon. We're never going to have a regular paycheck with benefits and a 401k for retirement. That means we have to be extra cautious."

"I know." I rested my head against his shoulder. "I promise, I'll be better."

You know how some people say they're going to change, but then they don't? Turns out, I'm not one of those people. Surprising even myself, I cleaned up my act. Rob opened a joint checking account and from that point on I gave him every penny I made. In return, he made me cut up all my credit cards—all fourteen of them—and set up payment schedules to pay them off. I became very financially responsible when I realized that I loved being with Rob more that I loved anything I could charge on a credit card.

When Jane called in the spring and asked if Rob and I would like to go back to Quisisana for another summer, we jumped at the chance. I opted to work in the well-paying dining room, so I could come back to New York in the fall with my debt paid off and some waitressing experience under my belt. In addition, Jane and the director Dwayne asked me to perform the lead in the summer musical, *Joseph and the Amazing Technicolor Dreamcoat*.

After a successful run in *Joseph*, I returned to New York with a fresh attitude. I'd nearly paid off all my debt and I'd landed a good waitressing job. I was ready to tackle the long audition lines. *This year I'm going to break through.*

les misérables

Any woman above a size 4 had better be pretty damn talented to get a good job.

That fall, Rob and I spent a lot of time exploring Times Square theater by theater, scrutinizing show pictures to see if there were any roles for me. I'd pose outside the theaters, mimicking the actresses in the pictures, asking Rob, "Could I be in this show? Do I look like them? Am I too fat?"

Rob would look at me as if I were crazy. "Sharon, you are beautiful and talented. They'd be lucky to have you!"

I loved Rob's constant upbeat message, but I knew the realities of New York casting better than he did. Any woman above a size 4 had better be pretty damn talented to get a good job. By then, I'd had many auditions where I'd walked in and the people had said "Oh my god! You are so great! I can't cast you in this show, but I just loved your audition!" Nine times out of ten, I knew why. I was too fat.

After studying the posters, the first Broadway show I decided I should be cast in was *Les Misérables*. At the time, I weighed about 180 pounds, but I'd checked out the pictures, and there were girls with my body type in the show. *Les Mis* was a huge show with some of the best singing actors in New York, and I decided I fit the bill perfectly. I was a shoe-in.

After some persuasive pestering phone calls to the casting office—*Hi, it's Sharon Wheatley calling again to remind you that I'm available to audition for you at any time*—I finally got my audition. It was a "screening" audition, which meant there weren't any jobs currently available, but they would consider actors for future work. I was thrilled to have the opportunity, but afterward I wasn't sure how I'd done. The casting director had barely looked up from her cup of coffee while I belted my brains out in the tiny room, except to say, "Wow. You have a voice of a bygone era. You don't have to sing so loud, hon, we use microphones now." I didn't hear anything from her for months, and I'd nearly given up hope, although I'd heard stories about people waiting for years for another chance to audition for *Les Mis*. I was waitressing at one of the restaurants at the famous Macy's in Herald Square, and one day the phone there rang. It was the very same casting director whose coffee cup I'd rattled a few months back. I took the call in the kitchen, where I could barely hear her over the banging of pots and pans.

"Sharon? This is Liz at Johnson and Liff Casting. There is an ensemble spot opening on the national tour of *Les Misérables*, and I was wondering if you'd like to audition for it? We are seeing people on Wednesday. Before you agree, though, you have to answer something for me honestly. Can you sing a solid high C?"

I said a short prayer of thanks to Miss Brown for all my classical training. "Yes. Absolutely. I can sing a high C."

Ecstatic, I called Rob immediately and told him everything. We jumped up and down together, because even the opportunity for a private audition for *Les Mis* was a big deal. Things were looking up.

The day of my audition, I was so confident I was going to get the part that I said goodbye to all the busboys at the restaurant and told them I didn't think I'd be back. I had a feeling that this job was mine. For years, I'd felt that my only true hurdle in show business was my weight, and since weight wasn't an issue for the audition, I thought I had an excellent chance.

Nervous but ready, I walked through the door with my hopes high, and that's when I first encountered Richard Jay-Alexander. I didn't know it at the time, but Richard Jay was famous in the Broadway world for being blunt, and the stories actors tell about auditioning for Richard Jay are part of Broadway lore. One memorable story involves a close friend of mine. During a callback, he said, "Eileen, lift up your hair and turn profile for a minute." She did. He looked at her for a few seconds before saying, "Thanks for coming in."

Eileen was devastated but walked out of the audition, got a nose job, and was subsequently cast in *Les Mis*, thus becoming part of Richard Jay's success stories. Later he told her, "You know, Eileen, I didn't have a problem with your nose; it was your chin I was looking at. But hey, look at the bright side, now you've got a cute little nose and you still got the job, right?"

Had I known Richard Jay's reputation, I would have skipped the audition. But instead, I went in full of hope and I sang my heart out. Richard Jay asked me to sing a lot of songs for him, and finally at one point, he closed the folder in front of him and said, "Okay. You don't have to answer this."

I braced myself for a personal question about my weight. "Around how old are you? Give me a ballpark idea."

Relief flooded through me that the number he wanted was my age, not my weight. "I just turned twenty-five."

He continued to look me up and down, and I felt a little drop of sweat roll down my back. "I don't know a thing about you. Who do you know that I know?"

I racked my brains. I'd heard a million times that show business was all about contacts, but this was the first time I'd ever seen it played out. I blurted out the first name that popped into my head. "Christa Justus!" Christa was in the Broadway company of Les Mis, and she had been a senior at CCM when I was a freshman. I didn't know if she remembered me, then or now, but I willingly dropped her name.

"Okay. I love Christa. Can you leave on Sunday? I need you in LA as soon as possible."

I was stunned. I'd heard stories that people auditioned for Les Mis for years, and Richard Jay had given me my first big break after only one audition—and I was a size 14! Even though I'd been very hopeful, being cast in Les Mis that day was a profound and wonderful surprise, and I will always appreciate his faith in me.

Four days later I kissed Rob goodbye and hopped a plane to Los Angeles where I joined the national touring company of Les Misérables as a "swing" (which means I understudied everyone except the young pretty girls). I was so excited, I would have sold T-shirts in the lobby if they'd asked me to. But to be onstage with this amazingly talented group of people was almost more than I could believe.

When I joined the company, I realized how different my attitude was from the other actors my age. On my first day of rehearsal, I met a girl named Sarah Uriarte. Like me, this was Sarah's first big job, but unlike me, she wasn't happy just to be in the ensemble. She was understudying two of the female romantic leads, Eponine and Cosette, and she made it clear from the first day that she wasn't content to sit out on a tour as the understudy. She wanted to play the big parts, on Broadway.

Shocked at her confidence, I took a step back and looked at my own situation. Why was I so incredibly grateful for my job, while Sarah thought of it as merely a stepping stone to better things? The answer came to me easily. Sarah was not only talented, but she was also beautiful and had a great body. There was no doubt in anyone's mind that Sarah was going to become a big musical theater star, and—in fact—she was promoted to Eponine on Broadway a mere six months later. When that happened, a lot of people were jealous, but I wasn't. My view of my place in show business was always starkly realistic. I was very talented, but I was not a beautiful, thin woman. Most jobs would be difficult for me to get, and I would never be cast in some roles. I accepted this as a fact of life and figured that it was not worth my time to fantasize about things that would never happen for me.

Even as I was coming to terms with the fact that I would never play a romantic lead, things were very romantic in my personal life. Rob and I had been dating for two and a half years, and my "let's get married" alarm clock was ringing loudly. Much to my dismay, Rob was not in the same "let's get married" time zone. I knew Rob wanted to establish himself as a music director before he settled down, but I didn't care. I was making enough money for both of us and I made it clear that I did not expect him to be the "provider." Still, Rob had goals he wanted to achieve before he made a lifelong commitment to me.

I respected that as best I could, although I wasn't always patient. I talked about getting engaged often, and I often dragged him into jewelry stores to look at engagement rings. "Rob, I don't want you to spend a lot of money on a diamond ring. In fact, a ring isn't that important to me. Just something symbolic would be great, even a ring made out of tinfoil."

"I am not going to make an engagement ring out of tinfoil. You are ridiculous." Rob repeated what became his engagement mantra. "I love you, but I'm not ready."

"Let me just show you what I like in case *at some point* you are ready." I tried to be sensitive and patient, but I didn't always manage well. My birthday, Christmas, New Year's, Valentine's Day, Sweetest Day, even the Fourth of July became potential "pop the question" moments in my head. I tried to hide my disappointment when the gifts were *just gifts,* but it was impossible. Rob could have presented me with the Taj Mahal, and still I would have been disappointed.

When *Les Mis* played San Diego, Rob flew in from New York and we spent a romantic day off together. After a trip to the San Diego Zoo, and a candlelit dinner in La Jolla, we ventured down to the oceanfront and found a cozy, rocky cove where we sat and listened to the waves crash around us. It was the perfect moment to propose. As we sat, I played out the entire scene in my head—Rob professing his eternal love while I smiled sweetly and accepted. I got caught up in my fantasy and before I knew what I was doing, I blurted out, "So is there anything you want to ask me?"

Rob knew exactly what I was saying, and he was furious. "I can't believe you just said that. If I propose to you, it will be when and where I decide to do it, not when you think it should happen. You know Sharon, you don't get to control everything." He stood up, looked at me with disappointment, and walked away.

I raced after him, scampering up the jagged rocks, a heartfelt apology pouring out of my mouth. After a few days he forgave me, but from then on I kept quiet on the topic of getting married.

Right after California, my *Les Misérables* company traveled for three months to Singapore. Rob was working another job, so we were separated for the first seven weeks, the longest we'd ever been apart. I missed him terribly. Because of the expense and the time change, we limited our telephone conversations, and corresponded via daily letters full of romantic pining for each other. When Rob finally arrived in Singapore, he was offered a job playing one of the keyboard books in the orchestra in *Les Mis.* He happily got to work, but almost immediately was sidelined by a nasty flu.

I'd planned to show him all of the interesting shops and restaurants I'd discovered, but instead we limited our tourism to the waiting rooms of several doctor's offices as we searched for a drug to lower his dangerously high temperature. I'd arranged a boat ride to a small island called Batam in Indonesia for our first day off together, which I assumed we would cancel, but the night before our trip Rob's fever broke and he declared himself well. I suggested we cancel and go another time, but Rob was adamant.

"I'm feeling great! Let's go, I don't want to waste any more time in bed. Look, I'll prove it." He did a long series of jumping jacks and toe touches to prove his point. "I'm healed." He really did seem completely better, so after taking his temperature multiple times, we packed an overnight bag and boarded a high-speed boat bound for Batam.

We stayed at a beautiful resort on the island, made of gleaming tropical hardwood and boasting numerous balconies overlooking the sea. We spent the afternoon swimming in the lagoon pool and the evening playing a long and competitive game of Monopoly with another couple.

We lost badly. When Rob suggested a midnight walk on the beach, I declined. "Let's just go to bed, okay? I need to sleep off our horrific defeat."

Rob had been so sick, I couldn't believe he was still standing. I assumed he was as ready to go to sleep in our little tropical hut as I was, so I was surprised when he laughed and pulled me down the stairs.

"You are such a rotten loser. Come on, I want to go see the beach at night."

I whined, but then Rob pointed out that I was turning down a romantic walk on the beach on a tropical foreign island with the man I love. I'm not stupid—I went.

After a few minutes of walking in the pitch-black darkness, we ran into a ladder ascending into the sky.

"It's a lookout tower. I saw it earlier when I was walking around. Let's go up and see it."

"We won't be able to see anything from up there. It's too dark." I put my hands out in front of me. "Are you there? I can't even see you!"

From the creaking sounds coming from the ladder, I guessed he was already halfway up it.

"Come on up and find me!"

At the top of the ladder, I felt my way out onto the lookout.

"I'm over here. Come and look at the lights."

The lights of Singapore were barely visible across the water. We stood and looked at the view, Rob's arm wrapped around my waist.

"It's beautiful." I felt very at peace in that moment in the trees with Rob. The only sounds were the rumble of the surf and the distant screech of monkeys.

Rob turned me away from the view and held both of my hands. It was so dark, I couldn't even see his face as he began to speak.

"Sharon, I love you more than I have ever loved anyone in my entire life. You bring me so much joy. I cannot imagine a day in my life without you. . . ."

Rob's voice morphed into an unintelligible sound, like the adult voices in the *Peanuts* cartoons. *Is he proposing?*

"*Muh wah, wah wah* forever, Sharon. *Muh wah wah* first day I saw you, *Muh wah wah*." *This sounds like a proposal. Have I really thought about this? Do I really want to get married, or was I just playing a game to get him to ask?*

"*Muh wah wah muh wah wah,* and I would like to ask you something."

I snapped back to attention just in time to hear the most important question anyone had ever asked me.

"Sharon Wheatley, will you marry me?" Rob lifted my arm and I felt something heavy slip onto my left hand.

I needed to clarify. "You got me a ring? Really? This is official? Are you really saying you want to get married?"

"I cannot believe you are surprised!" Rob laughed. "You've known this was coming!"

"I didn't think you were ready! I thought I'd bugged you about it too much and we would just date until we were eighty years old. I'm shocked! I'm thrilled! I cannot believe that you bought me a ring!" I couldn't see the ring on my finger. The fact that he'd been walking around with a ring in his pocket the entire trip really floored me. "When did you buy me a ring? You've been sick in bed since you got here."

"I bought it the second day I was here, before I got sick, and it's been hidden in my suitcase for eight days. Are you going to give me an answer?"

---

les misérables

"Yes! Yes! Yes! *Yes!*"

We set the date for January in Cincinnati.

After we got back from Singapore, I was asked to audition for a musical called *The Most Happy Fella*, which was being produced in Cleveland at a theater where Rob had worked the summer before. Rob was also the musical director of this production, and I really wanted to get cast so we could work together and be near Cincinnati to plan the wedding. I went to the audition prepared to sing for the wisecracking, sidekick role named Cleo, but when I got there, director Michael McConnell asked me to audition for the romantic lead role of Rosabella. I knew the show very well, and I totally disagreed with his choice, but I sang for him anyway.

While I auditioned, he walked around the theater. At first I expected him to stop me and say, "Oh well, I was just experimenting with this idea, but I'm wrong. Sing the funny stuff instead." But he didn't. He had me sing Rosabella's songs and do her scenes over and over, until I finally relaxed. Deep down I'd always wanted to sing about falling in love, especially at this point in my life when I was so in love with Rob. Michael seemed enthusiastic, and he said he'd call me soon with his decision.

As I waited for the call, I lectured myself: *Don't expect to play the pretty girl. No one in his right mind would ask you to do that. He'll go with someone more traditionally beautiful and thin. That's what audiences want to see.*

Then one day the phone rang, and to my disbelief I heard Michael say, "I want you to come and play Rosabella."

"Michael, I don't think I should play Rosabella." I was flattered, but I also thought he was completely out of his mind, and I tried to stop him from making a mistake. "I should play Cleo. I look like a Cleo."

"You know, Sharon, I actually think you will be a wonderful Rosabella." Michael seemed surprised at my resistance. "If you don't want to do it, you don't have to, but I've already hired someone else to play Cleo."

"But Michael, I don't look like a Rosabella!"

"What do you think a Rosabella should look like?"

I thought about this for a minute as I twisted the phone cord in my hand. "She should be skinny and pretty. I don't look like the kind of girl that men fall in love with, you know?"

"Sharon, this is my production of *The Most Happy Fella*, and I can cast whomever I'd like." Michael knew what he wanted, and he gave it to me straight. "In this production, I want Rosabella to look like you. Now I can understand if you don't want to take it because it's not nearly the money you are making on *Les Mis*, but I don't think you should turn it down just because you don't think you look like a girl that men can fall in love with."

How could I argue with that? Deep down I was *dying* to do it, so I took the job.

I gave my notice at *Les Mis*, left behind almost $1,500 a week, and flew to Cleveland where I spent the rest of the summer playing a character who falls in love (and kisses onstage, a first for me!). I'd never, ever, ever been given the opportunity to explore the soft, romantic side of myself onstage, and it was a wonderful experience. I wanted the summer to last forever. The only part of the show I had a hard time with was, during the second act, when I had to walk through the chorus as they sang "beautiful Rosabella." Every time I did it, I cracked up. Michael rolled his eyes and made me walk through them over and over again until I could hear "beautiful Rosabella" without even smirking. It was surreal. I was the only person in the room who thought I couldn't do it. Even when the reviews came out, the critics were kind. They talked about how good I was in the part, and that I breathed "new life" into the role. "Miss Wheatley may not look like your typical ingénue, but I promise that her performance packs an emotional punch. You'll leave the theater deeply satisfied."

I saved these reviews for years and read them over and over in a Sally Field "They liked me! They really liked me!" kind of way. I was ecstatic to know there were directors like Michael McConnell out there who'd risk casting a nontraditional ingénue like me.

A few weeks later, Richard Jay called again and invited me to join the Broadway company of *Les Mis* as a temporary replacement for Christa Justus, the woman whose name had gotten me the job in the first place. I was a swing again, not playing any of the pretty girl parts, but still I was ecstatic. *Broadway!* Getting cast in a show once could possibly be a fluke, but to get cast again made it real. I had a career!

The first day I reported to work, I walked right down the center of Times Square and breathed in the neon magic. It was the most exciting commute in the world. My first step inside the official stage door brought tears to my eyes as I remembered my trip backstage at *The Pirates of Penzance. I knew I'd get here,* I thought as I looked at my name on my dressing room door. *I just* knew *it!*

My first performance on Broadway was an amazing experience. Because I was an understudy, I didn't know I was performing until a few hours before the curtain went up. Fortunately I'd had a lot of rehearsal, which kept my nerves at bay, but my pulse still quickened a few beats when the stage manager made the announcement to the cast before the show started. "Good evening ladies and gentleman. At this evening's performance the role of the Head Whore will be played by Sharon Wheatley. This is Sharon's Broadway debut!" The women in my dressing room erupted in a cheer and the screams of support echoed through the stairwell from the other dressing rooms. Rob managed to purchase a ticket at the last minute and he had a dozen red roses delivered to my dressing room with a card.

> **Congratulations to my Broadway Baby. All your dreams are coming true! I'm so glad I will be by your side to see all of the amazing things in your future. I love you, Rob.**

After a three-month run on Broadway, my contract was up and I left to get married. Rob accepted a dream job as the associate music director on the national tour of *The Phantom of the Opera*. Although we were sad to be apart again, we were thrilled that the *Phantom* company gave him the weekend off in January to get married. With a little extra money in our pockets, we threw a fantastic winter wedding for 215 guests at an art deco train station in Cincinnati.

I still didn't have an agent, and I quickly discovered that most actresses on Broadway had proper talent agents so they could audition for more shows. I didn't want to be the only one without an agent, so I pulled a few strings and managed a meeting with a pretty famous musical theater agent. I'd been prepped by friends that he would probably only ask me to tell him about myself, and true to form, he left it up to me to keep the conversation going for the hour or so that I was in his office. I watched him smoke, telling him every stupid life story I could dream up to fill the silence. "Um, yeah, I had a lot of pets. We had something like eight dogs and twenty-two cats and a horse, although I didn't grow up on a farm. My mom just bought animals when she was mad at my dad. Uh, oh, and once my car caught on fire—that's a good story!" Exhausted, I was running out of subjects.

Finally, he put out his cigarette and spoke. "What roles are there on Broadway right now that you think you are right for?"

This is a common question, and one that agents love to ask prospective clients. I'd been warned to expect it, so I rattled off the short list I'd prepared. "I could do *The Phantom of the Opera* or *Beauty and the Beast* or, depending on the vision of the director, lots of the romantic roles. I just finished playing Rosabella and I got great reviews." I pulled out my dog-eared reviews, but he waved them away.

"You know, Sharon, I'm looking at you and I'm thinking, you are going to have a very tough time getting jobs at this weight. I'm sure you are talented, but unless you are an older character actress, you aren't going to get the kind of work you want. I'll tell you what. Why don't you think about losing twenty-five pounds or so, and then we'll talk again."

I was confused. I'd been cast in *Les Mis* after my first audition. I'd been selected for the Broadway company. I was currently employed on Broadway, and this man was telling me I wasn't going to get any jobs until I lost weight.

I tried to clarify. "Are you saying that you won't consider working with me until I've lost weight?"

"I'm simply saying that I think you should consider losing weight. I'm not saying that I think you should do it, and I'm also not saying that I'll sign you if you do lose weight. This is just a conversation, Sharon. I like you, and I want to give you my honest opinion."

I could tell that the meeting was over. I could also tell that he probably dealt out advice like this a lot, and that he didn't really expect that people would do it. But he'd never encountered me before. This wasn't a comment I was going to ignore.

For the first time in my life, I was comfortable with my body. So comfortable, in fact, that I hadn't lost any weight for my wedding, and I still thought I looked good in the pictures. Then I thought about Broadway casting. Was it really, really critical for me to be skinny in order to play roles like Rosabella in New York? Were producers or, for that matter, Americans in general, ready to see an overweight actress fall in love and get the guy in a musical? I decided that I would find out.

After I left that meeting, I decided that I would start thinking of my body not as a body at all, but as a product, like a box of Tide or a can of Coke. I took a widespread poll of what people thought about my weight.

"I just had a high-powered Broadway agent tell me that I would probably not work in my chosen profession because of my weight. I am attempting to redesign my body as a product in order to sell better. Like a box of Tide. Do you think that my product and my business would be more lucrative if I lost weight? Would you be more comfortable watching me as a love interest onstage if I weighed forty pounds less? I would greatly appreciate an honest answer. I like myself, and I'm okay with my body, but if I need to change in order to get better work, I will. What do you think?"

To their credit, my friends and family tried to answer questions about my body. My mom and dad tried to stay neutral because we'd had so many weight issues in the past. Most people said that they liked how I looked, but enough people said that I might get more work if I lost weight that I decided to try it. I called Rob to see how he felt about it.

"I'm going to try to get skinny. Are you okay with that? It will make me totally nuts, and I might make you nuts in the process, but I want to give it a shot. I don't want to look back on my life and wonder if I would have had a better career if I'd cut back on the Teddy Grahams."

"Listen, Sharon, you do what you want. I love you now, and I will love you just as much if you are thinner. This is totally your decision."

A couple of days later, I went to the doctor, had some blood work done, and then started a rigorous but very healthy diet, without any medication or supplements. I was amazed at how quickly the weight started to come off, and as I started to add in power walking and running, I got lean, then leaner, and even leaner yet.

After about seven months, I was forty-five pounds lighter, and officially a size 4, the right weight for my height. I hadn't been on a diet since high school, and even in high school I had not achieved this kind of success. It was an overwhelming experience on many levels.

First of all, I felt great. I could run the five-mile loop in Central Park and still want to do it again two days later. I could cross my legs and wrap my foot around my other leg, which is something only skinny girls can do. I could put on any article of clothing and look great in it—nothing made me look bad. I could wear a paper bag out the door and still look great. As a result, I wore all kinds of clothes I'd never worn before but always wished I could, from short skirts to bikinis. I had endless amounts of energy, and the most confidence I'd ever had. I felt like a superhero—all I needed was a cape.

Most of the people in my life were happy for me; some were ecstatic. My friend Vince worked at the TKTS booth in the middle of Times Square, and when he saw me, he made me stand on a big block of cement and turn in circles so he could see me from every angle while he screamed, "Where are your hips? They're gone! Turn around. Oh my God! Your ass! Where is it?" But there were downsides. Everyone seemed to want to talk about my weight all the time. I really felt as though I was stuck in some weird *Twilight Zone* where all conversations revolved around calories and workouts. I was called back into the Broadway company of *Les Mis* for a temporary replacement job while someone was on vacation, and I was shocked one day to walk into the dressing room and catch one of the girls trying on my jeans.

She didn't even seem embarrassed about it, and she spun around to show me. "You came back so skinny, and I wondered if you'd gotten thinner than me, but look! Your jeans are big on me! I can stick my fist down past the waistline!"

I was appalled that someone would actually try on my *clothes* to compare herself to me, but I had to get used to it. Girls get weird when someone loses a lot of weight; this girl wasn't the first person to try on my clothes—and wouldn't be the last. I wanted to scream, *This isn't a competition! Just be happy for me!*

Another downside: People around me scrutinized their own weight and became critical of themselves based on my success. It is really common for people to fall into this trap. I'd be rich if I had a quarter for every time someone said, "Sharon, you look fantastic! God, how did you do it? I feel like such a cow." I hate it when my weight loss makes someone else feel bad, especially when it is someone I love.

People also felt free to talk about how overweight you were before, and how you look so much better now. I wanted to remind people that I was losing weight as an experiment to see if I got more work. I didn't want to hear that I was fat and ugly before I lost weight.

The only person unfazed by my enormous weight change was Rob. In true Rob fashion, he just tried to help me as much as he could, and he loved me through the entire thing. He'd hug me and say, "You're just a concentrated version of yourself, and I still love you, whatever size you are."

As I was nearing my goal weight, I called Jane at Quisisana and asked her if I could come up and stay for the rest of the summer and climb mountains and run in the beauty of Maine to shed the final stubborn pounds. It worked, and by the time I left Quisisana, no one would have ever known I was a former heifer. Every trace of my old life was totally gone. I was a thin girl. I could have been the captain of the cheerleaders.

I hopped a plane to Cincinnati, arranging to meet my folks in baggage claim. I hadn't seen them in a few months, and I wondered what their reaction would be. When I spotted my mom, I didn't say a word, waiting for her to notice me first. She made eye contact with me, and then *my own mother walked right past me!* I said "Mary Jo!" and she stopped and turned around. She stammered and cried and said that she hadn't recognized me, and she couldn't believe it. She grabbed my luggage and dragged me outside so we could create the entire scene again with Dad. It was great moment for the three of us, a great accomplishment for me, and I was glad that my parents could share it with me.

My entire life I'd believed that forty-five pounds stood between a huge career in show business and me. So naturally, when I returned to New York with my teeny-tiny frame, I was expecting great career boosts. I needed a new wardrobe, and my good friend Sarah Uriarte, an undisputed girlie girl, offered to help revamp everything about my life in order to compete as a skinny girl. She helped me get new clothes (no overalls), new makeup (not too much and nothing too bright), new songs (love songs, nothing funny), and taught me the fine art of tweezing my eyebrows. I wore high heels, matching panties and bras, and never left the house without makeup. It was exhausting. My physical appearance had never been under such positive scrutiny, and I felt like I was living in a reality cable TV makeover show. Everyone had an opinion.

After I had my act together, I polished and powdered myself and knocked on the door of the agent who'd asked me to lose weight in the first place. He was stunned that I'd lost so much weight, and a few days later he agreed to come and hear me sing, which was a great sign that he was really interested in me. I sang love songs and sexy ballads, while wearing youthful makeup and skinny-girl clothes. It was my debut as an ingénue and I was a nervous wreck. He had to sign me. He just had to. It would change my entire career.

A few days later, he called and broke the news. "You know, Sharon, I never promised I'd represent you if you lost all that weight. You look great, honey, you really do, but I've got to tell you, I've got a ton of girls who are just your type. I don't think it's fair to them if I sign you, too."

I hung up and stood for a long time without moving. *You've got to be kidding me.* I was completely distraught. Sarah jumped to my rescue and sent me over to her agent. During our meeting he held up a sheet of loose-leaf paper with a list of thirty girls' names and said, "Why should I sign you? I've got a list of unemployed actresses a mile long and you're all the same type. I don't have room for another actress of your type."

And it went on from there. There were so many actresses of my "type" in New York that I couldn't get seen for anything. On top of that, these girls had spent their college years playing all the pretty girl roles, while I'd been stuck playing their mother, so I was at a huge disadvantage. At one particularly low point, I was in an audition for the ingénue in *Sunset Boulevard* when the director's assistant told me that my face wasn't pretty enough to play the role. "It's too thin," he said. I was devastated. Now I wasn't too fat, I was too ugly. Good God.

My weight had been my excuse my entire life, and now I didn't have that excuse anymore. Other thoughts started to creep into my head: *It was never your weight, Sharon; you just weren't talented enough. And now look at you. You're finally skinny, but you aren't pretty enough. You'll never be enough, no matter what you do. Never.* Some people might see a therapist at this point, but I made an appointment to see the only person I knew who would be totally honest with me: Richard Jay-Alexander.

We hardly knew each other, but I wanted his candor. My new packaging for my "box of Tide" wasn't working, and I needed Richard Jay to tell me why.

His eyes grew wide when he saw me. "Wow. You look great, honey. You didn't puke it up, did you? Were you healthy at least?"

I explained the whole situation to him, including my childhood weight problems.

He heard me out, and then leveled with me, as I knew he would do. "The problem is this. Some people really need to change themselves in order to make it in the business, and some people don't. It's like this actress I was just working with. She decided to get a nose job, and I'm telling you right now, she'll never work again. That nose was an important part of who she was. Look at Barbra Streisand. That nose of hers is legend. Look at Roseanne Barr. She gets a bunch of plastic surgery and suddenly she can't get a job. With you, it's harder to say. You got thinner and all of a sudden your eyes get a little too big for your face and it throws off the balance. You might look a little better heavier. Sometimes, Sharon, it's better to be a little unique. Maybe that extra weight matches your personality."

I was on the verge of tears, but he rescued me.

"How about if I hire you back into *Les Misérables* as the understudy for Eponine and Cosette." He was serious. "I just had a girl quit the tour, so why don't you take the job. You could go out and see how it feels to play the pretty girls for a while. Go do it for six months, then you'll know better if this is the right look for you."

Again, Richard Jay came through for me in a miraculous way. Thrilled, I packed my bags and went out to play the pretty girls.

I was nervous about rejoining a company of actors who'd only known me as heavy. Actors can be a relentlessly catty group; I was terrified that they were all going to judge me behind my back. In all my years with *Les Mis*, I'd never entertained the idea that I'd play the pretty-girl roles. I'd always thought they were about as right for me as a career in brain surgery. I was wildly, wildly uncomfortable with the idea of playing Eponine, described in the book as a "waif," and I was equally unnerved at the thought of playing Cosette, a classic teenage ingénue role, down to the big white wedding dress she wore in the finale.

The first role I went on for was Eponine. As I got dressed in her famous costume—a shredded, white, sleeveless shirt, and a long, sacklike brown skirt pulled in with a belt—my heart started to race. The word *waif* pounded in my brain. I smeared on some brown makeup as "dirt" and topped it off with her cute little cap, and looked in the mirror once again. There was *no way* the audience was going to accept me. I was a fraud. I was a heifer. I was a whale. I didn't belong here.

So scared I almost missed my cue, I went tearing up the stairs and raced onstage into eighteenth-century Paris. With each scene I relaxed, my confidence grew, and I ended up having a fantastic time. Moments flew by. Chasing Marius around the set (he's the character Eponine is in love with), pretending to be a boy, singing one of the great musical theater pop ballads "On My Own"—it was all magic. Of course, no one was waiting outside the stage door after the show to tell me I was too fat to play a waif and Richard Jay's words rolled through my head. "Go play the pretty girls. It'll be good for you."

One of the tour stops was a week-long stay in Cincinnati. As luck would have it, the girl playing Cosette got laryngitis, and they put me on for the whole week. My good friend Catherine Brunell, the other Cosette understudy, stepped aside so I could do the entire week for my family and friends. Everyone came, my aunts and uncles, my godmother, even some of my favorite teachers from high school. They ran a big picture of me in the newspaper with the headline "Weight Loss Gains CCM Grad Roles" and an article all about my weight loss and the opportunity Richard Jay had given me.

One of the things I managed to squeeze in that busy week was a trip to my alma maters, Ursuline Academy and the Cincinnati College-Conservatory of Music. I had a wonderful time teaching a class about theater at Ursuline and reminiscing with my faculty friends, including my guidance counselor, Carol Dettenwanger, and my music teacher, Judith Brown. I was thrilled to tell the Ursuline students all about the faculty members who'd meant so much to me in my high school years. I had an equally good time visiting old friends at CCM. It was great to see my old pal, Aubrey Berg, who was continuing to improve CCM's musical theater program with each passing year. He loved my weight loss and he twirled me around, showing me off to his current students as an example of success, which made me feel like a million bucks.

At the end of our day together, Aubrey and I ran into my acting teacher, Virginia. Her hair was almost completely gray now, and she was walking with a pronounced limp, and when I first spotted her, my first instinct was to walk in the other direction. But Virginia surprised me. She threw her arms open and embraced me, then looked me over with a big grin on her face. "Look at you!" she said. Then, in a booming voice, she proclaimed, "Pink pillar, no more!"

I was surprised she remembered calling me a pink pillar. I wondered if she'd felt she'd crossed the line with me, and if her "pink pillar, no more" was an apology of sorts. I decided to let it all go and I hugged her warmly and genuinely. After all, the truth was, I'd always wanted her approval, and I have to confess, it was nice to finally get it.

That week in Cincinnati was healing in many ways. I was at home, I was thin, and I was playing the pretty ingénue. By the time I left, I thought, *Okay. I've done that. I've been the skinny girl. Time to move on.*

The next time I saw Rob (he was still on tour with *Phantom*), I asked him a question that had been plaguing me for the past few months. "Rob, do you ever feel like someone is missing?"

"What are you talking about?"

"Do you ever feel like we aren't supposed to be two anymore, that maybe we are supposed to be three?"

Rob sighed. "I know you are dying for a dog, Sharon, but there is no way we can take care of a chow chow while the two of us are on different tours."

"You are so pigheaded. First of all, I'm not talking about a dog, but if I were, I would want a golden retriever, not a chow. I've heard chows are bad with kids." I paused, suddenly very nervous. "Speaking of kids . . . I think what we are missing is something that would sit in a car seat in the back of this car. I find I keep looking in the backseat while I'm driving, feeling like there is someone missing." I looked at his face, which had grown very flush. "Do you ever feel that way?"

His eyes never left the road, but I swear they got a little watery. "Yes. I feel that way, too, but it's really your decision, Sharon. It affects you a lot more than it affects me. But if you want to know how I feel, the answer is yes. I'd love to have a baby."

I'd never been the kind of woman who gushed over babies, but I also hadn't ever been the kind of woman who said I'd never have children because of my career. "I'm not absolutely positive that this is the right time, especially since I just got thin for the first time in my life, and I'm afraid pregnancy will make me look like a two-ton Tessie." Rob's brow furrowed as he concentrated on the road. I knew I sounded vain. Worrying about getting fat should be the last thing on my mind. "No, not really, I don't really mean that. Of course it'll be fine. You'll love me no matter what, right?"

"Of course I will. You know that. Sharon, don't do this until you are ready, okay? This is a huge decision for you."

I laughed and rubbed his arm. "For both of us. I'm ready. I promise."

I started to read up on the subject of ovulation. "Don't be disappointed if it takes a while to get pregnant," I told Rob. The plan was that I'd quit *Les Mis* and join Rob on the road to try to conceive. A couple of weeks later, Rob took a few days off to come and visit me in Iowa City. We were overjoyed to see each other, and in one particularly passionate moment, we decided to do something we'd never done before: We didn't use a condom. We knew we were officially "trying" to get pregnant, and it was joyfully romantic.

For the next few days I obsessed that I was pregnant, and I questioned Rob endlessly. "I really think I'm pregnant. I feel pregnant. Do I seem different? I think my boobs are tender. I think I'm craving a pickle." I scoured my reflection in the full-length mirror in my hotel room, looking for changes. "I already look bigger."

"Sharon, it hasn't even been twenty-four hours. Even if you were pregnant, which you aren't, there's no way you'd know already." Three weeks later my job with *Les Mis* was over and I was on a plane flying to Detroit to visit Rob on the *Phantom* tour. My period was four days late, my breasts were tender, and I was totally, totally convinced that I was pregnant. I'd purchased a home pregnancy kit so I could take the test with Rob—who had no idea that my period was late. Somewhere over Ohio I grabbed the test and rushed to the bathroom. I couldn't wait for Rob; I had to know now.

I'd never taken a pregnancy test before, and I'd like to go on record to say that it isn't as easy as it looks, especially in an airplane lavatory on a turbulent flight. I persevered, realizing that I wasn't sure how I was going to react if the little line showed up. While I waited for the results to appear, which was a very long three minutes, especially since someone was knocking on the door, I searched my soul for the truth. *Are you happy? Yes. Are you upset that your dream body is on the brink of ruin? Yes. Would you be relieved if it was negative? Yes. Would you be disappointed if it was negative? Yes.*

Three minutes later I emerged from the lavatory with the stick wrapped in several thick napkins. I needed to save it to show Rob. I was pregnant.

I sat down in my seat and the tears flowed. Tears of joy? Fear? All of the above? I was thrilled that I was pregnant, and I couldn't wait to tell Rob, but a little voice in the back of my head plagued me. *You're going to get fat again, Sharon. Big and squishy and fat.* When the plane landed, I put that voice on "mute" and ran out of the plane to tell Rob.

As my pregnancy progressed, my mood swings about my pregnancy continued. I never had a doubt about whether I wanted to be a mother. I was thrilled to have a baby. I could handle everything involved with becoming a parent—there was no doubt about that. My reservations centered around the actual state of pregnancy. I wasn't sure I could emotionally handle getting fat again, and no amount of saying to myself, *This isn't really gaining weight back. You are pregnant; it's different,* seemed to help. I became obsessed with what was going to happen to my body. I tried to avoid the conversation with Rob because I was afraid he would think I was the most superficial person in the entire world. The only person who would possibly understand was Maryday, and I called nightly after Rob went to work. Maryday and I were talking a lot these days because she was in the final planning stages of her wedding. In fact, she was marrying my brother, Buzz!

Once we got all of the wedding plan hoopla out of the way, I launched into my fears with my friend. "What if I can't lose the baby weight? What if I gain ninety pounds? That can happen, you know. I have a friend who gained that much weight and she never lost it again. I'm trying to really watch what I eat and I work out every day, but I think I'm bigger. I'm definitely getting bigger."

Maryday laughed on the other end of the phone. "Of course you're getting bigger, Sharon, you're pregnant! I think it's so fantastic that you are willing to put your career on hold for a while to have a baby. Most actresses won't do that, you know. They get too caught up in their careers to make the time for children. I'm so proud of you. Very few people in your profession would willingly get pregnant in the prime of their career."

I was surprised to hear her say that. I'd always thought the prime of my career would be later, in my late thirties and forties when I could play all the "broads" in musical theater like Mama Rose in *Gypsy* or Auntie Mame in *Mame.* I was constantly being told that I was too young for the parts I wanted to play. This was part of my decision to have a baby now, in my twenties. Her theory filled me with panic. "Do you really think this is the prime of my career? Was I an idiot to get pregnant now?"

"Sharon, you are going to have a very long and lucrative career. Why are you worrying about this now? You're pregnant! Enjoy it!"

I hung up the phone wracked with guilt. Why was I being so vain? What was wrong with me? I prayed that I would find the joy of being pregnant that so many women talked about. All I felt was panic. I worried that I had made a terrible mistake.

The best part of my pregnancy was Rob. His excitement was contagious. We talked endlessly about the practical things, which ranged from where we were going to live once we had this baby since his job moved from city to city every couple of months, to what we were going to name it. We were so excited we decided to tell our families, and we were routinely bombarded by phone calls from anxious family members inquiring, "How's she doing? How's she feeling? Is she nauseous? Is she tired?" Rob happily fielded these phone calls, assuring everyone that I felt fine, not too tired. No nausea.

About nine weeks into my pregnancy, I went into the bathroom and discovered blood in my underwear. I panicked. I was visiting my parents in Cincinnati for the weekend, and I quickly called Rob in Detroit to tell him. "Something's terribly wrong. I'm not supposed to bleed." I called my sister's ob-gyn, who ordered a blood test to check my hormone level. I was told I needed to have a series of blood tests to see if my hormone level was dropping.

My parents drove me to the hospital for the first test, and they tried their best to convince me the bleeding was normal. "You just sit with your feet up over the weekend and you'll see— the bleeding will stop," my mom said.

"Did you ever bleed with your pregnancies?" I asked her.

"No, I didn't. But don't worry. Lots of people do and they go on to have completely healthy babies. Next June you and I will be sitting in the family room, rocking that sweet little baby and laughing about all of this." I could tell by the worried looks on my parents' faces that they had a bad feeling about my pregnancy. After we got home from the doctor, I ran upstairs to the bathroom and sat on the toilet, crying. This was my fault. I'd been too vain and too worried about myself, and somehow I had caused this to happen. I hadn't been happy enough. I hadn't thought about the fact that this was a *baby. My baby.* And now I was losing it, which was my fault because I hadn't wanted it enough, I'd been too worried about getting fat again. I sat in the bathroom for a long, long time, crying and praying for a miracle. I prayed harder than I'd ever prayed in my life. "I promise that if you let this baby live, I will stop being so vain. I'm so sorry. I do want this baby." I said it over and over again. "I do want this baby, I do want this baby." All through the night I had intense cramps and I prayed for the bleeding to stop.

But the bleeding didn't stop. Over the next few days, the bleeding and cramping intensified to the point that another blood test became unnecessary. Rob drove down from Detroit to be with me when I went to the doctor. We sat and listened to the doctor's explanation of a miscarriage. "It's hard to say why miscarriages happen. Sometimes external factors can cause it, like dehydration or a massive fall, but it isn't anything that you've done."

Something he'd said rang a bell. "You said dehydration could cause this? I worked out a lot. Is there any chance that I dehydrated myself working out and that's what caused this?"

I wasn't very relieved by his answer. "It's not anyone's fault. There isn't anything you could have done to miscarry this baby. I promise you. I've delivered babies from mothers who were addicted to crack, and those babies come out fine. If the pregnancy isn't supposed to take, it doesn't, and there's nothing you can do about it."

Rob held my hand as we listened to the doctor talk. I didn't care what he said. It was a baby, my baby, and somehow it was my fault, probably because I'd worked out too hard. The doctor gave me the option of having a surgical procedure to discontinue the pregnancy, or he said I could just "bleed it out."

"I want to warn you, it takes a long time to pass a pregnancy naturally. I'd suggest having the surgery. That way it's over in one day and you won't have the emotional duress dragging on for weeks."

I made the decision to pass the pregnancy naturally. In my hormonally irrational state, I decided that was exactly what I deserved. I tried to explain all of this to Rob, but he thought I was unnecessarily torturing myself.

"You are being so hard on yourself. Millions of women miscarry pregnancies. You heard the doctor; it's very common. I'm not sure what is going on in your head, but you didn't cause this miscarriage by working out too hard, Sharon."

My miscarriage was a terribly dark time for me. I looked around for answers from the universe after that, long after the bleeding had stopped, wondering *how do women do this? How can someone miscarry and get pregnant again? How will I ever believe that my baby will be all right until I am holding it in my arms?* As I struggled with my loss, other aspects of my life carried on in wonderful ways. I was Mayday's matron of honor at her and Buzz's wedding. Soon after I was cast in Rob's *Phantom of the Opera* tour.

In the midst of all this sorrow and joy, I made a life-altering discovery about my weight loss. *It just doesn't matter.* It took enormous effort for me to be that thin; I had to eliminate a lot of food from my diet and work out constantly to maintain it. I was sick of thinking about dieting all the time, and I was sick of the more competitive world of size 4 actresses. Maybe Richard Jay was right—maybe my extra weight wasn't a hindrance; maybe it made me a little unique, like Barbra Streisand's nose. I decided that it was time to stop obsessing about my looks and that a little more weight wouldn't hurt me or my career. A few months into my time on *Phantom* I happily started to gain weight. To be exact, I gained thirty-eight pounds in nine months, and I had something wonderful to show for it. A baby girl named Charlotte.

Even though I carried Charlotte to term, I had a difficult pregnancy. In my first trimester I started to bleed, and the doctor ordered me on partial bed rest (I had to be in bed unless I was at work) until I was past the high-risk time. I sailed through my second trimester, and I stayed in *Phantom* until I was almost six months pregnant, returning to New York to be with Rob, who had taken a job with the Broadway company of *Les Misérables* as the associate conductor. We busied ourselves getting ready for the baby, creatively organizing our one-bedroom apartment. Five weeks before my due date I went into labor. I spent the night in the hospital, and the next two weeks flat on my back in our apartment. Rob was working a lot, so my dad came to New York to help take care of me. My dad is always entertaining, and

I loved having his cheerful energy around the house while I lay on the couch like a beached whale.

"Hey kiddo, what can I make you? I'm going to make myself a savory filet mignon and baked potato, but I might be able to rustle up a couple of saltine crackers and some water for you and that rotten little kid you're carrying." We laughed a lot while my dad was in town; we knew the baby was going to be all right, and my dad celebrated the happy life Rob and I had created for ourselves. "You've created a hell of a life for yourself, honey. You've got a great guy, you're a Broadway actress, and now you're having a baby. You've got life by the tail." We had a wonderful long weekend, and he cooked me more food than I could possibly eat.

When it was time for him to leave, I hugged him goodbye and cried into his shoulder. "Thank you so much for everything, Pops. Just think, the next time I see you, I'll be a mommy."

Two and a half weeks later, my water broke and I quickly delivered a healthy, full-term baby. As troubled as my pregnancies were, my delivery was letter perfect. Rob and I were delighted, thrilled, overjoyed, overwhelmed, everything that is impossible to put into words. To put it simply, we were parents!

My mom flew to New York the day after Charlotte was born. I had a car service pick her up at the airport and drive her directly to Lenox Hill Hospital, where Charlotte was swaddled and waiting to meet her JoJo. My mother spent a week in New York teaching me how to be a mother. We took care of Charlotte in a sleepy fog of joy, changing diapers and ordering in Chinese food. Five days after I delivered Charlotte, I got a call to audition for the Broadway show *Titanic*, so I threw on a big dress to cover my post-pregnant body, kissed Charlotte and my mom goodbye, and hustled down to Chelsea Studios.

Attending that audition was a huge mistake. I was still recovering from the delivery, I was exhausted, and I hadn't sung in months. Worst of all, Chelsea Studios was crammed full of hopeful actresses, all pretty and *svelte*. I ran into numerous friends and work colleagues who were shocked to see me at an audition so soon after birth. I was full of hormones and missing Charlotte, so my interpretation of the afternoon was that everyone was shocked to see me so puffy and gross. I sang poorly in my audition, and I beat it out of there as fast as I could. I cried the entire bumpy, painful car ride home and told my mother my fears. "I'm going to look like this forever! I'm so fat! My career is over!"

My mother gave me some much-needed perspective. "You'll lose the baby weight easily. Stop worrying about it." She placed sweet, sleeping Charlotte in my arms. "I completely understand how you are feeling, but right now, your only concern is healing yourself and taking care of your baby. The weight will come off. Take the pressure off yourself."

My mother was right. I smelled Charlotte's furry head and gave myself a break. I needed to trust that the right job would come along at the right time, and over the next few months, I did start to work. I performed *Into the Woods* at Lyric Opera Cleveland the next summer, and I was hired for a few months as a temporary replacement in the Broadway company of *The Phantom of the Opera*, which helped me finally land an agent. Mostly, though, I took care of my baby bundle of joy. That was the best job of all.

chapter 21

cats

They want me to be a *cat*. Look at my *butt*!

By the time *Cats* called with the big dance audition, Charlotte was fourteen months old, and I was ready to work again. I'd lost most of my baby weight, but I couldn't fathom putting on a slinky cat costume.

"Okay, seriously, it's funny, right? I mean, Rob, come on! They want me to be a *cat*. Look at my *butt*!" I twirled around so he could see me from all angles. "Now imagine this butt with a tail attached to it. It's ridiculous!"

"Sharon, why are you freaking out? If you don't want to go, don't go, but I think that if anyone could actually pull this off, you could."

"Rob!" I flopped down on the couch and collapsed onto him. "I'm too fat and I can't dance!"

Rob, ever the practical guy, replied, "Why don't you let them decide that?"

I figured he was right. Two days later, Rob packed up to go visit his brother and sister-in-law in Massachusetts. As he kissed me goodbye, he said, "Use this time to get ready for your audition on Tuesday. Charlotte's going to have a great time with her cousin, and it'll be good for you to have us out of your hair."

As soon as the taillights disappeared onto Ninth Avenue, I went inside and called my friend Liz. Liz had been a musical theater major in college, but her minor was tap dance, and I knew that she could help me out.

When she picked up the phone, I didn't even bother with *hello*. "Help! I have an audition for *Cats*."

Liz let out a huge whoop of laughter. "No!"

"Yes! And I need your help. I'm auditioning for the tap cat."

"Jennyanydots? That's a good part for you. Can you tap?"

"Yeah, about as well as I can perform brain surgery."

"Okay, you can do this. Come over." With that she hung up.

I had total faith, despite the fact that Liz wasn't a skinny dancer; in fact, she was more of a stand-and-sing performer like me. Still, if anyone could teach me to dance like a cat, Liz could.

I showed up at her apartment an hour later in dance clothes, holding a newly purchased copy of the *Cats* video in one hand and lunch in the other.

Three days later, I emerged from her apartment exhausted and sore. I was much more prepared, but still—I tried to be realistic. My final words to Liz were the same ones I'd been saying all weekend. "There is absolutely no way I'm going to make it past the dance call. Oh, have I mentioned? I'm too fat to be a cat."

The morning of the audition arrived. My dance clothes and shoes were so new, I looked like a plus-size model for Danskin. I looked around the theater and watched the other people warming up, immediately comparing my body size to theirs. I reminded myself, "Sharon Wheatley, you are not a plus size anymore. You are a respectable size 8. Okay, maybe a 10. Still, you are thinner than you ever were in high school, and not that much bigger than the other people here. These women are not dancers."

Apparently everyone's face read, "I'm not a dancer." I even caught one girl cutting the tags off her dance clothes. I felt better. At least I knew the dance combination, and I'd bet none of the other fifty girls here had sacrificed their Memorial Day weekend to learn dances off a DVD.

Someone has to get this job today, I reminded myself. *Why not me?*

Richard, the choreographer, clapped his hands—the universal signal for us to assemble on the stage. We climbed up the steps and stood facing him. I looked out into the theater and took a deep breath.

It's a common misconception fueled by the movies that Broadway auditions happen on the stage of the theater. In reality, almost all Broadway auditions are held in small, slightly dilapidated dance studios. This was the very first time I had ever auditioned on the actual stage of a theater. Thrilled, I remembered my dreams as a kid, how I had imagined myself onstage in a moment just like this, and the power of it almost moved me to tears. There was no denying the fact that even with two other Broadway shows on my resume, I still got goose bumps in a Broadway theater, and I wanted this job, cat or no cat. I pushed the nagging voice singing *You can't dance, and you're too fat* out of my head. I decided to go for it.

Richard's clapping snapped me back to attention as he started to talk to us. He stood at the edge of the stage in his dance clothes, with his legs together and his head slightly cocked, a smile on his face.

"Hello, ladies. How was everyone's holiday weekend? Some of you might be wondering why we are starting with a dance combination, so I'm going to remind you that *Cats* is a very strenuous dance show. That said, there are a few 'singer cats,' and Jennyanydots, the Gumbie Cat, is one of them. I'm sure you all sing beautifully, and we need that, but first we are going to need to see your dancing, since her big number in the show is a tap number. Everybody ready?" Richard got into the starting position, which was squatting on the floor with his left leg extended to the side. "Okay, counting one, two. . . . "

Forty-five minutes later we'd learned the opening number and performed it three dancers at a time for Richard, who took notes and kept repeating, "Remember, they are cats. Try to find your inner felinity!"

It was hard to do the steps in the first place, and it was even harder to do the steps while trying to remember to act like a damn cat. It took every ounce of chutzpah I had to do it, but I made it through with only one small mishap—I accidentally kicked the girl next to me.

"Okay, ladies, nice job." Richard clapped his hands. "Now we're going to concentrate on the tap. I don't care so much about the tap "sounds" because you are onstage with a whole group of people and they will make the tap noise for you. What I need is lots of personality."

Usually I show lots of personality onstage, but the minute someone asks for it, I become weirdly robotic, and my personality goes out the window. I tried to look energetic and friendly, which was my version of a cat with a lot of personality. "Stomp, stomp, pull back. . . . "

Somewhere around "Fan kick, pull back, pull back," things started to unravel. Richard started teaching new steps that weren't on the *Cats* video. I am very slow at picking up dance combinations, so even with my three-day dance seminar at Liz's, I still looked like a beginner. If we had to learn steps that weren't on the video I'd memorized, I was doomed. The girl next to me seemed to be picking things up very quickly.

"Hi, uh, excuse me?" I asked as we ball-changed and falaped.

"Uh-huh," she said as we marched along in a circle.

"Do you know the *Cats* video?" I asked.

"Yeah."

"Was this dance on it?" I asked.

"Uh, no. There was a lot of stuff cut for the movie, and the Gumbie Cat number was cut to almost nothing." We all stopped dancing for a minute while someone asked a question.

Oh God. "Is there any way you are wrong?"

"No, I don't think so. I played this part in Germany."

I was never going to make it through. I wanted to call Liz and demand a refund. Of course, I hadn't paid her anything, and she had sacrificed an entire holiday weekend to help me, but still.

Richard clapped his hands. "Okay, ladies, let's do it in groups of three."

I'd been so busy panicking I hadn't even paid attention to the final sixteen counts. I had no idea what to do. I tried to hide in the back, praying. *Please skip me; please forget I'm here. . . .*

"Wheatley!" Richard's voice boomed around the theater. I walked to my place and thought about that root canal I'd be willing to endure in trade for these two minutes of humiliation. At first I was fine. But when the new section started, I completely fell apart. I watched the person's feet next to me and tried to mimic them, but I was lost.

Then it hit me. Here I was—Sharon Wheatley, the girl who'd weighed 230 pounds in high school, the girl who'd been told never to sing a love song, the girl who'd been told that she needed to look like Marilyn Monroe to get a job—standing on the stage of the Winter Garden Theater attempting to dance like a cat. I stopped dancing and I started laughing.

I'd spent the majority of my childhood and early adulthood trying to fit into all of these roles that just weren't me—and I realized I was doing the same thing with *Cats*. I had gotten here because of who I was; I didn't need to pretend to be anyone other than that. If *Cats* didn't like me as Sharon Wheatley, I didn't need to be a *cat*. And just like that, the pressure lifted and I decided just to dance around like stupid, goofy me and have fun.

I made up my own dance until the music stopped, and I loved it—I laughed the entire time. By the time it was over, everyone else was laughing too, including several *Cats* managers and directors who'd stopped by to watch the auditions.

"Very nice interpretive dance, Miss Wheatley," Richard said with a wry smile. Then he asked everyone to line up on the stage for cuts. "Would the following people please stay to sing? Everyone else, thank you very much." As he called names, I stood in the back and started to strip off my dance shoes and pack up my bag. I'd been awful, and I didn't think I had a chance in hell of staying. I was about to head out the door to meet Charlotte and Rob for lunch when I heard my name.

"Sharon Wheatley."

"You've got to be kidding!"

Several people heard me and laughed out loud.

"Did he just call Sharon Wheatley?" I wanted to make sure I wasn't hallucinating. Their nods confirmed it. Somehow, I'd made it through the dance call!

About ten of the fifty original actors were kept to sing. Big ham that I am, this was my favorite part of any audition, and I sang my heart out, center stage of the Winter Garden. I sang a very obscure comedy song and it was appropriately funny and silly, just the way I was feeling. They liked it and asked me to come back in about an hour to dance again.

I called Rob during my break. "Okay, the strangest thing has happened. I actually made it through the dance call, got asked to sing, and now I have to go back and dance again. You know what's even weirder? I'm starting to think I might actually have a shot at getting this job!"

When I went back for the final dance call, there were three of us left. Pretty quickly, one of the girls was cut, and we were down to two. They asked us to sing from the score, which was very difficult given several ungodly high notes. I was starting to wonder if *Cats* wasn't actually a bizarre freak show created by evil British people. How could anyone actually do *this* eight shows a week?

Eventually, after more dancing and singing, they released the other actress. I'd liked her—she was a new mom too—and I was sad to see her go; but at the same time I could barely contain my excitement. I waved goodbye, feeling pretty damn good, and turned back to the people in the room, including the entire management team. I was the only person left, so clearly there was only one thing left to say. I smiled.

Instead of a job offer, however, there was an awkward pause, and Richard approached me. "Sharon, dear, would you mind walking with me for a minute?"

"Absolutely!" I was happy to do anything that did not involve dancing or singing, since I'd been at this audition for close to seven hours now.

As we walked, he put his arm around me. "Well, Sharon, I can't make any promises, but things seem to be going quite well for you today."

cats

253

I looked around the now nearly empty theater and resisted the urge to say something like, *Well, unless you are planning on hiring the theater ghost, it looks like I'm the only one left.*

"The thing is, well, you've seen *Cats*, and the dancers in our little kitty play are quite"—he struggled to find the right word—"fit."

Fit was an understatement. *Cats* had the most beautiful bodies on Broadway.

"The thing is, Sharon, we all like you very much, and we appreciate that you've recently had a baby, but we're going to need to ask you to lose weight for our show, and we're going to have to write that into your contract. Jennyanydots is the plumpest girl cat onstage, but we still need you to be a little thinner." He gave me a slightly nervous smile. "I hope you appreciate that this is uncomfortable, but necessary. Do you want some time to think about it?"

I kind of felt sorry for Richard. He was probably sent to talk to me because he knew me from another show we'd done together years before, but even so, this wasn't an easy thing to talk about with anyone. I smiled and went into the fat-talk mode that I'd developed during college when I was constantly critiqued on my appearance. I'd learned quickly that the more easygoing I was in a conversation like this, the quicker and better it went for everyone.

"Hey, listen, there is no reason this has to be uncomfortable. Don't worry about me. I'm totally fine talking about my weight, okay?" I laughed. "I've been doing it my entire life! I'm great at losing weight. I've done it before, and I think you'll be surprised at how effectively I can do it!" I was aware that I sounded like an enthusiastic infomercial, but I hated everything about this uncomfortable moment, and I wanted to just blow past it, so

I told him what he needed to know. I could lose weight and I would.

But somewhere deep underneath my good-natured reaction, my feelings were hurt and I was incredibly embarrassed. I ignored it and kept talking, trying to put Richard at ease, well aware that my reaction to losing weight was going to be as critiqued as my singing and dancing. If I got defensive and angry, they would decide I was "difficult" and offer the job to someone else. I gave him a friendly, enthusiastic smile and asked, "How much do you want me to lose?"

He looked relieved. I realized he'd probably thought I was going to cry, or throw my new dance shoe at him.

"Well, I don't know how much weight we need you to lose. We've never actually asked anyone to lose weight before. How about if we take tonight to come up with something fair, and we'll talk tomorrow?"

"Okay!" I was so perky. "Sounds great!" Richard and I hugged and he said a couple of nice things about my audition, and that was it. My *Cats* audition was over, and I'd gotten the job—with big conditions—but still, I'd gotten the job. I was ecstatic but disappointed that my first instinct had been so correct. I was, in fact, too fat to be even the "plumpest" cat onstage. It was a whole new level of humiliation.

The next day, I met with the production supervisor of *Cats* to discuss my weight. Rob and I had talked about it the night before and agreed that if the management team had never put a clause into a contract asking an actor to lose weight, I should be clear about what I felt was acceptable to ask. I'd come up with a list of rules, and I began the negotiations.

"Okay. Let me start by saying that I appreciate that this is a difficult subject, and I don't want you to feel uncomfortable."

I was dying to ask him why in the world they hadn't just hired someone skinnier if my weight was such a big issue, but I was afraid a question like that would make me seem ungrateful. I was happy to have the job. I also knew that if they were willing to hire me in spite of the fact that I didn't look the way they wanted, they must really want me. I tried to hang on to these thoughts as I forged ahead.

"I've given this a lot of thought, and I have an idea about how it might work. But I'm wondering if you have come up with any specifics overnight. My main question is, how much weight would you like me to lose, and how quickly?"

The supervisor looked uncomfortable. I wondered how he'd pulled the wrong straw and ended up having to talk about weight with a total stranger.

"Well," he said, "first of all, I want to say that I think you look great. I mean, in the normal world your weight wouldn't be a problem. It's just because this is *Cats*."

I smiled. He smiled. This was excruciating.

"I guess I haven't really thought about it. Why don't you tell me how much weight you think you can lose, and we'll go from there."

I wanted to throw my hands in the air and say, *I can't just guess! Give me a number! Five pounds? Ten pounds? Fifty pounds?* But I didn't. I raced through various numbers in my head, trying to figure out what he wanted. I remembered the "guess your weight, guess your age" games at the amusement parks, and I wondered if I'd get a stuffed animal if I guessed my future weight correctly. I made a stab in the dark. "Ten pounds?"

"Ten pounds?" He clapped his hands and blew out a sigh I could only interpret as relief. "That would be great! Are you okay with that?"

I felt as though I'd just written down the right number and won Final Jeopardy. I forged ahead with my rules. "Ten pounds is fine, but here's what I'd like for you to agree to. I don't ever want to be asked to weigh in at the theater. This all has to go through my nutritionist, okay?" I had a terrible vision of walking through the stage door and being pulled aside by some eighteen-year-old stage manager with a scale requesting me to step on and weigh in at any moment. Which wasn't going to happen. Ever. If they wanted me to do this, they were going to have to do it my way.

"And one more thing. No one in this building besides you and me can know that this is in my contract. Period. This is not to become show gossip, okay? I don't want everyone in the building watching my weight."

Then we hashed out the specific terms.

I told them if they wanted to know my weight, they would have to inform me in writing. I would go to my nutritionist's office within one week and she would weigh me in total privacy and fax the results to the stage manager's office. If I was more than five pounds overweight, I had two weeks to lose it or be fired.

He agreed and proposed a clause stating it was management's intent that I should practice medically safe weight-loss methods in order to maintain my ideal weight. They also added a clause that if I had not lost ten pounds by the end of my first four weeks of performances, I could be fired on the spot.

I then added a clause that my weight clause and my weight were never to be discussed at work. Then I signed it.

My rehearsals were held in a dance studio from 10 A.M. to 6 P.M. every day with the dance captain (the person responsible for teaching the show to new actors) and a pianist. Learning *Cats* was the most difficult thing I've ever done in my performing career, and at times it seemed impossible. I wasn't just learning a show—I'd done that before—I was learning to dance. Frequently I felt like there weren't enough rehearsal hours in the day to get me ready for my debut. After rehearsal ended I'd run up to the Winter Garden Theater and watch the show, starving and feeling my exhausted muscles tense up after a long day. I felt like I was in a marathon; I had three weeks of blood, sweat, and tears to turn myself into a dancing cat and lose ten pounds or get canned.

Our babysitter Julie would keep Charlotte awake until 10:45 P.M. so I could run home and rock her to sleep, humming whatever *Cats* song I'd drilled into my head that day. It was the only time I was able to spend with her, and I cherished each second, even if she was sleeping on my shoulder. It helped keep me in check every day; there's nothing like the perspective gained by having a child. Her presence in the world prevented me from worrying that I might get fired for being fat and uncoordinated. Charlotte didn't care if I was too fat to be in *Cats*.

As my opening night approached, things started to fall into place. The dances started to stick in my brain, and better yet, my body started to morph into a more feline shape. "Good! Good! You're getting it!" the dance captain said. "We're going to give you a put-in on Monday afternoon, and if all goes well, you will open in the show that night." A "put-in" is the final rehearsal an actor gets before the opening performance to put you in the company. Put-ins are very common for long-running shows, as actors are always leaving for other shows and other actors are always coming in to replace them. The goal for a put-in rehearsal is to replicate a performance as closely as possible. The actor being "put in" wears her costumes and works with all the actors she will be working with in performance. This is frequently the only opportunity you have to work with the entire company.

In my case, most of the cats are onstage the entire show; constant traffic patterns are closely followed to avoid head-on cat collisions. In rehearsal, the dance captain would constantly point to various places around me and say things like "Mungojerrie is going to be doing a cartwheel just to the left of you right here, so be sure you hit this spot exactly." Or "Grizabella will approach you on your right. Swipe away Syllabub the kitten as she tries to go through your legs, then turn to the left of Jellylorum and exit up right."

At first it seemed impossible, but eventually I mastered these traffic patterns by learning the makeup colors and costumes of the cats. I'd dance around the studio and yell things as I negotiated the imaginary traffic: "Alonzo is the gold cat and he is passing on my left. Macavity and Demeter are red and black and they are passing behind me." With this complete picture of the stage in my head, I felt confident going into my put-in rehearsal.

That is, until I realized that I was the only person who was going to be in costume and makeup. Without the costumes, I had no idea who anyone was, but I did know one thing: I was doomed.

My parents drove up from Cincinnati to watch my first performance of *Cats*. The buzzer rang their arrival, and I felt waves of nausea as they bustled through the door and I saw their excited faces. I was going to be a dancing cat on Broadway. Tomorrow. This was wrong, all wrong. I sat Rob and my parents down to explain the situation. "Please don't be disappointed, but I may get fired tomorrow and there may be no opening night. You have to understand that I have to make it through my put-in rehearsal in front of all of the supervisors. I have to be thin and I have to be able to dance. Unless there is a divine intervention, we may all be sitting here tomorrow night eating popcorn and watching reruns of *Sanford and Son*. There may be no Broadway opening."

"We're here to see Charlotte, that's all," my mother said. "Take the pressure off of yourself. We're just thrilled to be here."

"I don't think of you as anything but a total failure anyway," added Dad. "There isn't a single thing that could happen tomorrow to change my mind."

I threw a pillow at him and told him there was a ban on all mayonnaise in New York City, so he'd have to be off the smack for the duration of the visit.

He picked up his suitcase and headed for the door. "Well honey, it's been a really terrific visit, but we'll have to be going now."

I felt a little better. At least we were all still laughing.

The next day I got to the theater early to suit up in my cat costume—a hand-painted lycra unitard, a yak hair wig dyed orange and white, one arm warmer, two leg warmers, and a tail. Becoming a cat is complicated. The costume must appear seamless, so the only opening is at the top and you pull it on like a pair of pantyhose. There are no other zippers or hooks anywhere, so once you start to sweat, it is nearly impossible to pull the costume on and off quickly. It sticks to you like glue—so you plan your bathroom trips accordingly.

The costume, I quickly found out, was the least of it. The makeup had been designed for my face by the original makeup designer; because of its intricate detail it was nearly impossible to apply, and I had to do it myself. I tried again and again, but I didn't look like a cat at all. I looked like a cross between a clown and a chipmunk. I futzed with it as much as I could, until finally I had to let it go. Time for the put-in rehearsal.

Waves of nausea washed over me as I walked backstage. I could hear the cast chatting as they gathered in the house, and I heard the distinct voices of the supervisors who had hired me. I could just imagine them sitting in the audience, pens and notebooks in hand, waiting to critique me. I'd lost a lot of weight, eight pounds to be exact, but I wondered if Richard's very first note for the rehearsal would be: *Still too fat to be a cat.*

I stood in front of a black velvet curtain knowing that everyone was waiting for me on the other side. My mind swirled with negativity. *I look like a demented gopher. I'm fat. I can't dance.* I pulled myself together with a little pep talk. *There is great suffering in this world, and you walking through this curtain to do a put-in for a Broadway show does not rank as anything even remotely bad. This is a good thing! Go do it!* I raised my hand to part the curtain, and laughed out loud as I caught sight of myself. I had no hands anymore, only paws. I am a *cat* now.

Considering everything that could have gone wrong—the actors out of costume, the dancing traffic patterns, the supervisors' scrutiny, my weight, my bad makeup, and oh yeah, *the dancing*—things went reasonably well. I have attended put-in rehearsals when everyone in the building knows the performance is magical, and I've been around for the put-ins when you knew the person wouldn't last out the week. My put-in rehearsal fell squarely between those two extremes. I did just fine, but I still worried that I was too big.

Afterward, I met with all of the supervisors to get notes. I kept waiting for someone to mention my weight, especially because it was all we had talked about the last time we had seen each other. The supervisors gave me dance notes, vocal notes, and acting notes, but that was it. The note session ended with the decision that I would perform my opening night that night—a mere two hours from now. I felt like there was a huge pink elephant in the room, and I wanted to acknowledge it since it caused me so much stress. Even as the words came out of my mouth, I worried that I was wrong to say it. "So, how's my weight? Am I thin enough?"

Richard looked up from his notebook, surprised. "You look great! It's the first thing we all said when you walked out. You don't have to lose any more weight. We think you look great. Put it out of your mind."

They thought I was thin enough to be a cat. I was stunned.

Two hours later, the famous *Cats* overture started and I, Sharon Wheatley, former 230-pound heifer, came onstage with all those skinny dancers and became a dancing cat, proof positive that absolutely anything is possible. With my parents, Rob, and many friends as witnesses, I danced my way through one of the most famous dance shows in Broadway history. I still consider it one of the greatest accomplishments of my life.

Afterward, I greeted everyone at the stage door. After all of the hugs, kisses, and congratulations, we decided to go to my favorite theater restaurant, Joe Allen, to celebrate. Most people think of Sardi's when they think of Broadway actors and celebrations. But I prefer Joe Allen Restaurant. It has a similar feel to Sardi's—show posters on the walls and lots of famous people—but the food is a little less expensive and they serve fantastic cheeseburgers.

I wanted my parents to feel like they were experiencing a real Broadway opening night, so even though Joe Allen was packed, we decided to stay and squeeze around a small table. I'd been so nervous that I'd barely eaten a thing all day, so I ordered a cheeseburger and fries.

My mom and dad knew about the weight clause in my contract, and I became self-conscious about my cheeseburger. I should have ordered a salad. When my cheeseburger arrived, I whispered to my mother and pointed to my plate. "I haven't eaten all day."

"I was just thinking about how many calories you just burned off up on that stage tonight." Mom wrinkled her brow and made a funny face. "If I'd worked out like you just did, I'd be eating that, too."

"Here." I held out my cheeseburger. "Take a big bite. It's fantastic!"

One of the best parts of a successful performance is bragging about it afterward with people who love you. I kidded my friend Liz, the one who'd helped me with my audition. "How was my tapping? Not bad, huh? Can you believe how long that number is?"

My mom interrupted me. "Sharon, your dancing was amazing. I really had absolutely no idea that you could dance like that! You know what part I couldn't get over? The number you did with the boy cat when you did those amazing cartwheels at the end. When did you learn to do that?"

I didn't do any cartwheels, and I didn't do a number with a guy. I had no idea what she was talking about.

"She thinks you were Rumpleteaser!" Liz let out a scream and slapped me on the back. "Your mom was watching the wrong cat!"

Rumpleteaser is another *Cats* character with a similar costume to mine. In my mother's defense, all the cats really do look a lot alike, and it was nearly impossible to tell people apart. I'd never thought to tell my parents particulars about my costume—because I never *dreamed* that they would confuse me for one of the real cats, the dancer cats, the skinny cats. I just assumed they'd find me easily—the fattest one onstage.

But my very own mother thought I was small enough that she could confuse me with a dancer. *I'd come a long way, baby.*

Because *Cats* is basically a two-and-a-half-hour aerobics class, my weight remained steady and I never had to weigh in or even have a conversation about my weight with anyone in management for the duration of my time in the show.

You can bet, though, that on September 10, 2000, the night *Cats* closed for good at the Winter Garden Theater on Broadway, I celebrated at the closing night party with a *huge* piece of cake. It tasted great.

curtain call

"I arrived in Hollywood without having
my nose fixed, my teeth capped,
or my name changed.
That is very gratifying to me."

—Barbra Streisand

Photo by Jordan Matter.

Once *Cats* closed, I regained most of the weight I'd lost to look like a cat. The weight gain was gradual, and without a two-and-a-half-hour dance show to burn it off, kind of inevitable. Recently, my daughter and I got out of the subway in Times Square and walked north on Broadway. We held hands as I steered her through the hordes of theatergoers who could easily plow right into her as they stared up at the huge billboards. Since I work in the theater district quite a bit, Charlotte is used to bustling around on busy New York City streets and keeping up with my pace, so I was surprised when she stopped. She was looking at a large advertisement for a new diet drink. The billboard featured before and after photos of a female torso, clad in a white sports bra and underwear. The "after" picture featured a fit, trim body with six-pack abs, while the "before" picture was twenty-five pounds heavier and flabby. Charlotte looked at the billboard, cocking her head to one side. I could practically see the wheels turning in her head. I found myself bracing for her reaction, keenly aware that up to that moment, she was possibly the only person in my life who had never commented on my weight.

When we got to the corner, she turned to me and said, "Mommy, you know what? I like that you look like that one girl on that sign and not the other one because I think mommies should be soft."

I knelt down to her level and put my hands on her shoulders. Pedestrians swarmed around us. I asked, "Why do you think mommies should be soft, Charlotte?"

"Because then they are snuggly when their children hug them," she said, and put her arms around my neck.

It was so simple to her—and so sweet to me. *She's right*, I thought. Mommies shouldn't spend so much time worrying about being thin. Mommies are supposed to be soft.

"You know, Charlotte, I had a mommy who was afraid to be soft. It was very important to her to be thin, and I didn't like it. I wanted her to be soft, too."

"Like you?"

"Like me."

As we continued walking, I experienced a flood of conflicting emotions. I wish I could say that I was fine with being told that I looked like the "before" picture on a diet ad, but I wasn't. It stung to be looked at so truthfully. But I was also overwhelmingly proud of Charlotte for understanding something that so few American women understand. Mommies can be soft. Sometimes, when I look around at many of the mothers in New York City, dressed in their exercise clothes, looking taut and thin and worried, I wonder, *Do I want to work that hard just so I can be thin? Do I want my daughter to hear me talking about my desire to be thin, and do I want to pass self-criticism on to her? Can I eat a double-dip ice-cream cone every once in a while without talking about how long I'll have to be on the treadmill to burn it off? Can I look like this and still be happy? And most important, does it really matter if I am a size 12 instead of a size 4?*

Most people spend a lot of time thinking about all of the reasons they can't do something, rather than just going out there and doing it. Throughout my life, most people have underestimated me, which made me feel crazy, sad, and mad. And often it made me want to quit. But, above all else, it made me want to prove them wrong.

And I have. I've just learned a new skill—puppeteering— while performing in the original Las Vegas cast in *Avenue Q* at the Wynn Casino. My life is exciting and fulfilling, but like my Dad taught me, I'm still looking to overflow my glass.

My big plans were specific, and they started at a young age. One of my final assignments in the fifth grade was to write as if I were thirty-five years old, describing my life accomplishments. We were supposed to seal it in a time capsule on school grounds, but I kept mine. It has moved with me from dorm room to apartment, from house to house, and I check it like a crystal ball that foretells my future. I'm still impressed with how well I knew what I wanted to be when I grew up.

My Autobiography

I have always wanted to be an actress, but people always told me I'd never have the chance. This autobiography is about all the years of hard work it took me to reach my goal—show business.

I started liking acting when I was around three. I always said that I wished I was small enough to jump into the TV and do what the people did. My mother and father named me "Sarah Bernhardt" when I was around three. I did a lot of plays and I was in chorus. I started acting and singing lessons, and soon I joined The Playhouse in the Park group. I starred in some of the plays and was an extra for others. I really enjoyed it. My life stayed about the same until I was a senior in high school. I had to apply to some colleges. I applied to Yale, University of Pennsylvania, and UCLA. I got into all of them, and I went to Yale because my sister and brother had already been there, so it ran in the family. I had a great time in college, and when I got out I moved to New York to start my career.

I got a job at a nightclub entertaining at night, and during the day I looked for auditions. I finally made it. I was going to star in a Broadway play called Lucky Lady, and it was also a musical. After I did the play, I was offered a movie deal. Right away I accepted. I was now twenty-two and doing my first movie. After that I did two more movies, all starring roles. I enjoy my life on camera and I have my own Variety Hour. I am now making my sixth film, and at thirty-five enjoying California and my life very much.

The End

Some of it sounds a little far-fetched, but I've learned not to underestimate life. Who knows what tricks I've got left up my size-twelve sleeve?

Act One

Me as a fourth-grade Girl Scout. I quit as soon as the cookie sale was over.

Me and my sweet cousin Jennifer. I was about eleven.

Act Two

Christmas Eve with my Mom's family, my freshman year at Ursuline.

Sometimes it was hard to have such a pretty and thin mother, but we were all smiles even as I was close to hitting my top weight at age fifteen.

Act Three

Me in *Cats* on Broadway in 2000. I did the makeup myself every night and it took about an hour.

Photo ©2005 Carol Rosegg.

Me with Kate Monster in *Avenue Q*.